PIGS AT THE TROUGH

Lessons from Australia's decade
of corporate greed

Adam Schwab

WILEY
John Wiley & Sons Australia, Ltd

First published 2010 by
John Wiley & Sons Australia, Ltd
42 McDougall Street, Milton Qld 4064

Office also in Melbourne

Typeset in 11.3/13.8 pt Caslon

© Adam Schwab 2010

The moral rights of the author have been asserted

National Library of Australia Cataloguing-in-Publication data:

Author:	Schwab, Adam.
Title:	Pigs at the trough: lessons from Australia's decade of corporate greed / Adam Schwab.
ISBN:	9781742169903 (pbk.)
Notes:	Includes index.
Subjects:	Financial crises – Australia.
	Global Financial Crisis, 2008–2009.
	Executives – Conduct of life.
	Fraud.
Dewey number:	338.5420994

Cover design by Xou Creative

Printed in Australia by Ligare Book Printer

10 9 8 7 6 5 4 3 2

Disclaimer

The material in this publication is of the nature of general comment only, and does not represent professional advice. It is not intended to provide specific guidance for particular circumstances and it should not be relied on as the basis for any decision to take action or not take action on any matter which it covers. Readers should obtain professional advice where appropriate, before making any such decision. To the maximum extent permitted by law, the author and publisher disclaim all responsibility and liability to any person, arising directly or indirectly from any person taking or not taking action based upon the information in this publication.

Contents

About the author

ADAM SCHWAB was a corporate lawyer at one of Australia's largest firms before becoming a founding director of the privately owned diversified accommodation and services group AJ Capital. Since 2004, Adam has also been a financial journalist and business commentator for Australia's largest and most influential online publication *Crikey*, and a business contributor to Fairfax publications, including *The Sydney Morning Herald* and *The Age*. Schwab has also acted as a corporate governance adviser to Australia's largest institutions and fund managers.

Acknowledgements

A FEW people deserve my heartfelt thanks for their generous time and assistance. I am deeply grateful for the assistance of Jeremy, Lesley-Anne and Rosie, my outstanding proofreaders; and to Campbell for his wise guidance. I am also eternally thankful to Dean and Martin for imparting a mere fraction of their wisdom and knowledge to me, which hopefully was able to find its way into this book in some way.

To Mary, Brooke, Hannah and everyone at Wiley, my editor Michael and legal adviser Richard, your diligence, expertise and enthusiasm for the project throughout has been invaluable.

I am in the debt of the team at *Crikey*: Andrew, Thomas, Sophie, Jane, Leigh and Jonathan; and especially to Stephen for literally trailblazing the journalistic pursuit of corporate governance. Misha, my first editor, your faith in me and generosity have not been forgotten.

Finally, a special thank you to my family and close friends for their constant faith and support over the years; and to those executives whose greed and foolishness made this book possible.

Preface

The world is now caught in the worst economic crisis since the Great Depression. This crisis has been created by an ideology of unrestrained greed... turbocharged by unregulated financial markets, by obscene remuneration packages that maximised risk with no regard whatsoever to the impact of their behaviour on ordinary investors... this has been extreme capitalism writ large.

Prime Minister Kevin Rudd, 2008

FROM THE recession of the early 1990s until the global financial crisis of 2008, shareholders experienced almost two decades of unrestrained joy, punctuated only briefly by an Asian hiccup and burst dotcom bubble. Insatiable share price and earnings growth, coupled with billions of dollars of superannuation money, saw the Australian stock market explode.

But as good as the good times seemed, the boom was built on very shaky foundations. Generous use of debt created many paper fortunes. However, it is often said, the greater the bubble, the greater the deception — and there is little doubt that many of the fast-growing businesses were running on bluff and bluster, rather than sustainable and honest business models.

Throughout this period of excess there were several constants: the ever-increasing trajectory of executive remuneration, coupled with a new-found love of debt and widespread use of financial engineering. While real wages for ordinary workers barely kept up with inflation, executives received lucrative share options, performance rights and short-term cash bonus payments that contained very little alignment with long-term wealth creation (except for their own).

As executive remuneration skyrocketed, Australia also witnessed insatiable growth in companies that made very little of anything of value, but instead engaged in pursuits called 'asset origination' or 'asset recycling'. These companies (typically called 'financial engineers') would hide the nature of their businesses among an ever-growing cloak of complexity. Their Byzantine structures and opaque financial reports allowed executives such as David Coe and Phil Green to accumulate multi-million-dollar nest eggs. When the fall eventually came, these so-called masters of the universe would be well protected. Shareholders and creditors would not be so lucky.

The financial engineers, usually operating in the once staid, government-owned infrastructure sector, used layers of leverage and billions of dollars of shareholder capital to acquire assets and later pay income from that very capital and borrowings. The engineers —led by Babcock & Brown, Allco and MFS—would become the custodians of Australia's most important infrastructure and tourism assets. Their inevitable death, under the weight of burgeoning debt, would bear an eerie resemblance to the endeavours of the entre-preneurs of yesteryear—household names such as Bond, Skase and Spalvins would be replaced in 2008 by a new set of faces, with names such as Coe, Groves and Green.

The ease with which founders and executives enriched them-selves at shareholders' expense will long remain a case study for the importance of corporate governance.

Eddy Groves, the man who ran what was once the world's largest childcare company, paid his brother-in-law millions of dollars in untendered maintenance works, while Allco directors David Coe and Gordon Fell collected tens of millions of dollars after they sold their Rubicon property business to Allco—after the sub-prime crisis had taken hold. Only days after the sale, Gordon Fell's wife spent $27 million purchasing one of Australia's finest homes on Sydney harbour, the asset remaining safely out of reach of Fell's creditors and Allco's beleaguered shareholders.

Babcock & Brown's Phil Green and MFS's Michael King stood by while the empires they created crumbled. Both appear to have retained extensive private financial interests, often purchased with monies extracted from their companies during the glory years.

But it wasn't only the engineers who brought pain to shareholders.

The Village Roadshow troika of Robert and John Kirby and 'surrogate brother' Graham Burke would turn the notion of 'alignment' into a furphy. The Village executives received tens of millions of dollars over a decade while their bumbling management of Australia's largest cinema and production concern cost shareholders millions.

Telstra, once a staid, government-owned utility, would turn to a big-talking American to improve its fortunes. It took four years and many billions of dollars in lost market value for the Telstra board to realise the error of their ways.

Toll Holdings, one of Australia's most successful companies, became a pariah, paying its already wealthy executives millions for worthless options, right under the noses of shareholders.

Even two agribusiness companies, which sold woodchips to the Japanese, ended up being Australia's largest (alleged) Ponzi schemes, all the while costing taxpayers billions of dollars as Collins and Pitt street farmers collected tax deductions for upfront losses on revenue that would never materialise.

This is the story of how a generation of executives, under the apparent supervision of respected non-executive directors, duped millions of Australian investors, analysts and commentators.

From the carnage comes some valuable lessons. While the likes of Allco and MFS were complex, arcane entities, their financial statements gave warnings to investors to stay well away. But they were signals that were missed or ignored by almost all investors and analysts. At the same time, the business elite, the men and women who occupy the blue-chip boardrooms of corporate Australia, did little or nothing to rein in executives. On many occasions, non-executive directors were unwilling or unable to stand up to executives who enriched themselves while their companies burned.

This book is not merely a tale of greed, but of the clues that can be gleaned — important evidence that all investors who manage their own wealth should always be on the lookout for before trusting their retirement savings to the care of highly paid executives and boards of directors.

Pigs at the Trough will show you how to spot the next corporate car crash—and hopefully how to avoid becoming the next casualty. Santayana once noted that *those who forget history are doomed to repeat it.* Unfortunately for many investors, history is too often forgotten as soon as the next bubble appears.

CHAPTER 1

Telstra

Dialling up a loser

*Once I've developed a strategy, I want everyone to fall
behind it—you either catch the vision or catch the bus.*
Sol Trujillo, prior to his appointment as CEO of Telstra in 2005[1]

THERE HAVE been few more polarising figures in Australian
corporate history than former Telstra chief executive Solomon
Trujillo. He brought an American style of leadership to what was
once Australia's largest company. Despite being paid like a king,
Trujillo is widely believed to have left Telstra in a far worse state than
when he arrived four years earlier.

For critics of Telstra, the Trujillo experiment represented an
extreme case of a board of directors, appointed by shareholders to
represent their interests and reduce agency costs, utterly failing. As
business commentator Ian Verrender observed, 'between them, Trujillo
and [Donald] McGauchie in the past five years have infuriated and
alienated almost everyone who has come into contact with them;

federal politicians on both sides of the house, regulators, customers, even their own shareholders'.[2]

BS: BEFORE SOL (1992–2005)

Telstra under Trujillo was a long way from the government-owned monopoly that had been in existence for the best part of a century. Australia's pre-eminent telecommunications company grew out of the ashes of Telecom, the formerly government-owned phone carrier that was established in 1901 when the Postmaster-General's Department was created to run domestic telephone, telegraph and postal services. In 1992, Telecom merged with the government-owned Overseas Telecommunications Corporation, and the following year the company was renamed Telstra.[3]

Telstra was partially privatised in 1997 when the Howard government sold off one-third of the company as part of the global shift towards private ownership of assets.* At the same time as Telstra was being sold, the federal government opened the Australian telecommunications sector to full competition. (Telstra's full monopoly over telecommunications was gradually eroded from 1991 when competition began in the long-distance and international markets.)

From 1992, Telstra was led by American former AT&T executive Frank Blount. In 1996, shortly before Telstra was partially privatised, it earned $3.2 billion in profits and paid its American CEO $1.2 million in salary and bonuses. A decade later, Telstra managed to improve earnings by 59 per cent (to $5.1 billion) but saw executive remuneration skyrocket. In fact, over that time Telstra increased the amount it paid its senior management by more than 1000 per cent. (The Telstra directors did not fare too poorly either in the financial stakes. While former Telstra chairman David Hoare was paid $124495 in 1999 for his services, in 2008 outgoing chairman Donald McGauchie collected $602500 — an increase of 385 per cent in less than a decade. Similarly, Telstra director John Stocker witnessed his director's fees increase from $53500 in 1999 to $277370 in 2008.)

By late 1999 the federal government sold off a second tranche of Telstra (reducing the Commonwealth's stake to 51.3 per cent), with

---

* While private ownership has long been dominant in the United States, it was only in the early 1990s that Australian governments (both federal and state) undertook wholesale privatisations of publicly held assets.

the company then under the guidance of former Optus CEO Ziggy Switkowski, who had become CEO in March 1999.

The Switkowski era was highlighted by the internet boom which enveloped the IT and telecommunications sectors. Under Switkowski (and key lieutenant and former lawyer Ted Pretty), Telstra embarked on various failed endeavours, including the Reach joint venture with Pacific Century Cyberworks (which would culminate in a $1 billion write-down four years later). Telstra also acquired cornerstone stakes in local IT companies—including Sausage Software, Solution 6 and Keycorp—as well as overseas joint ventures such as Dutch satellite operator Xantic and New Zealand data services company Telstra Saturn. The vast majority of these ventures would prove to be financial blunders (Telstra had planned to merge Solution and Sausage, but the deal was scuttled after the share prices of both companies slumped), and would lead to a loss of confidence in Switkowski's leadership.

Switkowski's other problem was that, politically, he had lost his power base in the Telstra boardroom after former chairman Bob Mansfield was forced from his role in April 2004. (Mansfield, who had been with Switkowski at Optus, was a long-time supporter.)

By December 2004, the Telstra board had had enough. Led by a new chairman, former Farmers' Federation boss Donald McGauchie, Telstra terminated Switkowski two years before his contract was due to end.* While Telstra never outlined why Switkowski was sacked, many believe that the board lost faith in his ability to grow Telstra's revenues or facilitate the controversial sale of the government's remaining 51 per cent stake in the carrier. For that, they would need a showman.

Shortly after firing Switkowski, McGauchie publicly praised the former executive, stating that he had 'developed an outstanding executive team and Telstra is now well positioned as a competitive, full-service, integrated telecommunications company that is committed to delivering for its shareholders and the nation'.[4] McGauchie's comments would have surprised many of those outstanding Telstra executives, who were soon forced out of their roles.

---

* McGauchie had been appointed chairman of Telstra months earlier. McGauchie, a former Geelong Grammar student and head of the National Farmers' Federation, had minimal senior corporate experience but close links to the Liberal Party and former prime minister John Howard.

Switkowski's replacement would also certainly not deliver the solid returns for Telstra's shareholders that McGauchie foreshadowed.

YOU GOTTA HAVE SOL

At the time of Switkowski's termination, the Telstra board had not put in place any genuine succession plans. Speculation had mounted that the company would appoint an internal replacement, such as former IBM executive David Thodey or Sensis boss Bruce Akhurst. However, McGauchie and the Telstra board shocked onlookers by hiring a locally unknown US executive by the name of Solomon Trujillo. Trujillo almost didn't take the Telstra job, with the former US West boss earlier offered a role as head of Italian mobile communications carrier Wind, which had recently been acquired by an Egyptian telecom group associated with Trujillo.

The decision by Telstra to appoint Solomon Trujillo as CEO brought immediate and widespread publicity, much of it critical of the appointment of a 'Mexican' to the helm of Australia's dominant telecommunications company (Trujillo was actually born in the US state of Wyoming to Hispanic parents). Unlike Switkowski, Trujillo immediately embarked on a confrontational approach with government and regulators.* Trujillo's brash style made him a favourite target for the media. After Trujillo hired former close associates Phil Burgess, Bill Stewart and Greg Winn, commentators began calling the Telstra executive team the 'Three Amigos', a reference to Trujillo's allegedly Hispanic roots.

Even before Trujillo officially commenced his executive duties, he was described as possessing 'American brashness, even arrogance'.[5] While his self-confidence would allow Trujillo to negotiate one of the richest contracts paid to an executive in Australia, it is often forgotten that he was a very wealthy man before he set foot in the Telstra boardroom.

Trujillo had begun his career in the US telecommunications industry in 1974. At the age of 32, he was appointed an officer of

---

* Trujillo had previously been accused of maintaining anti-competitive activities at his former employer US West, which had allegedly kept a stranglehold on its own lines and local loop services to prevent them being accessed by several newer, smaller competitors, landing the company in court over alleged anti-trust breaches and monopoly activities.

US telco AT&T, before becoming CEO and president of US West in 1995. (US West was one of the seven 'Baby Bells' formed after the break up of AT&T in 1983.) Trujillo would later be appointed CEO and chairman of US West in 1998, before departing after the company controversially merged with Qwest in 2000.*

While Trujillo's Telstra biography hailed his time at US West, noting that 'innovation was the by-word for the company amongst its 30 million customers'[6], that view was not shared by US West's customers. US West faced legal action from AT&T, which had accused the company of starving its traditional telephone business while expanding its data and internet business. Allegations included claims that US West had failed to follow through on promises to connect services and neglected to develop facilities to handle new network traffic. US West also faced a 'slew of customer complaints' due to substandard levels of customer service.[7] Shortly after Qwest took over US West, it was forced to pay US$50 million to settle a class action resulting from poor services provided by US West. The company's shoddy customer service earned it the nickname 'US Worst'. (Perhaps coincidentally, Telstra customers also fared badly during Trujillo's reign. According to a report prepared by the Telecommunications Ombudsman, over Trujillo's four-year tenure complaints against Telstra increased by 241 per cent.[8] Many of the grievances related to Telstra's billing systems, a key area of focus for Trujillo.)

Not only was US West criticised for its levels of customer service, it was also maligned for anti-competitive behaviour (the company faced several lawsuits from the state of Oregon) and its share price performance left much to be desired. Shortly after Trujillo departed, the company's share price slumped from US$69 to less than US$11 per share. (Trujillo shrewdly sold a large amount of stock at US$89 per share prior to US West's merger with Qwest, reaping more than US$30 million.[9])

Controversially, only one day before Qwest took over US West, Qwest agreed to pay Trujillo what was a very golden goodbye. While never revealed directly to Qwest shareholders (the package was discovered accidentally after a lawyer for the US West retirees stumbled across court documents and released them to a Colorado

---

* Before being acquired by Qwest, US West had been endeavouring to merge with Global Crossing.

5

newspaper), Trujillo received a termination payment of more than US$72 million, largely in consideration for ending his contract but also as part of a deal by which Trujillo agreed to not make 'disparaging comments' about US West or its employees.

Trujillo also felt it necessary to clean out his office. Quite literally.

According to his termination agreement, the former CEO took with him the 'computer, monitor docking station, printer, fax machine, scanner, pager, wireless telephone, palm pilot [and] accessories'.[10]

Included in the golden goodbye was a US$36.9 million 'change-in-control' payment (ironically, the actual change in control that eventuated was orchestrated by Trujillo), US$13.7 million in pensions, US$10 million for signing the employment agreement and US$2 million for office space and administrative support. In addition, Trujillo also received perks such as country club memberships (worth more than US$900 000) and limousine services valued at more than US$320 000, indicating that Sol's driving abilities appear even less developed than his managerial skills. To ensure that he remained up to date with world affairs, Trujillo also demanded that US West continue to pay for his subscription to *The Denver Post*—at a cost of US$65 per year.

Even more controversial than the extraordinary amount of cash collected by Trujillo was the non-payment of a final dividend to US West shareholders; well, almost all US West shareholders.

Prior to its merger with Qwest, the US West board had determined to pay a dividend of US$270 million. Qwest later sought to have the dividend withheld (because the payment would effectively have been made by Qwest as the new owner of US West).

The US West board initially refused to withdraw the dividend, but shortly after it agreed to alter the 'record date' for the merger from 10 July 2000 to 30 June 2000—this had the practical effect of allowing Qwest itself to simply not pay the dividend.

While there may be no link between the two events, Trujillo's exceedingly generous severance package (which also was effectively paid by Qwest) was determined at around the same time as US West agreed to alter the record date of the merger.

While US West shareholders missed out on the dividend payment, their CEO was luckier. Trujillo's termination agreement revealed that he had secretly agreed with the company to receive a cash payment that equalled the value of the dividend not being paid to other shareholders. Known as a 'dividend equivalent payment', Trujillo's termination agreement provided for a US$1.5 million cash payment to compensate him.

In addition to cash payments, Trujillo also received three years of corporate jet travel (valued at US$5.5 million) and, somewhat amusingly, financial counselling (valued at US$10000) and 'career guidance'. Sadly for Telstra shareholders, it appears that the financial counselling did not lead to fiscal prudence at his new employer.

While Trujillo spent more than 26 years at US West, his termination payment appeared excessive given he had only served as CEO for less than four years.

Lesson #1: CEOs never change their spots

If a company hires an executive who has a reputation for self-enrichment at a previous company, don't expect that to change. An executive who is especially concerned about his or her own wellbeing is less likely to be concerned about the wellbeing of the company.

Investors should look closely at the work experience of executives. Before buying shares in a company, consider: if this were my private business, would I hire that person? If the answer is 'no', then you shouldn't be owning those shares.

It appeared that Trujillo's abrupt departure from US West was not only spurred by a generous severance package but by a personality clash with Qwest CEO Joseph Nacchio.* Trujillo was offered the co-chairman's role at the merged company, but rejected the job, instead opting to take the US$72 million termination package.

After departing US West, Trujillo was appointed CEO of technology company Graviton. With links to the CIA, Graviton had developed wireless technology and espionage applications. Not long after Trujillo quit as CEO in 2003, the company collapsed.

---

* Nacchio is currently in prison in the United States after being found guilty on 19 counts of insider trading. Nacchio was sentenced to six years' incarceration in 2007 and was forced to pay more than US$71 million in fines and restitution, after being convicted of selling more than US$100 million of Qwest stock while publicly forecasting strong growth.

Critics accused Trujillo of creating a 'top-heavy structure' involving numerous well-paid executives. Under Trujillo's leadership, Graviton burned more than US$66 million of capital funding before sliding into bankruptcy.[11]

Not long after his departure from Graviton, Trujillo accepted the role of CEO of UK-based Orange (he had joined the Orange board two years before). Trujillo's reign at Orange was equally brief. After only 13 months, he fell out with Orange's parent company France Telecom, ending his tenure as CEO. During Trujillo's short time at Orange, the company invested US$550 million to form the TA Orange joint venture with the Chearavanont family. Six years later Orange wrote off its entire interest in the venture.[12]

Despite his tumultuous business past, the Telstra board, led by McGauchie, embraced Trujillo, so much so that his contract provided for remuneration far exceeding his predecessors. Trujillo's employment agreement with Telstra promised him extraordinary riches for success and handsome compensation for failure. Trujillo received a 'sign-on' bonus of $1 million, plus a further sign-on incentive of $1.5 million. Trujillo would then receive a fixed salary of $3 million each year, regardless of how Telstra performed. Trujillo would also be able to receive upwards of $7 million annually in bonuses, much of which was at the discretion of the Telstra board. Trujillo's fixed salary alone was larger than the total remuneration paid to former executives Ziggy Switkowski and Frank Blount.

Even more unusual was the Telstra board's decision to pre-pay Trujillo 50 per cent of his 2006 'short-term incentive payment'. Onlookers could be forgiven for wondering how a payment could be deemed a 'bonus' when it is paid before any work is actually performed.

JOBS FOR THE AMIGOS (2005)

Less than two months after being appointed CEO of Telstra, Trujillo moved quickly to install long-time colleagues Phil Burgess, Bill Stewart and Greg Winn into senior roles at Telstra.

Winn had previously been Trujillo's chief operating officer at US West and also at failed technology company Graviton, while Burgess was the corporate affairs head at US West. (In October 2005,

Trujillo brought in another former associate, Jovan Barac, who worked with Trujillo at Orange, to head customer relations management at Telstra.) Burgess managed to create a furore only months after his appointment when he told the media that 'he would not recommend Telstra shares to his mother'.[13] Unsurprisingly, the comments did little to bolster Telstra's ailing share price.

Trujillo's next move was to bring in highly paid outside consultants from Bain and Accenture to undertake 'a comprehensive multi-year plan for the most rapid and dramatic ever transformation of a telecommunications company worldwide'. For Telstra shareholders, the consultancy certainly did not come cheaply. The transformation plan cost Telstra more than $54 million, a very high sum given the short time taken to prepare it. Telstra ended up paying its consultants approximately $45 000 per consultant per day. (As a comparison, other leading consultancy firms charge clients an average rate of around $10 000 per day.)

Lesson #2: Beware the helpers

Keep a close eye on how much a company pays its advisers such as investment banks and consultants. If fees are high, investors should ask: what exactly are management doing? Also, keep in mind that advisers are not responsible to shareholders like employees are (although they will be concerned about their reputation).

Bain and Accenture weren't the only winners from Telstra's largesse. As a result of simply producing a transformation plan, Trujillo was eligible to receive a $1.5 million bonus payment. (Trujillo would not be required to refund the 'bonus' even if the plan turned out to be a total failure.[14])

Telstra chairman Donald McGauchie claimed that 'Mr Trujillo's incentive payment for 2005–06 recognised that he led a detailed review of the company's problems, developed a comprehensive multi-year plan for the most rapid and dramatic ever transformation of a telecommunications company worldwide, assembled the resources including executive talent to execute the plan and achieved major milestones in the first year'.[15] Others noted that Trujillo's $1.5 million bonus appeared to be earned by virtue of his hiring of expensive consultants, but little else.

The decision to hire Bain, rather than one of the many Australian-based consultancy firms, would also surprise many. Because it was not based in Australia, Bain was forced to transfer staff from Singapore and the United States, accumulating considerable business class and five-star accommodation costs. Meanwhile, existing Telstra executives were sidelined from the planning process. Andrew Klein, a leading Bain partner, had previously worked with Trujillo at Orange.

Telstra under Trujillo was not only happy to lavish monies on consultants — senior executives also benefited. Only a month before Trujillo unveiled a plan to cut 12 000 Telstra workers, senior managers were treated to a $1.3 million junket to the exclusive Lindeman Island in the Whitsundays. Trujillo and his wife attended the $3500 per head getaway.[16] The retreat was provided as a performance reward for senior executives. Shareholders may have wondered exactly why Telstra management deserved rewarding, given the company's share price had slumped by 25 per cent in the past seven months.

When not hiring expensive consultants or running junkets, Trujillo's Telstra also fell foul of the corporate regulators after the company was accused of secretly briefing the federal government about its financial woes in August 2005, but forgetting to tell share-holders. In fact, Telstra did not issue a relevant profit warning to minority shareholders until the following month, leading to an investigation and public rebuke from the Australian Securities & Investments Commission (ASIC).

Trujillo's arrival at Telstra continued a marked downward spiral in the company's share price. At the height of the internet boom, Telstra shares had peaked at $9.16, before slumping to $3.92 in February 2003. By the time Trujillo was appointed, Telstra's defensive nature had led to its shares recovering to $5.06. Despite continuing to pay strong dividends from its billions of dollars of free cash flow, Telstra's share price slumped to $3.62 in June 2006, after Trujillo had been in the job for one year — a loss of almost 30 per cent. The company's share price woes partially emanated from its hostile approach to Australian regulators, specifically the Australian Competition and Consumer Commission (ACCC) and federal government.

Criticism also continued to mount regarding Trujillo's dealings with former associates. In May 2006, a leaked memo tabled at a Senate Estimates Hearing detailed a 10-year history of overcharging and underperforming on its obligations by French communications company Alcatel.[17] Despite the serious allegations, Telstra awarded Alcatel a $3.4 billion contract shortly after Trujillo's appointment, bypassing the company's usual procurement channels. Trujillo had been on the Chairman's Council at Alcatel from 2000 until commencing with Telstra. A former Telstra senior executive, Bill Felix, publicly questioned Alcatel's performance shortly after leaving the company.

The Alcatel contract was not the only instance of Telstra monies ending up in the hands of Trujillo's former associates. In another decision made shortly after Trujillo became CEO, the company awarded a $30 million annual contract to purchase more than two million mobile phones from a company called Brightstar—without any sort of formal tender process.[18] At the time Brightstar was handed the contract, it had not developed an implementation plan for Telstra. The deal was strongly criticised, with one Brightstar rival claiming that the process was 'a joke', noting that the prices paid by Telstra were more than 'three times the market going price'.[19]

One possible explanation for the Brightstar deal was that Trujillo and Brightstar's majority owner Marcelo Claure were former associates and allegedly long-time friends.[20] In July 2005 (around the same time Trujillo started work at Telstra), Trujillo, his long-time lieutenant Greg Winn, Claure and another associate pooled US$4.5 million to invest in Chinese telecommunications group Silk Road Telecommunications. Telstra denied that Trujillo and Winn were ever in partnership with Claure, claiming that there was no conflict of interest and that negotiations between the companies commenced in December 2004, prior to Trujillo's appointment.

However, Telstra's claims appear further contradicted by the subsequent revelation that Brightstar made a six-month US$5 million deposit with Los Angeles–based bank Proamerica in 2008. According to documents witnessed by *The Australian* newspaper, the loan required Proamerica to pay interest at a rate of only 2.25 per cent, well below the prevailing rate of around 8 per cent.[21] Undisclosed to Telstra shareholders was the fact that Sol Trujillo was also a board member of Proamerica. That Telstra appeared to be Brightstar's only Australian customer also did little to dispel suspicions of the contract being the 'back-door deal' alleged by Brightstar's competitors.

SOL CASHES IN (2006)

Apart from hiring expensive consultants and handing contracts to close associates, Trujillo was certainly digging in his heals with regards to his own remuneration. This was despite already being rich, courtesy of the US$72 million termination payment from US West shareholders

Telstra's remuneration structure changed markedly in 2006 after the company received advice from external remuneration consultants and management. (Remuneration consultants tend to have a highly inflationary impact on executive remuneration, which inspired legendary investor Warren Buffett to once dub them Ratchet, Ratchet & Bingo.) Telstra's new remuneration structure centred on the company's transformation plan, with the company's remuneration report noting that it had repositioned executive remuneration 'to drive the delivery of the transformation milestones that have been outlined in Telstra's business strategy. Over the next 3–5 years, the remuneration strategy will be based on performance measures that are strongly aligned to those transformation outcomes as well as on other traditional business measures'.

The change meant that qualitative metrics, such as 'individual accountabilities' and 'network transformation', would drive executive pay, rather than relying exclusively on more commonly used and transparent metrics, such as total shareholder return or earnings per share.

Therefore, despite Telstra's share price slumping by almost 30 per cent and its earnings dropping by 26 per cent in 2006, Trujillo was paid a short-term bonus of $2.58 million—86 per cent of the maximum bonus for which he was eligible. (Trujillo mysteriously did far better than fellow executives, with the average short-term bonus payment to Telstra management being 73.8 per cent.) Overall, the altered short-term incentive benchmarks appeared to benefit Telstra top brass. In 2005, senior managers received only 54.6 per cent of their potential short-term bonuses (2004: 31.4 per cent). In addition,

Telstra paid all 2006 short-term bonuses in cash, rather than Telstra shares, contradicting claims that the company was seeking to closely align executives and shareholders.

The increase in bonus payments is possibly explained by the bizarre metrics adopted by the Telstra board. Specifically, the bonuses were dependent on:

- *EBITDA (earnings before interest, tax, depreciation and amortisation):* this is a reasonable measure (albeit easily manipulated by executives). However, in 2006 Telstra's EBITDA actually decreased by 8 per cent, certainly not vindicating a substantial increase in short-term bonuses.

- *Cost reduction:* a noble aim, but arguably this is what executives such Trujillo are paid a fixed remuneration to achieve (in Trujillo's case, $3 million). In addition, reducing costs (such as slashing research and development or capital expenditure) can lead to a short-term profit kick, but will often be detrimental to long-term value creation.

- *The number of sites that are 3G equipped and receiving transmission:* Telstra shareholders have good reason to question why a telecommunications company would pay telecommunications executives short-term bonuses for simply setting up a phone network. This would appear similar to Burger King paying its CEO a bonus because its burger flippers didn't burn the meat.

- *Broadband market share:* another metric which may lead to detrimental results for shareholders. A preferred measure could have been 'broadband profitability'. Basing a bonus on a 'market share' benchmark may encourage executives to chase top-line revenue growth at the expense of the company's profitability. This would allow bonuses to be paid despite shareholder returns suffering. In this regard, during 2006 Telstra managed to increase the number of its broadband subscribers by 66 per cent, but suffered a decrease in revenue-per-subscriber of 13 per cent.

- *Individual accountabilities:* this appears to have been a completely illusory measure that justified the Telstra board paying substantial short-term bonuses to executives when financial metrics provided a different impression.

However, it was not Telstra's generous short-term cash bonuses that most raised the ire of shareholders, but rather its failure to properly disclose the hurdles attaching to long-term incentives payable to senior executives.

Spurred by criticism from proxy adviser Institutional Shareholder Services, a majority of non-government Telstra shareholders voted against the remuneration report. Had the government not voted its 51.8 per cent stake in favour of the resolution, the non-binding report would have been defeated.

The structure and lack of disclosure regarding Trujillo's long-term incentives led to a near revolt. Long-term incentives are usually paid to executives in the form of share options or the more nefarious performance rights (which are similar to options, but do not contain an 'exercise price', allowing executives to receive free shares if certain performance hurdles are satisfied without any share price appreciation). Not only did Trujillo receive a substantial amount of cash remuneration, he was handed 836 821 performance rights (valued by the company at $2.48 million). While Telstra outlined six different performance measures underlying the exercise of performance rights, it refused to provide any details pertaining to the 'total shareholder return' necessary for the rights to vest. (Telstra provided information to shareholders pertaining to other hurdles such as 'revenue growth' and 'operating expense'. However, those benchmarks have minimal correlation with shareholder return.)

When asked to provide disclosure of the total shareholder return benchmark, Charles Macek, the head of Telstra's remuneration committee, claimed that the company was unable to disclose such information as it was commercial-in-confidence, and would amount to the company commenting on its share price. Macek's reasoning appeared somewhat strange given that share price information is publicly known and virtually all companies provide details of total shareholder return hurdles.

Telstra revealed simply that the total shareholder return hurdle 'is a concrete number, it is reviewed by the board and it would only be paid in the event of gains that would make our shareholders very pleased'.[22]

Not only were the hurdles not explained to shareholders, but the terms of Trujillo's performance rights were far more favourable than for other executives. Telstra executives other than Sol received half of their performance rights if they achieved the 'minimum' levels of performance against the defined hurdles. Trujillo, however, would receive 75 per cent of his long-term bonus for such 'minimum' levels. Trujillo's vesting provisions were far less onerous than most long-term incentives provided to Australian executives.

Lesson #3: Beware the cult of the 'celebrity CEO'

Celebrity CEOs—such as General Electric's Jack Welch, Sunbeam's Al 'Chainsaw' Dunlap or even ABC's Eddy Groves—have a history of promising much but delivering little. Boards unfortunately fall in love with their celebrity CEOs, leading to substantially higher remuneration than other, less feted executives. When a CEO becomes more well known than the company he or she runs, investors should think carefully about whether the company's market price is based on expected future cash flows or overly optimistic expectations.

The best CEOs are more concerned about building shareholder returns than their own reputation.

In addition, Trujillo's long-term incentives were subject to an unusual 'change-in-control' provision. The clause allowed for Trujillo's options or performance rights to immediately vest if control of the company changed. In most cases, for a change-in-control provision to be triggered at least 50.1 per cent of a company's shares would need to change hands. In Trujillo's case, the Telstra board allowed for his performance rights to vest if a party gained control of only 15 per cent of Telstra.

This was either a monumental oversight by the Telstra board or a clear gift to Trujillo—largely because the federal government's Future Fund owned 16.5 per cent of Telstra.* Should the Future Fund ever sell its Telstra stake (which at the time was a reasonable possibility), Trujillo's performance rights would have vested in full

---

* The Future Fund was established in 2006 with the proceeds of the government's sale of 51.1 per cent of Telstra as part of the T3 process. In 2007, the federal government transferred its remaining 16.5 per cent stake in Telstra into the fund. The purpose of the fund is to meet potential superannuation liabilities to retired Australian public servants.

despite there being no actual change in control of the company. That Telstra, with a non-permanent 16.5 per cent holder, would set such a low threshold represented an appalling error of judgement.

The change-in-control provision was so poorly constructed that even if the Future Fund later sold its interest after losing faith in Trujillo's managerial abilities, that sale would have allowed Trujillo to cash in his long-term incentives, in spite of his performance.

Lesson #4: Read the fine print

Investors should carefully read the terms of options and other rights granted to executives. Hurdles should relate to long-term performance. If equity incentives are able to vest based on events that are outside the power of the executives (such as a change-in-control provision), those executives are not really incentivised to build long-term wealth for shareholders.

Unlike most other companies, Telstra shareholders were also never given an opportunity to approve of the terms of the performance rights granted to Trujillo and other senior executives. This was because Telstra did not issue new shares to executives as part of the long-term incentive scheme, but rather it purchased the underlying shares 'on market' (this was also the result of provisions in the *Telstra Corporation Act 1991* which prevented the company from issuing new shares). Due to an Australian Securities Exchange (ASX) Listing Rule loophole, companies are not required to seek approval for equity grants made to directors if the underlying shares are purchased on market, rather than newly issued shares.

Members of Telstra's remuneration committee which structured Telstra's remuneration scheme included McGauchie, Macek (who once claimed to have 'written the book on corporate governance' and also served as a director of Wesfarmers), John Ralph and John Fletcher. Fletcher, himself a CEO of Coles Myer, would have found himself in a difficult position when arguing the merits of lower executive remuneration. (Fletcher was, however, a relative pauper compared with Trujillo, receiving only $4.5 million in fixed and incentive remuneration from Coles Myer in 2006.)

Defending Trujillo's lofty remuneration, McGauchie stated: 'I vigorously reject any suggestion that Telstra's achievements are not substantial or that the board had not explained the basis of incentives paid to Mr Trujillo'.[23]

On both accounts, it appears that McGauchie's claims were not backed by evidence. Telstra's first year under Trujillo saw earnings drop by more than 26 per cent to $3.2 billion, largely due to costs associated with Trujillo's transformation plan. During 2006, Telstra's credit rating was downgraded by Standard & Poor's and Moody's, increasing the company's cost of capital. Most importantly, the company lost around $16 billion in market value.

Despite all that, Trujillo collected $7.3 million cash, compared with his predecessor Ziggy Switkowski, who was paid cash remuneration of $3.8 million the previous year.

TALKING DOWN HIS BOOK

During the 2006–07 financial year, the Telstra board changed tack and decided to grant Trujillo options, rather than any additional performance rights.*

In 2006, the Telstra board determined to make an almighty grant of options to Trujillo—10.3 million for fiscal 2007, followed by a further 5.2 million options in 2008 and 2009. According to the terms of the options, the exercise price would be determined during the five days prior to the date of the options grant.

In the case of the first grant, the exercise price would therefore be determined based on Telstra's share price in August 2006, not long

---

* A share option gives the holder the right, but not the obligation, to acquire the underlying instrument (which in this instance was ordinary Telstra shares). Options are considered preferable from a shareholders' perspective to performance rights because they have an additional 'exercise price' hurdle; that is, the holder needs to pay an exercise (or strike) price before being able to collect the underlying shares. (Performance rights are commonly referred to as ZEPOs—zero price options.)
   Most companies will require the exercise price to be at a premium to the prevailing share price —that way, for the executive to be able to exercise the option profitably, the underlying share price needs to increase. This provides a degree of alignment between executives and shareholders. (The alignment is not perfect because options allow executives to benefit from any appreciation in the share price, but not suffer any direct loss should the share price drop. In that case, the option itself becomes worthless, but the executive suffers no loss of capital.)
   The value of the options granted will therefore be highly dependent on the exercise price (which determines the 'intrinsic value' of the option). A lower exercise price will mean that an option will be 'in-the-money' at a lower underlying share price. The recipient of an option will therefore prefer a lower exercise price and will have a vested interest in minimising the underlying share price when the exercise price is being calculated. This creates a clear conflict: shareholders would prefer a higher share price (and resultant higher exercise price), whereas executives benefit from a lower exercise price.

after it announced its 2005–06 financial results. Only days before the results were released, Trujillo disappointed investors by announcing that the company would not proceed with the development of new broadband infrastructure following a dispute with the ACCC. The move cast doubt upon the company's full privatisation. Later, at an investor briefing on 10 August, the day Telstra announced its financial results, Trujillo added further doubts about the company's hostile regulatory environment.

Following its results and Trujillo's comments, Telstra's share price dropped to $3.60 per share, down from $3.94 earlier in August. The fall had the direct result of lowering the exercise price to be determined on Trujillo's options. (In response to criticism that Trujillo 'talked down' Telstra's prospects, remuneration committee boss Charles Macek claimed that Trujillo was simply giving an honest appraisal of the company's prospects and other analysts had low price targets on the company.[24])

It was perhaps another coincidence when on 9 August 2007 (shortly before Trujillo's second batch of options were being priced) Telstra's chief executive once again provided a negative outlook for the company, hinting that investors should not get excited about its future earnings. Following Trujillo's comments, Telstra's share price slumped by 4 per cent.

Not only was the hurdle for executives' options calculated from a low point in Telstra's share price, Trujillo's long-term options weren't really very long term. In fact, all going well, the first tranche would be able to vest as soon as 30 June 2008 — less than two years from their grant. Investors prefer long-term bonus payments be deferred for at least three years. This is to ensure executives are creating long-term wealth for shareholders, rather than indulging in short-term, extreme capitalist behaviour.

Further, Trujillo's options were not subject to an EBITDA hurdle (unlike the options granted to other Telstra executives). This cast additional doubt over the motives of the Telstra board. Trujillo's final contract, which included the terms of his options, was not signed until 9 August 2007 — after Telstra had finalised its 2006–07 financial results. Therefore, when Telstra agreed to remove the EBITDA hurdle, both the company and Trujillo would have been aware that the hurdle would not have been satisfied in 2007.

THE TELSTRA SHAREHOLDERS ARE REVOLTING (2006–07)

It appeared that the Telstra board (particularly its remuneration committee) were slow learners. Telstra announced a slight increase in profit for 2006–07 (up 2.9 per cent to $3.2 billion) due to improved mobile and broadband sales offsetting falling income from its fixed, copper-line network. During the year, Telstra's share price performed well after the government's successful sale of most of its stake in the company (with the remaining 16.5 per cent being parked in the Future Fund). Telstra also benefited from a global re-rating of telecommunications stocks in the second half of 2006.

However, the share price remained well below the internet boom highs and also below the level from when Trujillo was appointed in July 2005. Tepid shareholder returns did not, however, put any sort of dampener on Trujillo's remuneration, which skyrocketed in 2007 to $11.8 million — more than four times the pay received by Trujillo's predecessor only three years earlier. (When questioned on Trujillo's lofty pay packet, chairman Donald McGauchie glibly pronounced, 'I don't like paying US$75 a barrel for oil, but it's a market'.[25])

Again, Trujillo fared better than other Telstra executives, collecting 88.6 per cent of his possible short-term bonus (the average short-term incentive reward was 78.3 per cent). In total, Trujillo received a short-term bonus of $5.3 million (of which half was paid in cash, and the reminder in Telstra shares).

In its remuneration report in 2007, Telstra claimed that 'during fiscal 2007 the Board undertook an extensive review of the remuneration arrangements for the CEO. The revised remuneration arrangements reflect the importance of the transformation required at Telstra and of the competitive domestic and global CEO market. The new arrangements further reinforce the principle of linking significant proportions of the CEO's reward to company performance'.

While Telstra claimed its new remuneration structure better aligned executives with shareholders, it appears that the changes were designed to line Trujillo's hip pocket, rather than create any close link between remuneration and company performance. (Unsurprisingly, Telstra utilised the services of three remuneration consultants in devising the new remuneration structure. As Warren Buffett once noted, 'there are two classes of clients [that remuneration consultants] don't want to offend—actual and potential'.)

A major change to the structure of the short-term bonus payment calculation was the removal of the 'expense control' hurdle. In 2006, short-term bonuses were partly dependent on operating expenses increasing by less than 2.2 per cent per year. In 2007, the hurdle was changed to an EBITDA benchmark. While the expense hurdle itself was a strange metric, it is noted that between 2005 and 2007 Telstra's expenses increased by around 9 per cent annually, meaning it is almost certain that this hurdle would not have been satisfied.

Not only were the terms of Trujillo's bonus altered to his benefit, but the size of the bonus was also significantly inflated. While his fixed pay remained steady, Trujillo was eligible to receive far higher bonus payments in 2007. In 2006, Trujillo's fixed pay was 30 per cent of his maximum remuneration—in 2007 Sol's fixed pay was only 14 per cent of his total salary. This in itself is not a negative, as shareholders tend to favour executives' salaries being closely linked to performance. However, in Telstra's case, the company didn't reduce Trujillo's fixed remuneration at all (which remained at $3 million per year)—rather, it simply gave him the opportunity to receive a far higher short-term bonus of $6 million, compared with $3 million the previous year. The claim by McGauchie that 'executives will only benefit if our shareholders prosper' appeared to be very wishful thinking.[26]

Meanwhile, internal rumblings circulated regarding Trujillo's managerial ability. Leaks spread regarding Trujillo's incessant travel, with one Telstra insider noting 'he's never here [and] when he is, he often does all-nighters and demands staff do too, then he's off again, jetting around the world first-class'.[27]

In addition to increasing the scale of bonus payments, Telstra also refused to reveal the benchmarks which applied to the 10.3 million options granted to Trujillo other than the total shareholder return hurdle (strangely, Telstra revealed all but the total shareholder return hurdle in 2006).

The burgeoning remuneration paid to Telstra executives coupled with poor disclosure of hurdles relating to options, short vesting periods for 'long-term' incentives and the low exercise price for Sol's options led to a maelstrom of investor fury. Without being able to rely on the government's 51 per cent stake (the T3 sale resulted in the government's interest being largely sold to the public months earlier), the Telstra board faced the rare humiliation of having its (non-binding) remuneration report voted down by shareholders. In total, more than 66 per cent of Telstra shareholders voted against the resolution, a near record for an Australian company in what was dubbed by one commentator as 'one of the most embarrassing blows in recent corporate history'.[28]

Telstra's leading shareholder, the Future Fund, voted its 16.5 per cent stake against the resolution. The Future Fund chairman, former Commonwealth Bank CEO David Murray, noted that 'a critical principle in remuneration is that there is clear alignment between long-term equity-based executive reward and returns to share-holders...We believe this principle is not sufficiently evident in the Telstra arrangements'.[29]

Charles Macek, the man responsible for devising Telstra's remu-neration structure, refused to concede that the Telstra board were at fault. Instead of apologising to shareholders, Macek attacked proxy advisory houses (who provide advice to institutions regarding issues of corporate governance). Macek claimed that 'we have to recognise that the people who are advising institutions, the proxy groups, have no expertise whatsoever'. It is not without irony that, less than one year later, Macek was appointed by CGI Glass Lewis—one of the proxy advisory houses that only a short time earlier had 'no expertise whatsoever'—as the sole Australian representative on its Research Advisory Council.

Notwithstanding the near record repudiation by shareholders of the board's remuneration policies, Macek stated that the company would not be making wholesale changes to how it pays its executives, claiming 'you can't renege on a contract, otherwise you have serious litigation and significant loss of shareholder value'.[30] Macek made no reference to the fact that Trujillo's contract was determined after Telstra had prepared its financial statements, and his EBITDA bonus hurdle appeared to be tailored to ensure that Trujillo received the maximum possible remuneration.

The landslide rejection of Telstra's remuneration practices cer-tainly did not make Trujillo any less wealthy. In fact, the following year Trujillo walked away with even more money, despite shareholder returns continuing to stagnate.

THE LUCRE CONTINUES TO FLOW (2007)

While the rejection of Telstra's 2007 remuneration report marked a low point in board–shareholder relations, Telstra's remuneration committee did not temper the flood of money finding its way into Trujillo's obviously rather large pockets.

In early 2008, it appeared that Trujillo's transformation plan was on track. Mobile and broadband revenues grew strongly, outstripping the loss of earnings from slowing fixed-line sales. Telstra was also continuing to reduce headcount, incurring a sharp increase in redundancy costs (it appears that at Telstra, labour expense was to be reduced at all costs—except where that labour charge is being directed towards senior management). In total, for the 2008 financial year Telstra managed to increase earnings by 13.5 per cent and deliver a $3.7 billion profit (the profit was, however, still less than the $4.7 billion returned by former Telstra boss Switkowski in 2004).

Telstra's operating performance, however, again failed to keep up with Sol Trujillo's remuneration. During 2008, Sol's pay rose once more, with the Telstra boss collecting his usual $3 million in fixed salary, along with a $5.1 million short-term bonus (86 per cent of the maximum achievable), half of which was paid in cash.

If you're wondering why Trujillo consistently received such a high proportion of his short-term cash bonus (despite Telstra's shareholder returns being poor during his tenure), the answer perhaps lay in how Telstra determined the success of its transformation plan—a key element of Trujillo's short-term bonus. According to the company's annual report:

> [The Telstra] Board reviews the company's audited financial results and…assesses performance against each measure to determine the percentage of STI that is payable. *Transformation measures are tracked by an internal project office and reviewed by the COO and CEO before approval by the Board. (Emphasis added.)*

Cynics may suggest that the internal project office, which answered to senior executives, would tend to take a positive view of the performance of those senior executives.

Trujillo's fixed pay of $3 million was not only one of the highest base salaries in the country, it even exceeded the base pay of his successor David Thodey (whose contract provided for a base salary of $2 million). In its 2008 annual report, Telstra stated that the fixed salary for senior executives depended on the skills and experience of each individual, and also each person's role within the company.

Further, while Telstra's 2008 remuneration report trumpeted that the company's 'remuneration philosophy is designed to attract and retain world-class Board and executive talent...by driving and rewarding executive performance focused on the achievement of the company's strategy and business objectives [by linking] remuneration to the creation of shareholder value', much of Telstra's remuneration was geared towards short-term performance. This was all but confirmed by Charles Macek when he told a newspaper in 2007 that Trujillo and the other executives hired by Telstra from the US, such as the operations chief Greg Winn, 'clearly are not long-term Telstra employees—they are not 10-year employees'.[31]

The problem with remunerating employees with a short-term focus is that short-term cash bonuses and fixed pay do not get refunded should business performance worsen in subsequent years. This is what happened at many investment banks (including the collapsed Bear Sterns and Lehman Brothers) which paid huge short-term bonuses (in cash), but created no mechanism for aligning remuneration with long-term performance. Had the employees received equity that they could not dispose of, their remuneration would have been actually aligned with shareholders. While Telstra's shareholder return outperformed the market by almost 12 per cent during 2008 and the company appeared to be delivering its promised financial performance, within months Telstra's share price would once more slump to record low levels after it botched the National Broadband Network tender process (discussed later).

That Telstra's remuneration structure appeared to be generous in favour of Telstra executives would not be entirely surprising given that the company sought advice from remuneration consultants in structuring the plan. Specifically, Telstra told shareholders in 2008 that 'in developing the remuneration strategy the Remuneration Committee of the Board seeks the assistance of an independent remuneration adviser, Egan & Associates, who provides advice direct to the Committee on market practice, remuneration structure and competitive analysis of the executive market'.

Telstra executives wouldn't have been disappointed by Egan's appointment, given that firm's apparent long-held stance in favour of higher remuneration for executives. In 1999, Egan founder John Egan wrote an article in a leading broadsheet newspaper in which he 'made a plea on behalf of corporate executives, contrasting what he viewed as the public's reluctance to properly reward senior executives whilst being more than happy to shower riches on sports stars and entertainers'.[32]

Not only was Trujillo's remuneration almost double the median pay received by CEOs of similar-sized companies and it contained a short-term cash bias, but it is astonishing that Trujillo had any time to run Telstra, given how long he appeared to spend outside Australia. In 2008, Trujillo found the time to visit Davos (for the World Economic Forum, his ticket paid for by US West), Las Vegas, Barcelona, Phoenix, Nice, Beijing, Macau, Cairo, Paris, Washington and Denver.

The benefit Telstra shareholders received from Trujillo's lavish first-class trips abroad remains to be seen, especially given Telstra earned less than 10 per cent of its revenue outside Australia, and most of that was earned in Asia.[33] (This wasn't the first time Trujillo was missing in action. In 2006, the CEO was overseas during Senate Estimates hearings, requiring middle managers to attend in his place.[34])

Lesson #5: Beware the absentee CEO

CEOs should spend their time where the company generates most of its sales (or where they plan to generate sales in the near future). A CEO who spends most of his or her time overseas or giving speeches is not working for shareholders, but rather for him- or herself. The best example of this was GE's Jack Welch, the man once dubbed 'CEO of the Century' by business magazine *Fortune*. Welch's ability appeared badly overstated. Shortly after he departed General Electric's boardroom, the company's shares commenced a decade-long slump as GE's true predicament was revealed to investors. In his final year as CEO Welch allegedly spent 166 days (out of 252 working days) at speaking engagements, leaving barely a day and a half each week that hadn't already been 'spoken for'.

While the Telstra board continued to pay Trujillo handsomely, it was also secretly trying to save $50 million by transferring employees onto individual performance pay and introducing a productivity blitz for technicians.[35] To avoid potential problems, Telstra management also developed a strike mitigation plan which would be adopted should Telstra employees take industrial action. The plot involved the use of non-union employees and outside contractors. Despite the plans, shareholders would not see enormous overall benefits—the reduction in labour costs was almost entirely absorbed by Telstra's executive team, which was paid $46.3 million in 2008 alone.

WHO DARES WINNS

While Trujillo received much media and public scrutiny for his ever-increasing remuneration, one of Sol's amigos, chief operating officer Greg Winn, was also becoming a very rich man courtesy of Telstra shareholders. Like his boss, Winn certainly had a unique business style. A *Four Corners* report claimed that in a business meeting Winn allegedly told an associate that 'if you can't get people [employees] to go there [meet their targets] and you try...twice...then you just shoot them and get them out of the way'.

In his first year at Telstra as chief operating officer, Winn, a former protégé of Trujillo from US West, received $1.28 million in fixed pay, coupled with a $1.4 million short-term cash bonus and $1.1 million sign-on payment. In total, the American was paid $3.86 million for his first 10 months on the job. (Winn's base salary even exceeded former CEO Ziggy Switkowski's fixed pay for 2004, despite Winn only working for part of the year in a lesser role.)

Like Trujillo, Winn's remuneration leapt substantially during 2006–07, the second year of his two-year contract, with the COO receiving pay of $5.7 million. Due to the short-term nature of his employment agreement, Winn received virtually all his remuneration in cash, including a $3.2 million short-term bonus (88.6 per cent of the maximum possible).

Winn's contract was extended for a further 12 months in August 2007, with the chief operating officer receiving another substantial pay rise to $11.2 million. Winn's remuneration was again virtually all cash and included a $5.7 million payment for the completion of his initial two-year contract. In cash terms, Winn was among the highest paid executives in Australia, out-earning virtually all CEOs in 2008 with the exception of investment bankers from Macquarie and Babcock, and company founders such as Frank Lowy and Rupert Murdoch. Winn's remuneration was all the more remarkable given that, according to Winn himself, his presence was 'not that essential for the [company's IT] transformation'.[36]

For the largesse that flowed his way, Winn's predominant task was to streamline Telstra's IT systems (by reducing the number of networks used by the company from 1500 to 300). While Winn would later boast that he would depart the company with 'pride and satisfaction', other Telstra employees were not so sure. Despite lofty ambitions, only around half of Telstra's legacy IT networks were switched off during Winn's four-year tenure. Further, under Winn's guidance, Telstra's highly vaunted IT transformation ran hundreds of millions of dollars over budget and years behind schedule according to the company's chief financial officer.

The lack of success didn't prevent Telstra from handing Winn a final payment of $5.3 million for 2009. That payment included $666 666 for Winn to act as a consultant between 1 February and 31 March 2009. During that period, Winn received almost $12 000 each day.

THE NBN: SOL MEETS HIS WATERLOO (2008–09)

While Telstra gloated to shareholders about its strong performance in its 2008 annual report, that joy would be short-lived.

In December 2008, investors were shocked after Telstra was expelled from the tender process for Australia's National Broadband Network (NBN) after the company failed to submit a required plan on how to involve small- and medium-sized enterprises in the building of the high-speed broadband network.*

---

* Telstra's entire proposal was a mere 12 pages, compared with several hundred pages for Telstra's rivals, including Singapore-owned Optus and Canadian consortium Axia NetMedia. The small–medium business plan which was omitted by Telstra would have taken the company nominal time to compile.

The decision to submit an incomplete tender is believed to have been prompted by a split in the Telstra boardroom. Fearing that a successful bid may compel Telstra to once again share its broadband network, Trujillo is understood to have not wanted to submit a tender at all. By contrast, McGauchie is thought to have sought Telstra's involvement. Trujillo was not present at an emergency Telstra board meeting where the company finally decided to submit the non-conforming bid. Trujillo was in the United States with family.[37]

Regardless of Telstra's motivation or an alleged boardroom split, on 15 December 2008, the day it was excluded from the process for the NBN, Telstra's share price slumped by 11.6 per cent — from $4.13 to $3.65. In total, more than $6 billion was wiped off Telstra's market value in one day — the largest fall in the company's history. Not long after Telstra was excluded from the NBN process, Trujillo conceded that the company stood to lose $2 billion in sales should a competitor construct a broadband network. (In April 2009, the federal government announced that it would construct its own broadband network, at a cost of $43 billion.)

It was to be the last of Trujillo's long-running battles with the federal government and the ACCC. Shortly after the ill-fated NBN tender process, Trujillo exited Telstra — months before his scheduled departure date and well before his much vaunted 'transformation plan' was complete.

It was clear that Trujillo's attitude and hostility toward regulators backfired, badly. Fortunately for Trujillo, his remuneration was structured so that the majority of his pay was made in cash or short-term cash bonuses. As a result, he would be insulated from long-term underperformance. This is exactly what highly paid board members, such as Donald McGauchie and Charles Macek, are paid to prevent. In May 2009, shortly after Trujillo's NBN debacle, Telstra shares dropped to an all-time low of $3.06 per share — almost 40 per cent below the share price when Trujillo was appointed CEO.

Trujillo's stance towards regulators also received criticism from an unlikely source: his predecessor, Ziggy Switkowski. Switkowski stated that under Trujillo, a 'very adversarial strategy was played out in public through the media and involved extensive litigation [which] was never going to work because Telstra in Australia occupies a position like no other telco company anywhere else in the world … and to create enemies out of two successive governments is a world class effort and that is what Trujillo and his team succeeded in doing'.[38]

Lesson #6: Back a winner

When a company takes on the government, usually the government will win.

SOL DEPARTS (2009)

Amid the now usual media hype, in February 2009 Trujillo announced that he would be departing Telstra at the end of June. Trujillo's key ally, Donald McGauchie, was effusive in his praise, stating that Trujillo's 'vision, strategic direction and commitment to execution have positioned Telstra as a media communications company with a wide range of options for ongoing growth'.[39] Alas, with the share price down almost 30 per cent in four years, it appears that investors held a different opinion. It is not without irony that on the day of Trujillo's resignation, Telstra announced a downgrade in profit forecasts (largely caused by higher IT costs) and further job cuts — two hallmarks of Trujillo's tenure.

While Trujillo was expected to stay until the end of June, by late May 2009 he was gone, replaced by Telstra's government and enterprise boss David Thodey. Thodey, a former IBM executive, was preferred by the Telstra board for his cordial relations with the federal government and minimal links with the Trujillo regime.

As a final gift to Trujillo, the Telstra board decided to pay him a $3 million 'termination payment'. This was not only very generous, but also not legally required. Trujillo's employment contract specified that he was only entitled to a termination payment if he was to be terminated by Telstra or chose to terminate his own employment with 'good reason' (good reason is defined to include a change in responsibilities or a breach by the company).

Upon his resignation, Trujillo told the media that he was leaving to spend more time with family in the United States — such justification, however valid, would clearly not satisfy the definition of 'good reason' in relation to Trujillo's employment contract. Therefore, he was not legally entitled to the termination payment from Telstra.[40]

The Telstra board, led by Donald McGauchie (who left Telstra shortly after Trujillo's departure), and Telstra's remuneration committee, headed by Charles Macek, made the fatal mistake of falling in love with their celebrity CEO. Trujillo was paid far more than his predecessor and the man who followed him, but failed to deliver on his stated transformation objectives and destroyed shareholder returns through a myopic and hostile stance taken against regulators and government.

In the end, it was Trujillo who had the last laugh—collecting more than $40 million from Telstra shareholders in just four short years, before abruptly departing back to the United States in a blaze of shame. Not to mention the $3 million termination payment, even though he wasn't actually terminated. Adios amigos indeed.

CHAPTER 2

ABC Learning Centres

How Australia's richest man under 40 built a childcare empire on foundations of sand

I don't think I've ever done anything in
business that I've lost money on.
Eddy Groves to a local newspaper journalist in 1999[1]

THEY CALLED him Fast Eddy. The founder of what was once the world's largest publicly listed childcare company, Eddy Groves liked fast cars, crocodile skin boots and collecting assets, from Gold Coast waterfront real estate to basketball teams.

In 2006, Groves was dubbed the richest Australian under the age of 40. His company, ABC Learning Centres, had not only conquered the Australian childcare market, but also launched a major expansion into the United States and United Kingdom. Shortly before its collapse, the business founded by a former milkman from Brisbane would be the largest childcare company in the world.

It would turn out to be a mirage. Hundreds of millions of dollars of related-party deals to Groves's family, billions of dollars of debt and dubious accounting practices would lead to the collapse of ABC Learning Centres and the downfall of Eddy Groves.

THE EARLY DAYS

The dramatic rise of Groves represented near unparalleled wealth creation in a sector never before touched by corporate sensitivities. Born in South Africa in 1966, Groves moved with his family to Australia via Canada when Eddy was four. The Groves family chose to reside in Queensland, with Eddy being educated at Padua College, a Catholic high school founded by Franciscan monks.

After completing high school Groves briefly undertook a Bachelor of Business degree, but soon after dropped out to work as a teller at ANZ Bank, before acquiring a milk distribution business. That milk business, now known as Quantum Foods, would become the largest milk distributor in Queensland and provide the financial springboard upon which Groves created his childcare empire.

At the age of 19, Eddy Groves married Le Neve, who had a background in childhood learning (and would later obtain a masters degree and a doctorate in education). Le Neve was considered by some to be the intellect behind ABC's early growth and provided the educational bent to complement Groves's commercial sensibilities.

For many years, Eddy and Le Neve were dubbed 'joint managing directors' of ABC. However, the Groves marriage, like ABC Learning Centres itself, would later crumble, with the couple believed to have gone through a low-profile separation at around the time ABC listed on the stock exchange, eventually divorcing in December 2008. A month after the divorce was finalised, Eddy married former ABC employee Viryan Collins-Rubie, in a lavish ceremony at a Gold Coast golf course.*

Groves acquired his first childcare centre in 1988—at the age of only 22. It would be 13 years before he would make the quantum leap to listing on the ASX.

---

* Collins-Rubie was once employed by ABC but departed to become CEO of another childcare centre operator called Childcare Providers. Childcare Providers would later receive several million dollars from ABC in 2005 and 2007 and millions of dollars in loans from Groves's brother-in-law Frank Zullo.

GOING PUBLIC (1997)

It took more than a decade for ABC to really get started. By 1998, 10 years after Groves founded ABC, the company operated 22 centres, generating revenue of around $10.6 million. However, a change to the laws relating to childcare subsidies passed by the Howard government in 1997 significantly altered the childcare landscape. In a move that would have dire ramifications 11 years later, the Liberal government reduced the level of subsidies paid to not-for-profit centres and allowed commercial centres to receive federal funding.

Thanks to the change in laws and Groves's desire for scale, by the time ABC listed on the ASX in 2001, it managed 43 centres and had turnover of $22 million. This doubled again in 2002, to 94 centres and $44 million in total revenue.

ABC floated on the ASX in late 2001 at $2.00 per share, giving the company a market value of approximately $25 million.* Promising a bright future, ABC's prospectus noted:

> Increasingly stringent government regulations are driving smaller operators from the industry. This will continue to create growth opportunities for ABC through carefully selected acquisitions. Recent changes to Federal Government funding arrangements mean that low income families are reimbursed up to 110% of the cost of their child care.

> ABC has decided to list on the ASX to position the company to take advantage of future growth opportunities, to increase its public profile and to allow the Vendor Shareholders to realise part of their investment in ABC.

As part of its transformation to being a publicly listed company, ABC was required to appoint independent non-executive directors who would act as stewards to represent the interests of minority shareholders.

Strong corporate governance principles would dictate that a company's nomination committee consists of independent directors. It is the nomination committee who, in reality, appoint new directors. (What actually happens is that the nomination committee selects which board members are eligible for election by the company's

---

* ABC shareholders would later see their shares split into four, so the adjusted float price for ABC was 50¢.

shareholders. But due to the quirks of Australian corporate voting laws, it is virtually impossible for a board-nominated candidate to not be appointed to the company's board of directors.)

Lesson #1: Independence isn't only for countries

A strong, independent board is critical for publicly listed companies — it is even more vital when there is a dominant, founder CEO (or executive chairman), as was the case with Eddy Groves. While many successful companies remain dominated by their founder (such as Westfield's Frank Lowy or News Corporation's Rupert Murdoch), shareholders are effectively buying a stake in what is really a quasi-private company. Ultimately, without an independent board that is willing to act in the interests of minority shareholders, domineering CEOs will make the company a far riskier investment.

In ABC's case, corporate governance principles were given what appeared to be minimal consideration. Eddy Groves himself was on ABC's nomination committee; this allowed Groves to hand-pick the directors who were supposed to be scrutinising his performance.

Upon listing, ABC's board of directors included: Liberal Party identity Sallyanne Atkinson (who was appointed in October 2000); the chairman of ABC's broker Austock, Bill Bessemer; as well as Eddy and Le Neve Groves.* The only director who was deemed to be independent of ABC management was Sallyanne Atkinson.

Despite also serving as a non-executive director of Abigroup and APN News & Media, Atkinson had a political, rather than a commercial, background. Atkinson had previously been the Lord Mayor of Brisbane and had obtained an Arts degree from the University of Queensland.

While a shrewd political player, it would seem that Atkinson would not have the ability to control ABC's executive team, especially Groves. Such suspicion would later prove prescient — only months before the company was placed in administration, Atkinson would blame a downturn in the market and a loss of shareholder confidence for ABC's woes, rather than what appeared to be incompetent

---

* ABC executive (and former engineer) Martin Kemp would join the ABC board in November 2001, shortly after the company listed on the ASX.

management. It appeared that, despite sitting on ABC's board for almost a decade, Atkinson was completely unaware of what was actually transpiring at the company.

Shortly after listing, Groves and ABC commenced their rapid expansion. Throughout 2001, ABC continued rolling out new centres, largely in Brisbane and the Gold Coast, beating prospectus revenue forecasts by more than 15 per cent.

While ABC's financial statements indicated a rapidly growing company with healthy profitability, the ABC board paid little attention to any semblance of good corporate governance. Both Eddy and Le Neve Groves, the CEOs of the business, were also on ABC's audit committee (they remained on the audit committee until 2004).

The role of the audit committee is to ensure the veracity of reported financial information for outside shareholders. Critically, an audit committee should be independent of senior management, who may seek to influence the reported financial statements. In ABC's case, there appeared to be no delineation whatsoever between the company's executive directors and its non-executive directors.

At the same time, ABC's auditor, the small Brisbane firm of Douglas Heck & Burrell, was receiving more money from ABC for non-audit-related services ($83 549) than it was paid for actually auditing ABC's statements ($48 750).

ABC's growth continued in 2002, with the company increasing sales from $13 million to $24 million. In 2001–02, ABC acquired its first centres in New South Wales and Western Australia, although the vast majority of its operations remained in Queensland.

THE BIGGEST LITTLE COMPANY IN THE WORLD (2003)

By 2003, Groves and ABC were gaining speed.

Less than two years after listing on the stock exchange, ABC had grown into an empire of more than 200 centres (11 in New Zealand), providing daycare to more than 20 000 children.[2]

In 2003, ABC's revenues increased from $24 million to more than $40 million, with profits exploding to $12 million. The business was acquiring childcare centres individually and through acquisitions of other medium-size operators — taking over Educare in September 2002 and FutureOne and Brighter Future centres in June 2003. Strangely, between 2002 and 2003, despite ABC almost doubling sales, its employment expense remained constant (at $1.8 million). Perhaps ABC staff were suddenly working a lot harder.

The year 2003 also saw the appointment of a second independent director to the ABC board, with the election of former accountant David Ryan as a non-executive director. Ryan had previously been the CEO of Adsteam Marine (which had been spun off after the liquidation of the Adelaide Steamship Company). Ryan's time as CEO of Adsteam Marine was difficult, with some critics claiming that Ryan left the company in a perilous state after a series of ill-considered acquisitions (ironically, a fate that would later befall ABC). Adsteam was forced to write off more than $64 million after Ryan departed, as well as $24 million in restructuring costs. Fortunately for Ryan, it didn't appear that his reputation was a problem for ABC. Ryan was soon appointed chair of ABC's audit committee, responsible for appraising internal and external audit reports and reviewing financial statements and reports.

In early 2004, ABC acquired the Early Childhood Training College, located in Cairns in Northern Queensland. The college allowed ABC to train staff members and other, non-ABC workers in early childhood learning.

It was all systems go for Groves's team as ABC was fast becoming the largest childcare centre operator in the country and Groves one of the richest people in Australia under the age of 40.

LOSING FRIENDS

While ABC appeared to be a financial success, dark clouds were slowly appearing on the horizon.

As ABC grew it began to attract unwanted attention from media, community groups and unions, unhappy at the intrusion of a corporate player in what, until recently, had been a sector dominated by not-for-profit community centres.

In 2003, Groves launched a bizarre defamation action against the Australian Liquor, Hospitality and Miscellaneous Union (LHMU) after it handed out pamphlets outside an ABC centre depicting Groves as 'Uncle Scrooge', implying that he was 'trying to drive down low wages of child-care workers to line his own pockets'. Groves initially sought damages of $500000 and the matter was eventually settled out of court. The legal action appeared to have a lasting effect on the union—even years later, its members were too scared to publicly speak out against Groves.

Lesson #2: Beware the litigious

Executives who make a habit of trying to muzzle critics with defamation proceedings often tend to be hiding an inconvenient truth. Failed entrepreneurs Alan Bond and Laurie Connell issued hundreds of writs to silence journalists. More recently, City Pacific founder Phil Sullivan sued Fairfax for misleading conduct after it questioned the company's viability. Within a year, City Pacific had collapsed.

John Elliott infamously sued the National Crime Authority for prosecuting him for fraud in the 1980s. A few years later, Elliott's agriculture company Water Wheel would collapse and he was later banned from acting as a company director.

More concerning though for Groves was growing public anger at commercially operated childcare centres. For decades, childcare centres, like kindergartens, were run almost entirely on a not-for-profit basis. Any excess funds were reinvested in the centres themselves rather than distributed to shareholders or executives. With the growth of the commercial childcare sector, parents and community groups were growing increasingly concerned that companies such as ABC Learning Centres (and its rivals, Peppercorn Management Group and Child Care Centres of Australia) were placing the interests of shareholders before those of children.

This concern was magnified by the flood of taxpayer-funded subsidies finding their way into the coffers of the private owners. Allegations thrived regarding the quality of the food, care, level of training and standard of facilities at commercially operated centres. It was a charge that would continue to dog ABC throughout its existence, despite the ardent claims by Groves that ABC provided the best care and facilities for children. Among the allegations levelled against commercial centres was that only 50 per cent of the company's revenue was devoted to the payment of staff wages; not-for-profit centres, which had no responsibility to shareholders, were able to pay staff upwards of 80 per cent of income.

Speaking under the protection of parliamentary privilege in 2004, Victorian Labor parliamentarian Michael Danby was highly critical of ABC, accusing the company of '[refusing] to hire sufficient cleaners, [refusing] to pay staff a decent wage, and [requiring] staff to bring in their own music to play to children'.

ABC's sheer size also gave rise to inevitable safety incidents occurring at its centres. In April 2005, the company was prosecuted by the Victorian Department of Human Services and fined $200 after a toddler was able to climb a fence and escape from an ABC centre at Hopper's Crossing in 2002. ABC challenged the fine on the grounds that the company should not be held liable for the actions of low-level employees. The Victorian Supreme Court upheld the fine but did not impose a conviction on the company.

In another incident, ABC was fined $76 792 after an inspection detected mouse droppings on the floor and spiders in an area accessed by children.

In addition to criticisms regarding the standard of care provided by ABC, anger mounted at the company's willingness to exploit taxpayer subsidies by increasing fees. Between 2003 and 2006, the Australian Bureau of Statistics found that ABC had increased its fees by more than 60 per cent, despite federal government warnings against using increases in subsidies to raise fees for parents.[3]

THE BIG LITTLE AUSTRALIAN: ABC TAKES OVER ITS BIGGEST RIVALS (2004)

While continuing to acquire individual childcare centres across Australia, ABC's big break came in mid 2004, when it was approached by Michael Gordon, founder of rival listed childcare operator Peppercorn Management Group. Gordon owned a controlling 55 per cent stake in Peppercorn and possibly saw the writing on the wall for childcare companies.

Gordon offered to sell his interest (and by implication, the entire company) to Groves and ABC. It was an offer that the ambitious

Groves could not refuse. To cement the deal, ABC entered into an option agreement with Gordon for 19.9 per cent of his stake in Peppercorn and undertook a merger by way of scheme of arrangement with Peppercorn. Gordon eventually collected $130 million cash from selling his 55 per cent stake in Peppercorn to ABC, making him one of the few people in Australia to make serious money from childcare. Well, perhaps with the exception of Eddy Groves's brother-in-law, but more on that later.

At the same time as it undertook its merger with Peppercorn, ABC also acquired Child Care Centres of Australia (CCCA), another publicly listed company which was associated with Liberal Party figures Michael Kroger and Andrew Peacock. (Kroger was previously married to Peacock's daughter Anne and runs the boutique investment bank JT Campbell.) The transactions were complicated by the pre-existing cross-holding between Peppercorn and CCCA which required both mergers to occur almost simultaneously to follow the complex corporations laws. (CCCA entered into a management and cross-shareholding agreement with Peppercorn in 2003 after it encountered financial problems. In mid 2003, CCCA was forced to refund investor monies after announcing a surprise 90 per cent profit downgrade only months after completing a capital raising.)

The Peppercorn and CCCA acquisitions were 'company-making' deals for ABC—prior to its purchase of Peppercorn and CCCA, ABC operated 330 childcare centres in Australia (largely centred in New South Wales and Queensland) and New Zealand, providing approximately 23 000 childcare places. After swallowing its listed rivals, ABC owned more than 550 childcare centres and managed a further 228 centres (although the company was forced to divest 65 of the acquired centres for competition reasons). ABC noted in an information memorandum relating to the Peppercorn deal that 'the transactions will create Australia's leading provider of childcare centres and will provide further benefits to children and their families by increasing the availability of childcare places in areas of unmet demand'.*

---

* In 2008, the ACCC initiated legal proceedings against ABC for failing to comply with a 2004 court order demanding the divestiture of two Geraldton-based centres which it obtained through the Peppercorn merger. As part of the claims made against ABC, the ACCC alleged that the company interfered with the role of an agent who was appointed to sell the centres and that ABC failed to operate the centres in a fully operational and competitive manner to preserve goodwill.

To raise the funds to acquire Peppercorn (which was purchased by ABC for cash, rather than shares), ABC raised $400 million by way of a private placement and share purchase plan for smaller investors.

Not long after ABC completed the acquisitions of Peppercorn and CCCA, its boardroom ranks were boosted by the inclusion of former National Party politician Larry Anthony. The son of former National Party leader Doug Anthony, Larry Anthony had recently lost his federal seat of Richmond to Labor challenger Justine Elliott. Anthony had been the Minister for Children and Youth Affairs in the Howard government.

Anthony's quick transition from the minister responsible for the childcare sector to being a paid, independent director of the largest publicly owned childcare company in the country raised eyebrows. Tanya Plibersek, Labor's then Shadow Minister for Families, accused Anthony of having a conflict of interest due to his 'unparalleled access' to the federal government.[4]

Also questionable was the ministerial role Anthony played in the introduction of the Howard government's childcare policies. While almost certainly unrelated to Anthony's subsequent appointment to the ABC board, those policies did happen to substantially benefit ABC Learning Centres, specifically the 30 per cent childcare rebate to parents.

One month after Anthony was appointed to the ABC board, the company won a contract to operate 19 centres for the Department of Defence. The contract had previously been awarded to KU Children's Services, a not-for-profit operator.[5] A manager of KU Children's Services was shocked by the government's decision, suggesting that ABC would not be able to provide an acceptable standard of care based on the agreed financial arrangements.

Anthony's tenure at ABC would provide further proof that politicians tend to make poor businesspeople.

Lesson #3: Never trust a politician

Former parliamentarians, especially from the conservative side of politics, have had disappointing experiences in the boardroom. Aside from Larry Anthony, former politicians Andrew Peacock (MFS), Roger Pescott (Environinvest), Alan Brown (Traffic Technologies) and Jeff Kennett (Jumbuck) had poor records as non-executive directors.

At the same time as it was increasing the size of its boardroom was also significantly inflating the size of its balance sheet.

In its 2003 financial statements, ABC reported that it had 'contributed equity' (that is, funds invested by shareholders in the company through its initial public offering and subsequent capital raisings) of $71 million. That figure increased to $174 million the following year before ballooning to $677 million in 2005, after the capital raising to fund the Peppercorn acquisition.

However, the increased number of shares on issue did not stop ABC's relentless share price appreciation—from a split-adjusted 50¢ in 2001, ABC shares rose to $6.29 in October 2006. At that time, Eddy and Le Neve's stake was worth almost $200 million. A shareholder who invested $10 000 in ABC's 2001 float would have seen the value of this holding increase to $125 800 by late 2006.

But while most investors focused on ABC's stunning sales growth and its lucrative stream of government-protected earnings (approximately half of ABC's revenue was actually paid by Australian taxpayers in the form of childcare rebates), under the surface things were not quite so rosy. As the amount of ABC's equity increased, its profitability (usually expressed by analysts as 'return on equity' or ROE) slumped.

In 2003, ABC earned 18¢ for every dollar of contributed equity. This is a fairly good return. By 2005, ABC was earning only 7¢ for each dollar of equity—barely better than a term deposit. While ABC was increasing in size, the company was actually becoming less profitable—in other words, there were a lot more people trying to get a slice, but not much more pie.

Lesson #4: ROE, ROE, ROE your boat

While investors are able to consider many different metrics in determining how much a company is worth (such as price/earnings ratio or free cash flow), return on equity is a very important indicator of a company's ability to provide strong returns to shareholders and is a strong sign of the ability of management.

Put simply, companies exist to generate a return on equity for shareholders. If return on equity is falling, there may be problems within the sector (due to increased competition or changing consumer preferences) or management may not be up to scratch.

There are a lot of different businesses and sectors which you can invest in —don't waste your capital on a business whose profitability is shrinking. (However, investors should be wary of companies that use cheap debt to increase return on equity. Like beauty, low interest rates do not last forever.)

ABC's balance sheet was also starting to cause concerns—in 2003, the company listed total assets of $1.2 billion compared with relatively low debt levels of around $250 million (giving ABC a healthy gearing level of around 20 per cent). However, the vast majority of ABC's assets were 'childcare licences' and other intangible assets which the company valued at $942 million. In 2005 alone, ABC determined to increase the value of those licences by $165 million. While the company was prospering, the licences had some value, however were ABC to ever fall into financial difficulties or cease to operate as a going concern, the value of those 'intangible assets' would drop to almost nothing.

The other benefit of ABC 'writing up' the value of its childcare licences was that it would make ABC look like a 'safer' company, because its gearing (which is a company's ratio of assets compared with liabilities) would be lower. This would allow ABC to raise a further $1 billion in capital from naive investors in the coming year.

The audit firm that signed off on ABC's financial reports for 2005 was Pitcher Partners. Pitcher Partners was originally spun off from Big Four accounting firm KPMG back in 1991 to handle the firm's private business. Pitcher's Brisbane office, which audited ABC, was relatively small in size, especially compared with the major firms. The audit partner who signed off on ABC's reports (and, therefore, agreed with the company's optimistic valuation of its childcare licences) was a gentleman by the name of Russell Brown. (Brown had switched to Pitcher from ABC's previous auditor, Douglas Heck & Burrell.) Coincidentally, Brown was also the auditor of Quantum Food Services, Eddy Groves's private milk distribution company. Brown would later resign from auditing ABC, being replaced the following year by a more junior partner at Pitcher by the name of Simon Green.

GOING FOR BROKE (2005)

While ABC's acquisitions of Peppercorn and CCCA dented the company's return on equity, ABC was still a cash machine, generating net cash flow from operations of $47 million in 2005 (up from $20 million the previous year).

Seemingly oblivious to the fact that the more centres it managed the less profitable it became, ABC continued its breakneck expansion. In 2006, its number of childcare places under management rose from 46 164 to 112 179.

Just when it appeared ABC had reached its limit, Eddy once again surprised his critics, with ABC doubling in size once more, this time courtesy of a spate of overseas acquisitions. It was the overseas expansion which would make ABC the largest childcare operator in the world.

In November 2005, ABC Learning Centres announced that it would acquire the Learning Care Group from baby-food company Gerber, for $218 million. Learning Care Group operated 460 centres, predominantly in the United States, and was licensed to care for 69 000 children. At the time of the acquisition, ABC chair Sallyanne Atkinson told shareholders that 'North America is a natural area of growth for ABC Learning Centres and we believe we can successfully export our experience in Australia to the United States via Learning Care Group'.[6] Less than a year later, ABC made a second US acquisition when it purchased the Dallas-based Children's Courtyard, before undertaking the acquisition of Chicago-based Le Petite Academy from private equity investors for US$330 million.

The acquisition of Le Petite Academy (which had the capacity to serve 97 000 children and managed centres in 36 US states) made ABC the second largest childcare operator in the US and the largest globally. At the same time, ABC also announced it would pay £71 million to acquire the UK-based Busy Bees Group and $65 million to purchase 55 childcare centres from Macquarie Leisure Services in Australia and New Zealand.

ABC acquired Busy Bees largely for its unique childcare voucher system, which ABC had hoped to apply in other countries. Groves was never able to answer the question: why would the world's largest childcare company need to acquire a UK-based minnow for a voucher system? Was ABC unable to come up with its own voucher system?

ABC claimed that the acquisition of Le Petite Academy would lead to an EBITDA contribution after synergies of US$45 million, and elected to fund the acquisition through the use of debt rather than equity. ABC had almost solely funded its previous acquisitions of Peppercorn, CCCA and Learning Care Group using monies raised from shareholders (it was this hunger for capital that led to ABC's profitability falling substantially).

However, by late 2006 debt was very much in vogue and the private equity boom was in full swing—using this cheap money, ABC announced that it would fund the $680 million cost of the all-cash acquisitions through a bank debt facility. With ABC trading on a price/earning multiple of almost 40, and corporate interest rates well below 10 per cent, ABC sought to use borrowings to improve its dwindling return on equity.

It was this decision, above all others, which would contribute to ABC's downfall less than two years later.

A DEBT-FUELLED HONEYMOON (2007)

The acquisition of Le Petite Academy in the United States, coupled with the purchases of Australia-based Hutchinson's Child Care Services and Busy Bees in the United Kingdom, led to ABC announcing record revenue of $1.7 billion for the 2007 financial year. In the space of only six years, Eddy Groves's company had grown from 43 centres and turnover of $22 million to 2238 centres with sales approaching $2 billion.

But the rapid expansion came at a cost. ABC's contributed equity had increased from $20 million in 2002 to $1.7 billion in July 2007. ABC had also taken on a mountain of debt to fund its US and UK acquisitions, with total borrowings of $1.8 billion. ABC's assets also continued to be largely intangible, consisting primarily of childcare licences ($2.9 billion)—its tangible assets of $900 million were dwarfed by the company's growing debt burden.

The childcare licences largely represented what accountants call 'goodwill'; that is, when one company is acquired by another company, the amount paid over and above the 'book value' of the assets of the target is deemed to be goodwill. The acquired goodwill will remain an asset on the buyer's balance sheet unless it is deemed to be 'impaired' by the company itself or its auditors. Calling the excess purchase price 'goodwill' is a polite way of saying someone paid more than the acquired company previously thought it was worth (in its books). Sometimes, the goodwill is perfectly legitimate; for example, if the acquirer is able to obtain revenue or cost economies of scale. Most of the time, however, it is a proxy for the hubris of a CEO with a Napoleon complex.

In ABC's case, its goodwill related to childcare licences which it hoped would turn a handy profit in years to come. Of course, this is never certain, and in many cases the goodwill is later quietly written off when a new management regime is appointed. Whenever a company has a lot of goodwill on its balance sheet and a dwindling return on equity, investors would be advised to run the other way.

Lesson #5: Goodwill gone bad

Unless a company is able to glean substantial cost savings or revenue 'economies of scale' from an acquisition, 'goodwill' isn't really an asset at all. While some intangible assets are incredibly valuable (a brand name such as Coca-Cola or McDonald's or Google can be worth tens of billions of dollars), investors should focus on assets which directly contribute to cash flow, rather than what appears on a balance sheet.

Despite its weaker balance sheet, ABC's share price didn't suffer, with analysts still believing in Groves's ability to profit from the company's overseas gambits. While falling from an all-time high of $8.80 (reached in December 2006), ABC shares were still trading at around $7.34 in July 2007.

ABC also received a boost in May 2007 when Temasek, the investment company wholly owned by the Singapore Government, became its second largest shareholder.* The $100 billion sovereign

---

* Temasek already owned a large number of Australian-based assets, including Optus (via its interest in SingTel), Tiger (through its holding in Singapore Airlines) and SP Ausnet.

fund invested around $400 million in ABC Learning Centres as part of ABC's $1 billion capital raising to fund its recent US and UK acquisitions. Temasek's purchase amounted to approximately 12 per cent of ABC's listed equity. (The sovereign fund would, ill-fatedly, increase its shareholding in ABC to almost 15 per cent the following year, shortly before ABC's collapse.) It's fair to say Eddy Groves won't be rushing to Singapore for a holiday any time soon.

Not long after Temasek announced its stake in ABC, institutional investor Lazard Asset Management obtained a 5.1 per cent equity ownership.

With ABC shares flying high and the addition of well-heeled investors on the share register, Groves was quickly gaining a reputation in Australian business circles. In August 2006, Groves paid $3.95 million to acquire the Distinctive Homes Dome—the basketball stadium that is home to the National Basketball League side the Adelaide 36ers. The acquisition would complement Groves's ownership of basketball team the Brisbane Bullets.

Groves was also being recognised by *BRW* magazine, which compiles an annual list of the wealthiest Australians. In 2005, the business magazine estimated Groves's wealth at $272 million. The following year, Groves was dubbed the richest Australian under the age of 40, replacing the late 'Crazy' John Ilhan. *BRW* deemed Groves to have a net worth of $260 million in 2006, based largely on his stake in ABC Learning Centres but also his holding in his milk distribution business in Queensland, Quantum Food Services. (The 2006 Young Rich List represented the zenith of the fast-money 2000s—also listed in the top 10 were GMC founder Peter Hosking, whose company has since collapsed, failed Queensland property developer Craig Gore and bankrupt former Billabong CEO Matthew Perrin.)

The flamboyant Groves showed the trappings of wealth—in 2006 Groves paid $675 000 to purchase a black Ferrari Superamerica (then the fastest convertible sports car in the world).* Groves also owned an Augusta 109 seven-seat corporate helicopter, until it crashed into the Brisbane River in June 2004 with Groves inside. All passengers managed to escape from the damaged helicopter safely.

---

* Groves's fondness for fast cars continued even after the collapse of ABC. After Groves departed from ABC he continued to drive a new Mercedes Kompressor automobile in Queensland and was seen behind the wheel of a luxury Audi in Melbourne.

However, while Groves was living the high life, his dream run would soon come to a very abrupt end.

The collapse of two Bear Sterns hedge funds in July 2007 triggered what would become known as the global financial crisis. A downturn in the US residential property market led to a global re-pricing of risk across the financial world. Whereas in 2006 debt was all the rage, by early 2008 highly geared companies with low levels of tangible assets were being punished by investors. No longer was it fashionable for companies to be carrying a large debt load on their balance sheets. ABC Learning Centres, with billions of dollars of short-term liabilities and little cash, was not a company suited to this new, somewhat less gilded age.

From $7.48 in July 2007, ABC's share price commenced a downward spiral, dropping to $5.00 in November, before steadying in January 2008. The sharp fall in ABC's share price would have been causing a degree of nervousness in the ABC boardroom. As discussed later, ABC directors, including Eddy Groves and Martin Kemp, had amassed large margin loans attached to their holdings in ABC. If the share price continued to fall, there was a chance that Groves and Kemp would be 'margin called' and forced to sell their sizable stakes in the company.

If that were to happen, all hell would break loose.

CATASTROPHE (2008)

The year 2008 started well enough for ABC Learning Centres. While world stock markets were reeling from the actions of a sole rogue trader at Société Générale, ABC shares had remained relatively stable, finishing January at $4.41—well down from their high, but still valuing the company at more than $2 billion, up from $25 million when the company floated seven years prior.

However, the good times were almost over.

ABC's first death knell came on 25 February 2008, when the company released its half-year financial statements for the previous period. Until then, ABC—much like infamous Ponzi scheme operator Bernie Madoff—had rarely disappointed investors, delivering reliable revenue and profit growth.

This time was different.

While ABC reported increased revenue, it shocked the market by revealing that headline profit had fallen by 42 per cent to $37 million. ABC also recorded a negative operating cash result.

While the 42 per cent drop in profit was bad, the fine print was even worse. The notes to ABC's financial statements revealed that the company's $37 million earnings figure had been inflated by various items, including the payment of liquidated damages of $26.2 million by developers for non-performance of agreements. Most companies would treat the liquidated damages payment as an 'extraordinary gain'—but ABC was not like most other companies. It simply slid the damages payment into the ordinary earnings. This was at best questionable judgement, and at worst misleading.

Also included in the profit figure was a $51.1 million gain from the purchase of Leapfrog Nurseries. This gain represented a fine piece of accounting chicanery, and essentially involved ABC claiming that it purchased another company (Leapfrog) for $51 million less than what the company was actually worth. Accordingly, ABC would then claim that the $51 million bargain was really 'ordinary profit'.

Lesson #6: Look for exceptions, not rules

Struggling companies will often bury bad news below the 'headline' results. While 'extraordinary gains' are usually deemed to be a part of ordinary profit, large losses are often dubbed 'abnormal' and hidden deep within the notes to the financial statements. Poorly performing companies will report abnormal or extraordinary losses on regular occasions. If a gain is a one-off, assume it won't be repeated—if a loss is due to management, assume it will be.

Accountants have a funny way of dealing with discounts on acquisitions compared with overpaying for businesses. As discussed above, in most cases acquirers pay more for a business than what the target's book value of assets indicates. When that happens, the purchaser labels the difference 'goodwill', which sits as an asset on its balance sheet until it is impaired. This would generally have a minor effect on the acquirer's profitability, but will hopefully be overcome by the profit increases due to synergies or economies of scale.

By contrast, when a company pays *less* for another company than the target company's book value, that difference is allowed to be claimed as a 'discount on acquisition', resulting in a direct increase in the company's profit for the current year. It is a good deal for acquirers—if they pay too much for an asset then that overpayment sits on the balance sheet while the business is able to claim to possess a larger asset base. If the acquirer claims to have underpaid for a business, it can immediately (and arbitrarily) increase its profits for that year—which is exactly what ABC did.

Stripping out the extraordinary gains from the damages claim and discount on acquisition (but adjusting for the $36.5 million loss ABC incurred from its stake in toy seller Funtastic), ABC would have actually made a loss for the period ending December 2007 of approximately $4 million.

However, that was far from the end of the story—the worst was yet to come.

In a footnote buried deep in ABC's notes to its financial statements, the company revealed that it had also been adopting questionable accounting practices with regard to how it recorded 'development revenue'. The footnote stated that ABC's 'services revenue' of $970.7 million for the period included 'fees paid by childcare developers of $73.3 million (2006: nil) to support centres during occupancy growth. This agreement expires on 30 June 2009'.

This seemingly innocuous footnote (included for the first time in 2008 only after ABC changed auditors from Pitcher Partners to Ernst & Young) was the straw that broke ABC's credibility among investors, destroying any remaining vestiges of trust that the market placed in Groves's managerial abilities. The $73 million in payments which ABC booked as normal services revenue were actually payments from developers.[7]

Essentially, what happened was rather than acquire childcare centres directly, ABC would get an adviser (most commonly, Austock) to arrange for the purchase of the property underlying the centres (usually through a third party such as the Austock-managed Australian Education Trust). The childcare centre itself would be constructed by yet another party, usually a property developer.

After construction of the centre was complete, ABC would buy the business from the property developer. The amount paid by ABC to the property developer would be recognised as an asset by ABC, specifically 'childcare licences'. Essentially, the more ABC paid for the centre, the greater its 'asset' balance would be. The problem was, these so-called assets were not really assets at all—they were not generating satisfactory returns to vindicate the lofty valuations that ABC claimed.

ABC was one step ahead though. When it bought childcare centres from the developers, those property developers would be forced to agree to promise ABC a budgeted level of revenue. If the childcare centre was only half full, the developer would make up the shortfall by paying cash to ABC. ABC could then turn around and tell shareholders and creditors that its new centre was 80 per cent full.

This is similar to what property developers offer to purchasers for 'off-the-plan' apartment sales in which they guarantee a specific rental amount. If the apartment isn't rented, the developer would be legally obliged to pay the owner out of its own pocket for the term of the rental guarantee. The developers who built ABC's centres did a very similar thing—if the childcare centre was below a specific capacity, the developer would make up the shortfall to ABC. The problem with receiving these monies is that it is only a short-term fix.

In the December half of 2007, ABC received payments from developers which amounted to $73.3 million.

While ABC claimed that the payments were revenue, in actual fact they were little more than an accounting round-robin which served to inflate ABC's earnings figures. In essence, ABC would pay cash to the developer (but record that cash payment as an asset, 'childcare licences') and later receive a portion of that cash back.

ABC would book the cash it received back as ordinary sales. In effect, what was happening was that ABC would over-pay for childcare centres and receive a portion of that over-payment back as revenue—this would provide a short-term kick to ABC's financial statements.

Until 2008, when Ernst & Young demanded disclosure of the 'developer payments', ABC's investors and lenders would have been blissfully unaware that almost 10 per cent of the company's revenue was effectively derived from itself.

Excluding development fees, the discount on the Leapfrog acquisition and the liquidated damages (and adding back the

Funtastic loss), ABC would have actually lost almost $80 million for the six months ending December 2007, not made a $37 million profit as claimed.

ABC also reported a $108 million 'exchange difference on translation of foreign operations'—this amount did not affect annual profit. The foreign exchange 'difference' was, in reality, a foreign exchange loss (it resulted from adverse foreign exchange movements which reduced the earnings of ABC's US operations in Australian dollars). However, instead of reducing profit, ABC was able to shift the loss directly to an equity reserve. While the loss could be deferred to the equity account for the time being, were ABC ever to sell its US operations, that amount would need to be recognised on the company's profit and loss statement.

Even before the accounting irregularities are considered, ABC's earnings per share fell by 51 per cent and the company was unable to fund its 8¢-per-share dividend from ordinary earnings. The problem for ABC was outlined by long-time critic and value investor Roger Montgomery, who noted that 'ABC generates a lower rate of return on the owner's equity than a term deposit. ABC was once a very profitable small business. It's now a less-than-mediocre large business'.[8]

Despite ABC blaming the result on the seasonality of the US childcare sector, the market was not impressed. When ABC shares resumed trading on 26 February 2008 investors fled, with the scrip dropping from $3.74 the previous day to $1.15. Two days later, ABC shares bottomed at 88¢ as margin lenders sought to close out their clients' positions and regain what they could from their diminishing security.

ABC was hit by a perfect storm—its dirty financial laundry was finally being aired, and when combined with fears that the company may have breached lending covenants (which could lead to administrators being appointed) and that various ABC directors, including Eddy Groves, were at risk of being 'margin called' out of their sizable stakes in the company, even true believers in ABC started to have very serious doubts about the viability of the company.

SKIRTING THE MARGINS

As ABC shares continued their downward spiral, the situation facing ABC executives, especially Eddy Groves and Martin Kemp, was becoming increasingly dire. Groves and Kemp (along with non-executive directors Larry Anthony and David Ryan) had secretly borrowed millions of dollars through margin lending facilities to acquire additional shares in ABC Learning Centres.

Margin lending is often a route to quick wealth during economic boom times, but can lead to a rapid descent when the value of the underlying security falls. That is because, while the value of the loan remains constant, the shares which were purchased using the borrowed funds are dwindling in value. While margin loans will require a 'buffer' (of usually around 50 per cent), if the share price falls dramatically, the borrower could be in the situation where the value of the debt owed exceeds the value of the securities.

On 25 February 2008, just before ABC announced its poorly received results, Groves had a relatively large 'buffer' in his margin loan account; that is, he had more than enough equity in his margin loan account to cover the amount of money borrowed.

However, ABC's falling share price had already been problematic for another ABC executive director, Martin Kemp. Kemp was originally ABC's director in charge of special projects and acquisitions, before becoming its CEO of operations. An engineer by profession, Kemp had earlier founded his own childcare company, Premier Early Learning Centres, which he eventually sold to ABC in 2002.

It was Kemp who was ABC's executive point of contact for its acquisitions of Peppercorn and CCCA. When ABC shares traded at $8.80 in late 2006, Kemp was a very rich man, with his shares worth almost $100 million. However, while the equity value of Kemp's share had grown substantially, he had used margin loans to increase his holding—this was causing problems as ABC's share price fell.

On Christmas Eve 2007, ABC confirmed that Kemp (or more likely, Kemp's margin lender) had sold 1 000 000 of his ABC shares at an average price of $4.72. While some companies specify in their announcement whether the shares were sold pursuant to a margin call, ABC did not provide such information.*

Not long after the sale of part of Kemp's stake, ABC company secretary and legal counsel Jillian Bannan shocked investors by

---

* While Martin Kemp was offloading ABC shares, Eddy Groves was frantically raising funds to prevent his stake being sold by his margin lender. In December 2007, Groves sold his exclusive Gold Coast waterfront property for more than $11 million. He also sold a three-bedroom property to Katie Page, the wife of Harvey Norman founder Gerry Harvey, for $2.1 million.

announcing her resignation. Bannan had been Eddy Groves's loyal legal counsel for more than four years. Her departure should have raised eyebrows, with the company claiming that Bannan departed ABC to 'pursue other opportunities'.

The departure of the diligent and ethical Bannan did not appear to be related to money. Despite being the chief legal counsel at a leading ASX company, Bannan had until recently been relatively poorly paid by ABC. While most solicitors who switch from private practice to an 'in-house' counsel role receive a rise in salary, Bannan was paid a mere $81 250 in 2004 (despite being ABC's second most senior lawyer). That increased to $157 400 the following year and $343 109 in 2006. In 2007 Bannan earned $465 000, almost triple her wage two years prior. That she would depart in mysterious circumstances should have further raised alarm bells for ABC investors. It didn't.

Lesson #7: Beware of rats and sinking ships

The abrupt resignation of a senior, long-term executive without proper explanation is often a talisman for impending bad news. This is especially the case when a CEO resigns and does not take a position elsewhere; for example, the abrupt and unexplained departure of Enron CEO Jeffrey Skilling occurred a short time before the company's collapse.

However, it was ABC's dramatic share price plunge on 26 February (at one stage, ABC shares had slumped by 70 per cent to only $1.15, before recovering to finish the day at $2.15, down 40 per cent) that led to a wave of margin calls upon ABC directors.

A furious Groves would later accuse short-sellers of selling down ABC stock to force leveraged stockholders into margin sales. There may have been a small grain of truth in Groves's claims, however it was most likely that ABC's dire financial results, coupled with its highly leveraged balance sheet, caused investors to abruptly lose all faith in the stock.

Some investors feared that ABC would breach debt covenants on its $1.2 billion in debt. The fears stemmed from the fact that covenants attached to ABC's loans required that the company maintain shareholder funds of more than $2 billion. 'Shareholder funds' is defined as a company's net assets (or its total assets less its total debts).

The problem for ABC was that the vast majority of its assets were not cash or real property, but rather intangible childcare licences which the company built up during its mad acquisition dash. Therefore, a drop in the company's profitability would have the effect of casting serious doubt on the underlying value of the licences. It was a vicious cycle for ABC — lower earnings meant that the company's licences were worth less, resulting in a further drop in earnings as the carrying values of those licences were written down. Even worse — if ABC's auditors required that ABC reduce the value of its childcare licences (by as little as $223 million), it may have been required to immediately repay loans, effectively forcing it into administration.

While ABC shares were plunging, the directors' margin lenders were furiously selling shares. On 26 February 2008, David Ryan, the chairman of ABC's audit committee, had his entire shareholding of 249 101 ABC shares sold by his margin lender, at an average price of $1.89 per share.

Fellow director Martin Kemp, who had already seen a large slab of his shares sold two months earlier, could merely watch as his shareholding was decimated. Lenders briskly sold 2 million of Kemp's shares at an average price of $3.73, and a further 5.6 million of Kemp's stake at a price of only $1.67 per share. Kemp's ownership of ABC, worth more than $100 million only 14 months earlier, had dwindled to $3 million (less the associated debt).

The third victim of the margin call purge was non-executive director Larry Anthony. Anthony — you would recall — was the man who went from making laws relating to childcare into the ABC boardroom. Anthony's stake in ABC was worth more than $1 million at the company's peak, however as the company's share price fell, the value of Anthony's stake dwindled to less than $250 000. Anthony could, however, take some small solace in the lucrative consulting fees of $125 000 which he received from ABC in 2007.

While Kemp, Anthony and Ryan saw their stakes sold off, hardest hit were Eddy and Le Neve Groves. While ostensibly Eddy and Le Neve held their interests in ABC Learning Centres separately, most analysts and the media tended to view the stake as belonging solely to Eddy. In any event, the combined Groves's interest in ABC shrank from more than 37 million shares to around 18 million shares. The value of the fall was extraordinary—Groves's stake in ABC had shrunk from approximately \$325 million in December 2006 to around \$25 million.*

Two days later, ABC requested and obtained a voluntary suspension from trading on the stock exchange as it frantically tried to sell assets to repay debt and soothe investor concerns.

EDDY'S LAST ROLL OF THE DICE

On 6 March 2008, it appeared Groves had pulled off a remarkable coup, with ABC announcing the sale of 60 per cent of its US businesses to Morgan Stanley Private Equity, in a deal that valued ABC's US assets at US\$775 million. ABC would use the proceeds of the sale to repay senior debt under its syndicated banking facility.

However, as with most things that Groves did, the sale was one part smoke and another part mirrors.

Groves claimed that the sale placed ABC in 'a strong financial position' with the company 'readily able to fund [its] future growth path and, at the same time, maintain a low risk capital structure'.[9] While the deal was praised by the media and sharemarket, the agreed sale (which would later be renegotiated to a lower price) represented a near complete repudiation of ABC's growth strategies.

No longer would the company be an aggressive acquirer of global childcare assets; instead ABC would be forced for the first time to address some of its problems closer to home, most notably that childcare wasn't really the profitable business many had thought it was.

Not long after completing the Morgan Stanley deal, Groves gave a remarkable interview in which he attacked an analyst who accused ABC of breaching its debt covenants. Groves claimed that an analyst from Citigroup did not undertake proper research and failed to check facts with ABC. Groves then accused Citigroup (who was also his margin lender) of selling his shares without first consulting him, alleging, 'If I had a phone call on that particular day saying "can

---

* ABC chairwoman Sallyanne Atkinson would later claim that she was unaware Groves's stake had been funded by margin loans, stating 'I didn't know and perhaps I should have. Perhaps we should have as a board…in all the companies I've ever been on, nobody's ever asked directors "how are you financing your shares?"…You assume that people are taking care of things'.

you reduce your exposure because the shares have fallen", I could have written out some money for cash and reduced the stock. I never got that opportunity. We never even got a phone call. The stock was sold before I even blinked an eye'.[10]

A day after Groves's interview, ABC revealed in an announcement to the stock exchange that Groves's entire stake in the company had been sold by Citigroup. On 6 March 2008, the day ABC shares resumed trading after the US asset sale, Groves's lender sold the remainder of his holding — 12.1 million shares — at an average price of $2.14. Le Neve's stake was also sold, with her 6 million shares sold at an average price of $2.21. (Martin Kemp also saw almost all of his remaining 3 million shares disposed of for an average price of $2.02 per share.)

The sale of Le Neve Groves's shares by margin lenders Citigroup and BT Securities (a subsidiary of Westpac) would later lead to a legal stoush. This was because Le Neve herself did not take out margin loans against her stock — rather, Le Neve's shares were used by Eddy as security for his margin loans. When ABC's share price collapsed, the lenders seized Le Neve's shares (which had allegedly been offered as collateral) and used the proceeds from their sale to repay Eddy's loan.

In January 2009, Le Neve initiated legal action in the Supreme Court of Queensland alleging that she never provided guarantees for Eddy's margin loans, claiming that the signature on the loan documents was not her own. In other words, Le Neve effectively alleged someone forged her signature on the loan documents to obtain the margin loan (given that Eddy appeared to be the only person to benefit from the loans, the implication was reasonably clear).

Le Neve Groves is seeking to recover more than $64 million, which includes the loss of value of her ABC shares (which had been used as collateral for Eddy's margin loans) and dividends paid by ABC.* BT Securities alleged that Le Neve Groves was fully aware of the nature of the guarantee provided, with the former co-managing director of ABC allegedly attending a meeting in which the guarantee documents were executed.

---

* Le Neve Groves alleged that while the dividends paid on the shares held were paid into a joint account, she had no access to that account, despite repeated requests to Eddy for access.

By 22 April, remaining vestiges of hope for a recovery had diminished. ABC announced that the sale of 60 per cent of its US operations to Morgan Stanley had been finalised for the reduced price of US$700 million—US$75 million less than what had been agreed to in March (then again, ABC were hardly in a position to be making demands). ABC also stated that instead of turning a profit from the sale of its US business, the company would actually record a loss from the deconsolidation of $280 million, along with restructuring expenses of $30 million.

ABC also announced the departure of directors Martin Kemp, Bill Bessemer and Sallyanne Atkinson.

While ABC's share price continued to weaken, Groves retained the faith. In early July, Eddy reached a deal for him and Le Neve to sacrifice almost 90 per cent of their salaries in exchange for options in the company. The options would cost Groves 23¢ each, and would contain an exercise price of $1.15. That meant Groves would significantly benefit from any appreciation in ABC's share price above $1.15 per share (ABC shares were trading at 84¢ at the time).

The options had the potential to catapult the Groveses back to extreme wealth. That, of course, was dependent on the company's survival.

Less than a month later, ABC issued a formal profit warning, telling shareholders that as a result of write-downs in the carrying value of assets (specifically, childcare licences), worsening operating performance and a downgrade on the expected return from the sale of its UK business, the company would lose $437 million for the year. This figure was four times greater than the guidance ABC had provided in April, and easily exceeded all the alleged profits that ABC had reported in its 20-year life.

THE SWORD FALLS

On 25 August 2008, two days before ABC was due to reveal its 2008 financial results, the company requested and obtained a suspension from trading on the ASX on the grounds that it had not yet finalised its statements. Those financial results would never be revealed—nor would the company's shares ever trade again.

Just over a month later, the Sword of Damocles would finally descend on the necks of Eddy and Le Neve Groves.

Eddy Groves was replaced as CEO by Rowan Webb, a former executive from clothing group Colorado. The man who was forced to give Groves his marching orders was ABC chairman David Ryan, who noted that while Groves was 'emotionally attached to the business...he's acting in the best interests of the business to his own personal regret'.[11]

One suspects ABC shareholders and gullible lenders were even more remorseful.

On 6 November, with the company's financial statements more than two months overdue, the remaining directors of ABC finally gave up and appointed administrators.

The impact of ABC's collapse was immediate and far reaching.

The true predicament of ABC was worse than even the most cynical of onlookers would have suspected. ABC's receiver, Chris Honey of McGrathNicol, initially stated that 386 of ABC's 1042 centres were under operational review. This placed the care of more than 30000 children in jeopardy. (Ultimately, ABC's receivers would shut 55 centres, leading to the loss of more than 100 jobs and necessitating the switch of 4000 children to alternative centres.)

The diabolic nature of ABC's cash balances also forced the administrators to rely on government funding to continue operating the centres. At the time of ABC's collapse, the federal Minister for Education, Julia Gillard, publicly committed to spending millions in taxpayer subsidies to ensure that ABC centres remained open, stating that 'the Government's priority is to ensure working families reliant on ABC Learning Centres can continue to access child care for their children and ABC employees have some immediate stability'.[12] (Taxpayers ended up pumping more than $108 million into ABC before receivers were able to offload ABC's unprofitable centres to smaller, mostly not-for-profit operators.)

The collapse of ABC attracted the attention of the corporate regulator, with ASIC believed to be investigating various facets of ABC's business and whether Groves, or other ABC executives or directors, may have breached corporations laws.

Former ABC chief financial officer James Black and Eddy Groves were questioned by ASIC in late 2008 regarding potential breaches of the continuous disclosure rules. (Public companies are required to keep the market continually informed as to any material items that would be deemed by a 'reasonable person' to have an effect on the company's share price.) ASIC is also understood to have been investigating whether any ABC executives provided false or misleading statements with regard to the company's profitability.

At the time of publication, while no civil or criminal charges had been laid against Groves or any other employee or director of ABC Learning Centres, in June 2009 ASIC took legal action in the Federal Court to freeze the assets of Eddy Groves, his wife Viryan Collins-Rubie and Groves's brother-in-law Frank Zullo.

RELATED-PARTY TRANSACTIONS

While Groves received a relatively low salary from ABC (he was paid $268 468 in 2003, rising to $336 546 in 2005 and $697 000 in 2007), he benefited in other ways from his unique position as founder and CEO of the largest childcare business in the world. Despite ABC being a public company for more than seven years, Groves's personal affairs remained closely intertwined with ABC's.

ABC had maintained a very close connection with Melbourne-based investment house Austock. Former Austock chairman Bill Bessemer sat on the board of ABC since before ABC listed on the stock exchange. Coincidentally, Eddy Groves obtained a major shareholding in Austock of 4.1 per cent in January 2005. Austock effectively served as ABC's house broker, underwriting its original listing on the ASX in March 2001, and advising ABC on its later equity raisings and takeovers.

In 2002, ABC paid Austock $944 000 for financial advice relating to capital raisings; this increased to $1.2 million in 2003 and $3 million in 2004. It was not until 2005 that the money really started flowing though (shortly after Groves obtained a 4.1 per cent ownership interest in Austock). In 2005, Austock advised ABC on its complex dual mergers with Peppercorn Group and Child Care Centres of Australia, as well as an associated capital raising to fund the acquisitions. In 2005, ABC paid Austock fees of more than $16 million. That amounted to more than 30 per cent of ABC's total earnings for the year (which were $52 million).

The following year, ABC was even more generous, paying Austock more than $27 million, largely for 'payment and commission' on ABC's capital raising.

Not only did Austock provide financial advice and capital raising services, an Austock managed fund, the Australian Education Trust, also owned almost 400 properties which were leased to ABC. For another fund, called the Austock Childcare Fund, major assets were properties leased to ABC. Austock earned fees for managing these funds.

While ABC lavished fees upon Austock, it was even more generous in payments to Queensland Maintenance Services (QMS). QMS provided maintenance and construction services to ABC in work that was not submitted to a public tender process. The owner of QMS was a gentleman by the name of Frank Zullo. Zullo happened to be married to Eddy Groves's sister.

In 2002, ABC paid QMS $1.4 million. That figure rose to more than $6.3 million in 2003, $13 million in 2004 and $15.4 million in 2005. However, it was in 2006 that the relationship between ABC and QMS really flourished, with the childcare company paying Groves's brother-in-law more than $74 million for maintenance and capital works. The number was especially high given that ABC reported a total profit of $81.1 million (what's more, that profit result would later be revised downwards).

When questioned as to why such large sums were paid to a related party without any tender process, Groves claimed that 'the reason why we don't tender out is because we are satisfied of its independence and because they give us the best price by far, from the point of view of reliability and pricing … everyone (also) has to have police checks (due to work near children), so you just can't go and tender this out to a building company and then expect them to all run through the police checks'.[13]

Given ABC was spending the equivalent to almost the entire year's profit on maintenance to a related party, shareholders may have been justified in demanding a legitimate tender process. Presumably, QMS was not the only maintenance and construction company in Australia capable of having police checks conducted upon staff. Admittedly, QMS was the only maintenance business which was owned by Eddy Groves's family.

In 2007, ABC declined to tell shareholders about its dealings with QMS, claiming that as a result of changes to accounting standards it was not obliged to disclose the extent of its relationship with QMS.

Lesson #8: Watch for the relatives

A company with a high proportion of related-party transactions should be avoided by investors. Related-party transactions, even when ostensibly on an 'arm's-length basis', are usually to minority shareholders' detriment and executives' benefit. If they didn't benefit executives, it is fair to suggest that the executives would not undertake such deals in the first place.

In addition to paying QMS upwards of $100 million of ABC's money, Groves and Zullo maintained a wide-ranging commercial relationship, investing in other businesses together, with documents also indicating that the pair purchased and sold property to each other.[14] QMS once even listed its 'principal place of business' as Eddy Groves's Brisbane apartment.

Intriguingly, profits earned by QMS flowed through to another company, called Gelding. Eddy Groves was, until 2003, a beneficial shareholder and director of Gelding. In 2003, Groves's interest was transferred to a gentleman by the name of Tony Martin. Martin had once served as a director of ABC. (He resigned as a director of ABC in 2000, shortly before the company floated on the ASX.)[15] Martin was later a director of one of ABC's regional management companies which ran ABC's childcare centres. It was later alleged that these regional management companies were primarily intended to minimise payroll tax.

However, that wasn't the end of the links between ABC, Groves and Zullo. In June 2007, it was reported that a company owned by Zullo provided a $10 million loan to another childcare company, called Childcare Providers. The CEO of Childcare Providers was Groves's soon-to-be new bride, Viryan Collins-Rubie. Zullo would later acquire Childcare Providers through another company called Neighbourhood Early Learning Centres.[16]

ABC's generosity would also extend to its sponsorship of the Brisbane Bullets basketball team, which played in Australia's National

Basketball League. ABC paid the Brisbane Bullets $200 000 in 2002 and 2003, increasing to $255 000 in 2004 and 2005 and $352 000 in 2006.

It is unclear exactly what value ABC received from its lucrative sponsorship of the Bullets, however the owner of the Bullets would have appreciated the company's generosity. That person happened to be Eddy Groves. (Groves would later claim that ABC's sponsorship of the Bullets involved providing basketball tickets to 'ABC families'. A more independent observer may have deemed the sponsorship as a form of payments by the publicly owned ABC to the Groves-owned Brisbane Bullets.)

SELLING STOCK (2006–07)

Not only did Eddy Groves arguably benefit from the myriad related-party transactions he had with ABC Learning Centres, but Eddy and Le Neve were also able to sell a sizeable stake of ABC shares before the company collapsed.

Groves's net share sales were in stark contrast to his public support for ABC. Even after his eventual removal as CEO, Groves told the *Australian Financial Review* that he 'always believed fully in this company, I didn't just take it for a ride and take shares and think this is good. I bought tens of millions of dollars worth of shares at $7.00 ... I have lost that whole shareholding and I am still here to make sure that we take this to where it needs to go because of the responsibility I feel for shareholders, the banks, the staff and the families'.[17]

Groves did purchase numerous blocks of ABC shares between May 2006 and November 2007. In fact, Eddy and Le Neve acquired more than $32.6 million worth of ABC shares in 12 different purchases, at prices ranging from $5.29 to $7.25.

It was these purchases of ABC shares that led to Groves professing his faith in his company, noting in a 2008 speech that 'I left with my pants on but I've got holes in my pants. At the end of the day, I'd bought shares at probably nearly their highest point because I thought the company was undervalued then, and most of the shares were sold out from me somewhere between $1 and $2 so

I think I took the heat with everybody else...when the share price started to slide, I wanted to show them I was with them, so I bought $40 million worth of stock'.

While Groves did buy around $32 million worth of ABC shares, he neglected to add that the purchases were eclipsed by the sale of almost $40 million worth of ABC shares over that same period.

In total, over the last two years of ABC's existence (before their stake was subject to a margin call), Eddy and Le Neve were actually net sellers of ABC stock—collecting more than $7 million cash from the net sales. Groves bought only $32.6 million worth of shares, and sold nearly $40 million worth.

While his stake in ABC was reduced to nothing after receiving a series of margin calls, Groves did not leave ABC destitute. Despite Eddy being forced to hand back the Brisbane Bullets basketball licence, he still retained an interest in Quantum Food Services—the Queensland milk distribution business. Financial statements indicate that Quantum sold its milk business in September 2006, with its most recent public filing revealing that the company had net assets of $1.6 million and produced a profit of $413 798 for the year ending 30 June 2006 (the business did manage to generate operating cash flows of more than $1.3 million).*

Groves is also understood to have retained his ownership of the Distinctive Homes Dome in Adelaide (which was purchased for $3.95 million), a $2.5 million French mansion, as well as maintaining close links to the internet betting agency Sports Acumen. It is understood that Groves had a 25 per cent ownership interest in Sports Acumen, through his shareholding in parent company Bet Worldwide Pty Ltd.

A director of Sports Acumen is Groves's former personal accountant James Black. Black and Groves have a long association; Black served as ABC's chief financial officer, and his former accounting firm (Harris Black) was the registered office of another childcare business called Bright Horizons. Bright Horizons was owned by none other than Frank Zullo, Groves's brother-in-law and

---

* Quantum's financial statements were audited by Simon Green of Pitcher Partners—the same auditor who signed off on ABC's accounts in 2006. Those ABC accounts did not provide any indication of the existence of upfront developer payments (which were not revealed until Ernst & Young audited ABC the following year) and which, according to a class action being funded by IMF, had the effect of artificially inflating ABC's reported earnings by $30 million.

recipient of more than $74 million in untendered maintenance works from ABC.

Another of Groves's surviving financial interests is in ABC's former broker Austock. Groves is believed to have retained five million shares in Austock (the value of those shares has slipped from $11 million to $1.1 million).

After ABC's collapse, it also appeared that Groves suddenly developed a taste for philanthropy. ASIC alleged that Groves transferred a $5 million Palm Beach mansion to a trust called Perfection Too in March 2009. The sole director of the trust happened to be Groves's new bride Viryan Collins-Rubie. The beneficiaries of the trust are Groves's children.

That's not all though—Eddy was also busy transferring overseas property interests to close associates. In 2009, Groves sold a US$2 million property located in the United States to a man called Grant Caddee. Caddee, a sports agent and former CEO of the Melbourne Tigers basketball team, was an old friend of Groves and once served as a marketing executive with ABC.

WHAT WENT WRONG?

The collapse of ABC was more than just another corporate collapse. With the help of an unpopular federal government policy (partially implemented by former ABC director Larry Anthony), Eddy Groves revolutionised the childcare sector. ABC Learning Centres became the McDonald's of childcare—ubiquitous, consistent and almost universally detested.

As the company grew, its profitability and return on equity declined. From being a small and profitable private company, ABC came to resemble somewhat of a pyramid scheme. The company needed to continue acquiring centres to maintain its sales and earnings growth. Meanwhile, every time ABC added another centre, it became less profitable. Eddy Groves was furiously trying to remove water from a sinking ship. But every time he threw a bucket-load overboard, even more water would seep in.

In desperation, as its return on equity fell, ABC turned to debt to fund its overseas expansion—a decision which would prove fatal. ABC obtained billions of dollars in debt and equity while its financial statements were arguably misleading (a fact that may be the subject of lengthy arguments in any legal action). It appears that ABC, under the so-called watchful eye of auditor Pitcher Partners, was not adequately explaining to investors and lenders the true nature of its income.

While entrepreneurs need a large degree of self-confidence to build a successful business, it is that innate belief which may lead to their ultimate downfall. Only months before ABC's insolvency, Groves claimed that 'this is all about a rebirth and takes us back down a pathway that we can go down...[ABC is] a very good company. We made a mistake in a year out of 20 years. I don't think that's too bad. I am not saying that lightly. I am disappointed with what we did but we need to change that around and I know we can'.[18]

But ABC was not a company that could be changed or turned around. It was a company which grew too quickly using too much debt in an industry simply not suited to the harsh realities of the commercial sector.

Despite the eventual collapse of ABC and the loss of wealth suffered by investors and directors of the company, Eddy Groves appears to have survived the fall with many interests across the globe. Groves still owns millions of dollars worth of assets, including property and operating businesses, while he also appeared to hurriedly transfer other assets to friends and family. Meanwhile thousands of children, parents and childcare workers had their lives placed in turmoil by ABC's collapse.

If the rise and fall of ABC Learning Centres proved anything, it's that some businesses are just not made for profit.

CHAPTER 3

MFS

How the Gold Coast white shoe brigade got a second chance—and blew it

We don't actually need the equity… We could stay as we are and keep going. Our earnings guidance is unchanged and there is no change to our debt position.

MFS CEO Michael King to analysts on 18 January 2009, three days prior to MFS shares being suspended from the ASX, never to trade again[1]

OF ALL the collapses that occurred during the height of the financial crisis of 2008, few stand out more for sheer incompetence and unmitigated greed than the sorry saga of MFS. At its height, MFS was valued at more than $3 billion, while its managed funds and satellites owned billions of dollars of tourism and financial assets, including stakes in Australia's largest ski resorts, a swathe of hotels and apartments as well as commercial and residential property interests. Its founders, two small-time lawyers from the Gold Coast, would own a stake once valued at more than $436 million.

And then, almost overnight, it was gone—along with virtually the entire senior management team that caused the debacle.

NEVER TRUST A LAWYER (LATE 1990s–2002)

Anyone who believes that history repeats would never have invested a dime in MFS or any of its satellite funds. The co-managing directors of MFS, Michael Christodoulou King and Phillip Adams, were solicitors who had been partners at a small Queensland law firm called McLaughlins Solicitors, based on the Gold Coast (MFS stood for McLaughlins Financial Services).

The two lawyers began a small funds management business before launching a $440 million pooled mortgage fund in November 2000, called MFS Capital Insured Income Fund (later renamed MFS Premium Income Fund).

In July 2001, MFS would acquire the management rights to the MFS Leveraged Investments Group (MLIG). It was this vehicle that provided King and Adams with their first foray into the magical world of the ASX.

MLIG listed on the ASX in December 2002. That was back when leverage was considered a good thing as it allowed investors to receive turbocharged returns through the generous use of debt. It was only after the financial crisis of 2008 that risk premiums were rediscovered and the word 'leverage' would become about as popular as Richard Dawkins at Sunday mass. (MFS was the manager of MLIG and the entities would merge in 2004.)

The board of MLIG included MFS directors such as King and Adams, as well as financial planners Michael Hiscock and Paul Manka, and hedge fund manager Spencer Young. Financial planners (especially Avenue Capital Management, of which Hiscock and Manka were partners) would later prove vital to MFS's growth, with clients' monies pouring into MFS's satellites and managed funds.

Investors acquiring units in MLIG (and investing in the MFS Premium Income Fund) would have been well advised to have done some digging into King and Adams's past before handing over their hard earned. McLaughlins Solicitors had been embroiled in a national mortgage scandal in the late 1990s. In 1999, ASIC was forced to crack down on the practice that involved law firms investing clients' monies into risky loans to property developers. The managing partner of McLaughlins Solicitors would later describe King as having a 'very aggressive risk profile'.

Consumer advocate Denise Brailey noted that 'investments with McLaughlins Solicitors were the first ones mentioned almost every time' and 'investors...were having huge problems with McLaughlins, with people [noting that] their income payments had stopped and they couldn't recover their capital'.[2] A decade later, near identical claims would be levelled at a fund managed by King and Adams, with equally disastrous results.

Lesson #1: History repeats

There are tens of thousands of businesses you can invest in (through local or international sharemarkets or privately). It is not advisable to buy (part of) a company that is run by someone who has been involved in dubious behaviour or was previously part of a collapsed company.

MLIG's prospectus outlined the cauldron of risky assets in which the trust would invest unitholders' funds, including 'property-linked high yield secured loans', including 'mezzanine, bridging and non-confirming loans' and 'interests in unlisted investment vehicles'. The prospectus noted that MLIG was prepared to provide second mortgages based on a loan-to-valuation ratio of 95 per cent. That meant should the value of the security underlying the loan fall by 5 per cent and the borrower be unable to repay the loan, MLIG would have been forced to take a loss.

It appeared that MLIG, and its manager MFS, were following the well-trodden route favoured by Queensland's infamous white shoe brigade, providing what appeared to be high returns to investors in exchange for inordinately high risk.

THE EARLY DAYS (2002–04)

After listing in 2002, King and Adams rapidly expanded MLIG's business. By 2003, the firm had more than $1 billion of funds under management across a range of listed and unlisted managed funds.

While MLIG's performance appeared rosy, a closer inspection of its financial results would reveal it wasn't as safe as the houses in which it purported to invest. For a start, MLIG was funding its expansion largely through expensive, borrowed monies. Even during 2003, back when debt was plentiful and cheap, MLIG was paying interest of more than 10 per cent on its short-term borrowings and unsecured notes. It would then lend those monies on at interest rates of above 15 per cent, largely for second mortgages on Queensland residential and commercial properties. Very quickly, King and Adams were creating the foundations for what would become one almighty house of cards built on foundations of debt.

While MLIG represented the public face of MFS, MFS itself (then still privately held and controlled by Adams and King) was frantically expanding its assets under management. The company would acquire the Mount Hotham and Falls Creek ski resorts in Victoria and purchase an 18.5 per cent stake in the ASX-listed BreakFree Limited. BreakFree had been founded in 1989 by former Sydney Swans footballer Tony Smith, and managed Queensland holiday rentals and serviced apartments. In total, through an aggressive series of acquisitions MFS had accumulated funds under management of more than $1.7 billion by 2004.

MFS was also the responsible entity for other listed funds, including MFS Living and Leisure (which had an option to acquire MFS's ski resort assets) as well as MFS Diversified Trust, a listed property trust with a market capitalisation of around $47 million. In September 2003, MFS entered the lucrative hedge funds business when it purchased HFA Asset Management Limited (the founder of HFA, Spencer Young, was also on the board of MFS).

In late 2004, MFS announced that it would merge with MLIG. The merger was effectively a 'back-door' listing of MFS (which was considerably larger than MLIG). The deal came at a convenient time for MFS—in 2004 the business had lost $2.9 million (before tax benefits), compared with a profit of $2.8 million the previous year. The major difference was a substantial increase in borrowing costs based on its ever-increasing debt.

RAPID GROWTH (2005–06)

After the merger was consummated, the new MFS ran a remarkably diverse array of businesses, with interests in fund management, structured finance and advice and tourism. MFS had even acquired the downtrodden Sheraton Mirage Resort at Port Douglas. The Mirage had originally been developed in the mid 1980s by failed entrepreneur Christopher Skase, whose empire was later crippled by mounting debts.

During the 2005 financial year, MFS enjoyed an 81 per cent rise in assets under management to $2.8 billion. MFS acquired the remainder of BreakFree and vastly expanded its tourism assets through the purchase of the Mirage, as well as the Peppers and Bale luxury accommodation brands. Its shift into tourism would be consummated when MFS combined all of its tourism assets into a vehicle which it would name Stella Resorts Group.

Lesson #2: Buying and selling stuff isn't a real business

In the 1980s, entrepreneurs such as Alan Bond, John Spalvins and Christopher Skase were known as 'paper shufflers'; that is, they bought and sold assets, but didn't make or do anything in particular. The same can be said for MFS (as well as Allco and Babcock & Brown).

It is usually preferable to invest in a company that makes money by doing something (such as BHP Billiton which digs stuff out of the ground, or Google which sells advertisements and provides accurate search results) rather than a company that buys and sells assets (a notable exception to this rule is Warren Buffett's company Berkshire Hathaway).

The rapid expansion was not accompanied by an immediate rise in profit, with MFS losing $6.3 million in 2005 based on sales of $94 million (the laggard was MFS's ski fields, which reported a loss of $11.8 million). Despite the deficit, MFS's share price remained buoyant, with King and Adams's joint stake in the company rising to be worth more than $107 million.* Tony Smith, who vended his BreakFree business to MFS earlier in 2005, would hold a $15 million stake.

Investors were happy to shrug off the earnings performance and buy into MFS's growth story. In its 2005 annual report, directors noted that they expect 'MFS Limited and its subsidiaries will continue to experience significant growth in the underlying businesses and expect

---

* Adams and King were paid meagre salaries in 2005, of $276 554 and $282 645 respectively. Even Jonathan Pain, the chief investment officer of MFS's hedge fund subsidiary, received remuneration of only $180 376—an extremely low income in an industry not known for wage restraint.

to take up any new business opportunities as they arise'. However, while MFS appeared to be on a growth trajectory, the seeds of its failure had already been planted.

A closer inspection of MFS's balance sheet would reveal that it was being propped up largely by intangibles, specifically more than $300 million of goodwill. An intangible asset is something which you can't touch, unlike, say, plant and machinery. While intangibles sometimes have a negative connotation (analysts will often tout a firm's 'net tangible assets'), it is foolish to suggest that intangibles have no value. For example, a brand name can be worth billions if it is Coca-Cola or McDonald's.

However, not all intangibles are income-producing assets. One of the most common intangible assets is known as 'goodwill'. As was explained in the ABC Learning Centres chapter, goodwill appears on a company's balance sheet when it acquires another business for a price which is greater than the other company's 'book value'. (A business will pay a premium above book value when it thinks it can extract synergies from the acquisition.)

Accounting goodwill therefore is only an asset in the sense that the acquirer believes it can do a better job of running a business than the previous owner or can reduce costs by 'economies of scale'. Sometimes it can; however, often it can't and the goodwill is quietly written off in later periods. Generally, a company with large levels of goodwill is considered 'riskier' than a company with significant tangible assets which can be easily sold. The other problem with goodwill is that if the company ceases to be a 'going concern', the value of the goodwill will generally shrink to zero.

While MFS had tangible assets worth $400 million, it had accumulated $385 million in debts. When its $300 million in intangibles were ignored, the company would appear far less attractive.

In 2005, an MFS managed fund would be awarded the annual Standard & Poor's Mortgage Fund of the Year award. It is not without irony that Standard & Poor's, which would later be heavily criticised and face multiple legal actions for its generous rating of sub-prime debt in the United States, would deem an MFS managed fund to be worthy of such an honour.

For MFS, 2006 would be its 'break-out' year. It turned a $6.3 million loss into a reported $97.4 million profit. MFS was certainly riding the financial boom with gay abandon; some even compared the Gold Coast–based fund manager to Australia's own investment banking superstar Macquarie Bank. However, investors who were paying close attention would have realised that MFS's profit was far from sustainable.

In early 2006, MFS sold its troubled ski field assets to another one of its listed satellites, MFS Living and Leisure, for approximately $110 million (including debt). The purchase price appeared to be exceptionally generous given that MFS had acquired the ski field assets for $75 million the previous year and had done only minor renovations and expansion to improve their value (some would argue that their value had actually dropped with skier days falling at the resorts under MFS's ownership). The pesky issue of global warming and recent poor Victorian ski seasons would also do little to bolster the value of the ski assets. Further, given the ski fields generated earnings before tax of only $4.6 million in 2005, the purchase multiple appeared at best lofty, and at worst a complete rip-off.

The sale to Living and Leisure (which was managed by MFS) generated a $15 million 'profit' for the mothership.* One suspects a more independently minded manager would not have been so willing to pay such a high price to MFS (fortunately for MFS, it was not averse to the conflict). Two years later, Living and Leisure would be forced to write down the value of the ski resorts by $29.1 million after seeing profit slump to $680000 in 2007 and $2.3 million in 2008. Living and Leisure also wrote off another $10.7 million in 2009, meaning that Living and Leisure effectively overpaid $40 million to MFS for the ski resort assets.

The benefits to MFS from the sale of its ski assets were twofold. First, MFS would be able to book a profit that year on the grossly inflated sale price. Not only that, MFS would receive an enlarged management fee from Living and Leisure on the basis of Living and Leisure having greater assets under management. The following year MFS not only booked a profit from the sale of its ski assets, but it also charged Living and Leisure a $2.9 million 'acquisition fee' for

---

* An independent expert's report prepared by Ernst & Young found that the sale was fair and reasonable for MFS Living and Leisure securityholders, valuing the ski assets at between $104.5 million and $121.1 million. Ernst & Young's view was based on very generous future revenue and cost-of-capital assumptions. These assumptions would be repudiated by Living and Leisure in 2008 when it wrote down the value of its ski assets by $29 million based upon higher cash outflows and an increased cost of capital. Ernst & Young was paid $150000 by MFS to prepare its independent report.

the privilege of effectively overpaying by $40 million for the resorts. That year, Living and Leisure also paid MFS management fees of $1.1 million, up from $59000 in 2006.

In 2006, MFS also booked an $88.5 million profit from 'other income', of which $83.6 million related to a 'profit on disposal of assets'. The vast majority (approximately $67 million) of those 'profits' was due to the partial sale of MFS's stake in hedge fund manager HFA. HFA shares would later slump by 90 per cent as investors ran from hedge fund assets in 2008. A further $8 million profit would be booked on the sale of part of MFS's New Zealand subsidiary MFS Pacific Holdings (MFS Pacific Holdings would later collapse, with investors losing more than NZ$450 million).

In any event, without the bonuses of the related-party sale of its ski field assets and the disposal of part of its HFA and MFS Pacific stakes, MFS would have made a pre-tax profit of $18 million, rather than the reported $116 million.

Lesson #3: Treat 'related-party' sales with great caution

When a company sells an asset to a related party (especially where the related party is 'managed' by the seller), investors should treat any profit on the sale as 'extraordinary'. Often the asset will be sold for more than it was really 'worth'. That is because the seller is more concerned about its earnings than it is about its satellite or subsidiary. While selling assets to related parties may be a successful business model in the short term, eventually shareholders in the buyer will realise they are being duped.

A company is required to specifically disclose when it sells an asset to a related party. It is always worth looking very carefully through the notes to the company's financial statements (of both the buyer and the seller) to determine what related-party sales occurred during the year and how this affected profitability.

Aside from reporting what many thought was a fine profit result, during 2006 MFS would also increase its public profile by sponsoring popular events, including the Australian Golf Masters in Melbourne. While the sponsorships represented a good chance for MFS directors such as Michael King to enter polite circles, the benefits for MFS shareholders from the $3 million naming deal appeared somewhat more vague.

MFS's higher profile may, however, have assisted it in receiving favourable coverage from stockbroking analysts. Admittedly, analysts tend to have one eye on the company they are appraising and the other on potential investment banking business which might be forthcoming. One particularly fawning analyst from ABN AMRO noted that 'MFS now has the ability to leverage off its established business model to increase recurring income streams via management, transaction and performance fees'.[3]

MFS's earnings result would also hide other somewhat dubious investments. In January 2006, MFS Diversified (another of the satellite companies that was spun off and then managed by MFS) spent more than $6 million acquiring a 14 per cent stake in struggling retirement home operator Village Life. Less than two weeks after it acquired the stake, the retirement home company requested a two-week suspension from trading on the stock exchange, as its managing director was unable to guarantee it would be able to continue as a going concern. (In June, MFS Diversified would write down the value of its Village Life holding by almost $3 million.) When an investee company doesn't last two weeks before its CEO questions its very existence, questions need to be asked about the competence of MFS Diversified's due diligence process. If it even had one.

The following year MFS Diversified was forced to cut ties with Village Life, leading to what was described by some as an 'absolute disaster' for residents who were evicted from their homes.[4] Ultimately, management of the 10 retirement homes was taken over by another provider.

What wasn't a disaster were the bank accounts of MFS founders Michael King and Phil Adams. In April 2006, their combined stake in MFS was worth more than $250 million. Not bad for a couple of lawyers from the Gold Coast. However, King and Adams would err by not cashing in their chips — instead they chose to double down.

A TOURISM GIANT (2006–07)

In September 2006, MFS upped the ante once more, announcing a cash and scrip takeover bid for accommodation provider S8, valuing the accommodation business at more than $900 million. S8 was a hotel management group (S8 had previously attempted to acquire BreakFree prior to that company's takeover by MFS) which also owned the travel agencies Harvey World Travel and Gullivers Travel Group. Shortly after the S8 acquisition, MFS spent $120 million acquiring Australian and New Zealand accommodation provider Outrigger.

S8 was founded by colourful entrepreneur Chris Scott. Scott would later emerge as a key player at MFS, along with S8's deputy chairwoman Jenny Hutson. Both Scott and Hutson assumed MFS board seats following the merger, which created Australia's second largest accommodation business. In a decision that he would later live to regret, Scott accepted MFS shares, rather than cash, for virtually his entire holding in S8.

In March 2007, shortly after the S8 deal was consummated, MFS announced that its public face and co-founder Phil Adams would relocate to the United Arab Emirates to lead an international expansion (perhaps sensing the danger, Adams also resigned from the MFS board). At the same time, chairman Terry O'Dwyer would be replaced by former politician Andrew Peacock.

The changes didn't appear to hamper MFS's share price ascent. In May, MFS shares would peak at $6.85, valuing the company at more than $3.2 billion, an astonishing figure considering the previous year MFS had earned only $18 million from continuing operations (which was equal to less than 10 per cent of the company's reported profit figure).* By financial year-end 2007, MFS had amassed more than $5 billion in assets under management. The future, according to MFS anyway, was bright, with the company telling shareholders in its 2007 annual report that 'the Directors of MFS expect substantial out-performance in the near-term and over the next few years. The Company is in an excellent position to capitalise on the many opportunities before it'. It would appear that the MFS directors were a tad optimistic—six months later, the company collapsed.

---

* At its peak, King and Adams's combined stake in MFS was worth more than $400 million, while long-term directors Michael Hiscock and Paul Manka had each amassed holdings worth more than $30 million. It would be revealed after MFS's collapse that the directors all had substantial debt attached to their holdings in the company.

THE DARK CLOUDS GATHER

MFS's 2007 results showed signs of dark clouds on the horizon. While the company reported a net profit of $184.9 million, almost double the previous year's earnings of $97.4 million (2006 earnings had been substantially enlarged by the sale of HFA and the ski resort assets), the profit was once again somewhat mysterious.

While MFS's tourism assets accounted for half of the company's revenue, they delivered $60 million, or around one-fifth, of total profits. It was MFS's fund management and 'investment banking' businesses which would prove to be its key profit centres. The investment banking division, which effectively bought and sold assets (and charged fees along the way) would make a profit of $132 million on sales of $159 million. The financial services assets delivered earnings of $75 million on only $103 million of sales. MFS did not explain the actual origins of its investment banking profits in its financial statements, nor did it provide a detailed breakdown of financial services earnings.

A disinterested onlooker would most likely conclude that the MFS financial statements indicated a company in solid health — $1.53 billion in net assets, strong operating cash flow and a relatively small level of current liabilities due within the next year.

The headline profit allowed MFS to spread the wealth among its senior executives. CEO Michael King, who had in the past received a relatively low salary, saw his base pay increase from $505 000 to $800 000. King also received a $1.6 million cash bonus. In total, King's remuneration increased by more than 220 per cent to $3.1 million. Stella boss, Rolf Krecklenberg, also received a substantial pay rise, with his remuneration tripling from $527 139 to $1.6 million. MFS's new head of Corporate & Investment Banking, Luke Gannon, was paid $2.9 million, although Gannon unwisely elected to receive $1.9 million of his pay in soon-to-be-worthless MFS scrip.*

MFS's 2007 financial results would prove to be its zenith. As the global financial crisis began to take hold, MFS's share price slumped, falling from more than $6.50 in June to $4.40 in December. However, the weakening share price was little more than a shudder

---

* Gannon had previously served as MFS's outside council while working at a large national law firm. The vast majority of Gannon's former legal practice related to servicing MFS.

compared to the earthquake about to devastate MFS and its CEO
Michael King.

THE PHONE CALL FROM HELL
(JANUARY 2008)

MFS had spent the best part of 2007 trying to offload its Stella
tourism business. In November 2007, King rejected an offer from
private equity firm CVC Capital Partners which valued Stella at
approximately $1.8 billion.

MFS appeared to be travelling swimmingly through choppy
financial waters, until January 2008. Just after New Year, King told
shareholders that the company would need to refinance $150 million
in short-term debt by March. Soon after, MFS would receive a
surprise merger proposal from fellow Queensland-based fund
manager City Pacific. The offer involved City Pacific acquiring all of
MFS's business, except the Stella travel group, in exchange for City
Pacific shares. (Only five months prior, MFS had made an offer to
acquire City Pacific.) Pending shareholder reaction, MFS shares were
suspended from trading.

MFS shareholders gave the offer short shrift, and two days
later MFS announced another proposal to separate Stella and its
financial services businesses into two separately listed entities. While
MFS's presentation to investors and analysts appeared upbeat,
King also noted that Stella would undertake a rights issue to raise
$550 million. While the separation of the two distinct businesses was
expected, the market was shell-shocked by MFS's sudden need for
new capital—according to the company's 2007 financial statements,
it had net assets of $1.5 billion and generated $211 million cash from
its operations and apparently only needed to refinance $150 million
of debt in coming months.

To explain the deal and rights issue, on 18 January 2008 MFS
boss Michael King held what would later become one of the most
infamous conference calls in recent Australian corporate history.

During the 67-minute presentation, MFS shares reopened
and securityholders exited in droves. MFS's share price, which had
previously closed at $3.75, would fall to only 71¢—a drop of more

than 80 per cent in the space of an hour. The precipitous share price fall was especially destructive for MFS directors, including King, Hiscock and Manka, who had substantial margin loans attached to their shareholdings. (Long-time director Hiscock had resigned from the MFS board earlier in the week after receiving an earlier margin call.) At the conclusion of the call, King would make one of his few accurate observations, noting that 'it seems this proposal today has not been well received'.[5]

One analyst covering MFS noted that it was 'a ridiculous time to do a capital raising. It's suicidal...I just can't understand why you would have to do a capital raising unless you have an urgent need to do so at this point of time'.[6] King's credibility was fatally wounded after stockbroker and former MFS supporter Charlie Green called for his resignation, noting that 'the share price is telling you that nobody believes you at the end of the day'.[7]

The conference call would mark the beginning of the end for MFS.

Three days later, King would fall on his sword, resigning as a director and CEO of the company he founded a decade earlier. King was replaced by his young deputy Craig White, whose first public utterances would be to criticise investors for departing the share register. White noted that MFS's 'share price does not represent what the company is worth'.[8] White was correct in one sense—there was no way MFS was worth anything near $300 million. The true figure was closer to zero.

On Wednesday 23 January MFS shares would once again be suspended from trading on the ASX. MFS as a listed company was dead. Many would soon feast on its withering corpse.

SHARING THE PAIN: THE MFS SATELLITES COLLAPSE

By early 2008, securityholders in the MFS headstock weren't the only ones to experience the cold chill of MFS's follies. Listed satellites MFS Diversified (which invested in property assets and retirement homes) and MFS Living and Leisure were also embroiled in the turmoil.

While MFS was flying in 2007, so too were Diversified and Living and Leisure. Diversified boss Guy Farrands gloated to the fund's securityholders in its 2007 annual report that 'the 2007 year demonstrates the Group's ability to execute efficiently and decisively across a range of areas. The full benefits of the business model we have built have only begun to be extracted and we are confident we are on the right track to achieving all the goals for the business outlined to Securityholders'. Farrands may have been a little optimistic— within two years, MFS Diversified's security price fell by more than 90 per cent.

While MFS Diversified recorded a strong improvement in profit, the devil was in the detail. The entity, which had merged with retirement home operator Villa World during the year, reported a large operating cash loss, burning more than $65 million cash. The major problem lay in a substantial rise in debtors (accounts receivable increased by $94 million in 2007). While MFS Diversified was reporting sales revenue, in many cases its customers hadn't actually paid anything.

Lesson #4: Increasing 'accounts receivable' is not a good thing

While 'accounts receivable' (also known as debtors) is classified as an asset on a company's balance sheet, it is not an asset which should usually be increasing. Rising debtors (especially as a percentage of revenue) may mean that a company is having difficulty getting its customers to pay. This could be because its customers are in financial trouble, or the sales were not legitimate in the first place.

Notwithstanding the poor cash flow result, MFS Diversified paid more than $8.5 million in fees to the MFS mothership during the year. Arguably, MFS Diversified unitholders were overpaying for MFS's management expertise—the fees paid to MFS actually exceeded the $6.1 million net profit the business earned.*

In a somewhat perverse state of affairs, in 2008 MFS Diversified would pay MFS (which by then was known as Octaviar)

---

* Fees paid by MFS Diversified to MFS included a base management fee, performance fee, asset acquisition fee, asset disposal fee, development management fee, debt arrangement fee and reimbursement of other costs. It is somewhat surprising that MFS didn't charge Diversified a fee for calculating the myriad fees.

a management fee of more than $5 million—that was despite the entity losing $66 million and its security price slumping by more than 70 per cent. In May 2008, Diversified (which had since been renamed GEO Property) cut all ties with MFS, paying $10.5 million to buy out the management rights. The following year, GEO announced a $131 million loss, largely caused by write-downs on dud investments acquired under MFS's management.

MFS's other major satellite, MFS Living and Leisure, was an even bigger abomination. You may remember Living and Leisure as the sucker which appeared to pay too much for MFS's ski resort assets in 2005. Living and Leisure had managed to perfect the strategy of buying high and selling low, with its security price slumping from more than $1.00 in 2006 to only 2¢ in 2009. Living and Leisure would ultimately be forced to turn to Australia's former richest man James Packer, whose hedge fund Arctic Capital provided an emergency $100 million lifeline to the entity in late 2008. Despite its poor performance, Living and Leisure paid the MFS mothership management fees of more than $4.7 million.

THE FALLOUT (FEBRUARY 2008–09)

As MFS grew, so too did Michael King's riches. By the time of the company's collapse, King had developed a five-field polo complex near the Gold Coast which he named 'Elysian Fields'. According to Greek mythology, Elysium was a heavenly place where the righteous are made immortal by favour of the gods. Sadly for MFS shareholders, about the only thing that had anything to do with King which was immortal was the name of his polo field—everything else was dying a slow, painful death.

On 23 January 2008, MFS announced that King's ally and long-time director of MFS Paul Manka had his entire stake in the company sold by his margin lender. Manka's holding in MFS was once worth more than $30 million. For a financial planner, it appears that Manka's financial affairs were not especially well planned.

MFS directors weren't the only ones whose phones were ringing —MFS itself revealed that it had been forced to offload its stakes in satellites MFS Diversified and HFA, as well as a smaller holding in retirement home operator Babcock & Brown Communities, to pay off associated margin facilities. MFS reaped around $60 million from the sales. The sales were made in a desperate bid to repay $150 million to US-based hedge fund Fortress Investment Group, a creditor not known for its patience with debtors.

By early February, MFS reached an agreement with Luxembourg-based CVC Asia Pacific to sell a 65 per cent share of the Stella travel business for $409 million (valuing Stella at $630 million). CVC had the advantage of being the only legitimate bidder for the assets, which had the previous year been valued by MFS at $1.5 billion. Based on the sale price, MFS overpaid for its tourism assets by $830 million — even with global stock markets crashing, few businesses can lay claim to destroying so much shareholder value in such a brief period.

With King at the helm, MFS truly was a money-losing machine. (MFS would eventually sell its remaining 35 per cent stake in Stella to CVC for $3.5 million, ultimately reaping only $412.5 million for assets which it paid more than $2.2 billion for.)

MFS shareholders were somewhat aggrieved by its performance — none more so than former S8 boss Chris Scott, who had vended his accommodation business to MFS the previous year in exchange for $220 million worth of MFS shares.* With his consideration being now virtually worthless, Scott wasn't especially happy. In March 2008, Scott threatened an extraordinary meeting of MFS shareholders unless he and his two associates were appointed to the MFS board. (At that meeting, MFS was renamed Octaviar, after receiving a settlement payment from a US-based fund manager also called MFS.)

Scott was especially critical of the decision to sell 65 per cent of Stella to CVC, attacking the board led by Andrew Peacock and dubbing the deal the 'scandal of the year'; Peacock appeared to be no fan of Scott's either, noting that 'for reasons well known to Mr Scott, I have no respect for him whatsoever'.[9] (The sale to Stella would later be vindicated with the business's profitability falling drastically. In fact, its performance was so bad that CVC ended up taking legal action against MFS for misleading conduct in overstating the profitability of the tourism group.)

---

* Scott had begun his business career as a truck driver, before moving to Singapore in the late 1970s and creating several transport companies. Scott would then build his travel business, S8, to be worth $700 million before making the fatal mistake of selling it to MFS in exchange for MFS scrip.

Peacock's feelings towards Scott may have also had something to do with Scott's upcoming appearance in the Southport Magistrates Court in August that year to answer charges relating to commissions deducted in relation to S8 apartments. If found guilty, Stella would have been liable to pay $44 million in fines while Chris Scott himself faced a possible two-year jail term.

Peacock's enmity for Scott would not last long. Several weeks later, Scott, along with two business associates, was welcomed onto the MFS board. By May, Peacock had resigned as chairman of newly renamed Octaviar (for the sake of consistency, Octaviar will generally be referred to as MFS throughout). Scott's joy would be short-lived; the following year, Scott would be sued by his margin lender for failing to meet a $9 million margin call on his MFS shares.

When MFS finally released its December 2007 preliminary results in April 2008 it didn't make for pleasant reading. MFS directors noted that there was 'material uncertainty' as to whether it would be able to continue to operate as a going concern. The directors wrote off $590 million from the book value of its Stella accommodation business. Directors would also write off $90 million from the value of its Gersh property investment business and would not even try to quantify the impairment to goodwill on the balance sheet. In August 2009, MFS administrators sold the company's remaining 35 per cent stake in Stella to CVC for only $3.5 million.* (In return, CVC agreed to drop legal action relating to the alleged inaccurate profit forecasts originally made by MFS.)

In what appeared to be very wishful thinking, directors claimed that MFS still owned net assets of more than $1.2 billion. Even before the massive write-downs, the entity managed to lose more than $46 million from its operations during the past six months compared with positive cash flows of $211 million the previous year.

MFS would never release its 2008 financial results. Administrators were appointed to the company in September, and the following April receivers would be assigned to the company's Sunleisure subsidiary, one of its few profitable businesses. In August 2009, Octaviar was removed from the official list of the ASX after being unable to pay its listing fees. Formal liquidation proceedings began.

---

* CVC is also understood to have undertaken a debt-for-equity swap with major creditor UBS, which was owed approximately $600 million.

THE PAIN SPREADS

While MFS was suffering an agonising death, its satellite funds were also having a torrid time. MFS's largest managed fund was the MFS Premium Investment Fund (PIF). The PIF was meant to be a relatively safe investment fund whose brief was to provide a steady income stream, largely through financing and property investments. The fund claimed to provide returns ranging from 8.25 per cent to 9.25 per cent with investment terms of 6, 9, 12 and 24 months, and investors having the ability to withdraw funds when their investment term expires.[10]

As with everything to do with MFS, the PIF reality was quite different.

On 28 January 2008, PIF announced it was freezing redemptions for its 11 000 unitholders for 180 days. In March, the fund also suspended interest payments. The suspension was particularly painful for PIF unitholders—PIF was not a hedge fund for sophisticated investors who could afford to be without their money for an extended period; rather, it was supposed to be a sturdy, income-paying fund relied upon by thousands of retirees for their livelihoods.

Unbeknown to many PIF investors, the fund had been making all sorts of risky investments, including a $40 million punt on an apartment development in the Sydney suburb of Sylvania (which would fall through) and the acquisition of substantial holdings in other MFS satellites, such as MFS Living and Leisure and MFS Diversified. PIF also made a $50 million 'loan' to the MFS mothership, another $62 million loan to Diversified and lent a further $50 million to another MFS satellite called Causeway. PIF also acquired a 19 per cent stake in MFS Diversified.* One suspects the aged pensioners who thought they were investing in a safe property fund would have received quite a shock when they were told that their savings were being handed about the MFS empire like a slab of beer at a barbecue.

As the manager of PIF, MFS received more than $16 million in fees during 2007. (The MFS headstock also reaped more than

---

* PIF was the major shareholder in Diversified, while the second largest unitholder was another MFS managed fund known as MFS Optimizer One, which owned 14 per cent. In July 2009, a Joint Parliamentary Committee would investigate the allegations that Octaviar improperly dealt with PIF funds to prop up its other operations.

$3 million in management fees from MFS Diversified in 2007.) The management services undertaken by MFS appeared to largely consist of diverting PIF funds to prop up the value of its other satellites. Those other satellites would also then pay management fees to MFS.

Given that it appeared PIF investors were paying MFS management to use their funds as a moneybox for the mothership, the obvious question arises: why would anyone invest in such a risky managed fund, especially when they depend on a steady income stream for their livelihood?

The answer is that the majority of unitholders invested in PIF based on advice provided by financial planners. Mostly unsophisticated investors, unitholders would rely on their financial planner to provide honest, unbiased guidance for achieving the highest returns for their risk tolerance. One of the largest sources of funds for PIF was clients of one particular financial planning firm, Avenue Capital Management.

In what appeared to be a remarkable coincidence, two of the principals of Avenue Capital Management were none other than Paul Manka and Michael Hiscock. Those names may sound familiar. Both Manka and Hiscock had been directors of the MFS mothership since it listed in 2002. Manka would later become chairman of MFS, and served as a director of MFS Diversified and MFS Living and Leisure. As noted, PIF had not only lent $62 million to MFS Diversified, but it was also a major equityholder.

Avenue started recommending that clients invest their retirement savings into PIF in 2005 after the fund was rated by managed funds research provider Lonsec. Within three years, more than $50 million of Avenue clients' funds would find its way to PIF. That money would then be funnelled into MFS Diversified and MFS Living and Leisure, as well as the MFS headstock—entities which Hiscock and Manka were directors of. Despite the apparent conflict and the disaster which befell PIF and MFS, no action was ever taken by ASIC or the Institute of Financial Planners against either Manka or Hiscock.*

---

* Allegedly dubious financial advice to clients wasn't Hiscock and Manka's only problem—the pair lost a Supreme Court bid to have a debt owing on margin loans to Citigroup extinguished. Hiscock and Manka claimed that they had instructed Citigroup to sell MFS shares to ensure that their margin account was kept in a positive balance. The argument failed, and in June 2008 Manka and Hiscock were required to repay $4.9 million and $5.7 million respectively.

Lesson #5: Don't trust your money to someone being paid a commission

Car salespeople, real estate agents and (some) financial planners have one thing in common—they are paid based on how much they sell. Financial planners who work on a 'commission basis' are not so much planners but rather investment salespeople. Before you follow the advice of a financial planner, ask: 'How much commission will you make if I buy this product?' (It is also worth asking the planner what 'soft commissions' they receive as well.) If the answer is more than 3 per cent, don't buy it. Even better —hire a financial planner who works on a 'fee-for-service' rather than a commission basis.

The PIF tragedy would continue after MFS's collapse but with a new set of characters.

In May 2008, Jenny Hutson's Wellington Capital acquired a call option over MFS Investment Management, the responsible entity of PIF and several other MFS funds. While the deal appeared to have all the hallmarks of a related-party transaction (no other interested parties would be permitted to conduct due diligence on PIF), MFS did not seek shareholder approval, nor did it obtain an independent expert's valuation on the sale. While the MFS board approved the sale, such auspices would not have been difficult to obtain given that three of MFS's five directors had close links to Hutson (MFS boss Chris Scott was even a former owner of the investment adviser).*

In May 2009, the Public Trustee of Queensland (which represented Octaviar noteholders owed $359 million) claimed that Hutson's Wellington Capital was able to snare the management rights to PIF for nothing. Documents filed in the Queensland Supreme Court would allege that Hutson's close association with Scott allowed the two to work out a complex payment scheme which effectively transferred ownership to Wellington for free.[11]

Within days of taking over management of PIF, Hutson sold PIF's stake in MFS Diversified (since renamed GEO Property Group) for a substantial 35 per cent discount to its prevailing market

---

* The new board of Octaviar Investment Management included Hutson, Robert Pitt and Craig Wallace. Shortly before, Wallace had been a part of Chris Scott's 'ticket' for the MFS board. In the space of less than two months, Wallace had gone from potential co-director and close associate of Scott to a director of a supposedly independent company that had been sold on an 'arm's-length' basis.

price to a company called Trojan Equity. Trojan was chaired by a gentleman by the name of Andrew Kemp. Kemp just happened to be a former associate of Chris Scott, having served on the board of S8 prior to its merger with MFS.

WHO WAS WATCHING THE WATCHERS?

MFS's abrupt collapse would have no doubt come as somewhat of a surprise to shareholders—less than six months earlier, MFS's financial statements painted a far rosier picture. Those statements had been audited by accounting firm KPMG—one of the Big Four global accounting practices.

In its 2007 financial statements (audited by KPMG), MFS failed to correctly identify short-term liabilities and almost certainly provided a grossly inflated book value of its assets.

However, it was in its auditing of PIF that KMPG would face its most serious problems. In 2008, a class action would be launched against the firm (and also former MFS directors) by 10 000 PIF investors alleging a failure to exercise reasonable due care, skill and diligence in its review of the fund (the PIF class action would also be aimed at MFS directors for allegedly providing misleading information in its product disclosure statement). KPMG and MFS were also accused of failing to adhere to the fund's compliance plan in allowing loans to various MFS entities which were allegedly not on commercial terms satisfactory to the fund, did not comply with the fund's investment guidelines and did not adequately protect the fund in the case of a default.

Not only did KPMG fail to detect anything was amiss at MFS, but the firm had numerous close links with the collapsed group. MFS's chief financial officer David Anderson was formerly a partner at KPMG, while MFS company secretary Kim Kercher was previously a KPMG manager. The presence of former senior KPMG staff at MFS should have raised alarm bells. In corporate governance terms, it is strongly suggested that former employees of the auditor not work at a company being audited by their old firm. That was one of the problems which pervaded Arthur Andersen's infamous bungled audits of Enron in the United States and HIH Insurance in Australia.

In 2002, Justice Neville Owen stated in the Royal Commission investigating the collapse of HIH Insurance that he recommended 'a mandatory period of four years following resignation from an audit firm before a former partner who was directly involved in the audit of a client can become a director of the client or take a senior management position with the client'. The findings of Justice Owen were never adopted after strident lobbying by the accounting industry.[12]

Not only was MFS infiltrated by former KPMG employees, but KPMG also earned large amounts of revenue from non-audit-related services provided to MFS. In 2006, KPMG received $447337 for audit work but charged almost $200000 for other assurance and tax services. In 2007, KPMG received $483600 in audit fees but more than $700000 for taxation services and due diligence services. KPMG also earned $665600 for non-audit services to MFS Diversified in 2007 (KPMG was also the auditor of Diversified).

In the wake of the Enron collapse, legislators sought to impose restrictions on the levels of non-audit work which could be undertaken by a company's auditors for fear of their independence being compromised. It has been said that where an auditor provides other services to a company it is auditing, it can hardly claim to be independent and it is less likely to be critical or do anything that might embarrass management.

While KPMG's repeated failures to detect any problems in MFS's reporting may have been due to simple incompetence, its close relationship with MFS executives and the quantum of non-audit fees earned by KPMG gave rise to the thought that it turned a blind eye to the company's woes, to the significant detriment of creditors and shareholders.

Lesson #6: Auditors are fallible

Corporation laws require companies to hire auditors to review financial statements—auditors are effectively paid by shareholders to make sure the data is not fallacious. If an auditor is being paid by the company to perform other services (such as tax consulting or due diligence), their independence may be compromised. The risk is greater when the value of the non-audit services is relatively significant, or if former members of the auditor are widely employed by the company. Investors should review the notes to a company's financial statements to determine the relative level of audit and non-audit fees. It is also worth checking to see if any executives once worked for the company's auditor.

One of the worst examples of audit conflict was at collapsed US utility and trading company Enron. The company's former auditor, Arthur Andersen, was paid tens of millions of dollars in non-audit fees while allowing flawed financial statements to be presented. Andersen's failure to fulfil its responsibilities in relation to its audit of Enron and its subsequent attempts to cover up its mistakes resulted in the firm being found guilty of obstruction of justice and being forced to surrender its right to practice.

TO THE LOSERS GO THE SPOILS

Despite presiding over a plethora of dubious related-party transactions and signing off on misleading financial statements, no civil or criminal action has been instigated by regulators towards MFS or its former directors.

Former CEO Michael King was able to quietly retire to his 230-hectare Queensland polo complex (King is understood to have sold only a small fraction of the $20 million property), and was even able to keep his multi-million performance bonus which was paid only months prior to MFS's collapse. MFS also forgave a $25 million loan made to MFS Alternative Asset Management, which listed King as a major shareholder. MFS shareholders weren't the only ones hit by King—the former lawyer is understood to have owed more than $100 million to margin lenders, with the security for the debt being worthless MFS scrip.

MFS's other founder, Phil Adams, re-emerged from hiding in 2009 as the managing director of Dubai-based boutique investment bank Agilis Global. Agilis's website noted that Adams had 'co-founded an Australian investment banking business, which within 2½ years of listing and from a market capitalization of less than $200 million, grew to be an ASX listed Top 100 company with a market capitalization of $3.5 billion'.[13]

Agilis's website appeared to make no mention of the fact that this same business would collapse a short time later, appearing to contradict the website's claim that Agilis's 'business is conducted with ethics and integrity, with a corporate governance structure that underpins a sustainable business and enhances our reputation'.[14] In October 2009, Adams's former margin lender, Lift Capital, moved to bankrupt him, after Adams failed to repay debts of more than $13 million.

MFS directors (and financial planners) Paul Manka and Michael Hiscock, who advised their clients to invest in PIF, would continue to provide financial advice and were not disciplined by ASIC, or any other professional body. Former MFS CFO David Anderson (who had previously worked at KPMG) was paid almost $1 million to assist MFS's liquidator after the company's collapse—around double the fixed pay Anderson received while MFS was still a going concern.[15]

Meanwhile, MFS investors would lose virtually their entire holding in the company (including BreakFree founder Tony Smith, who lost $60 million), while creditors are expected to receive a nominal return of less than 4¢ in the dollar.

Investors in MFS's managed funds, including PIF and MFS Pacific Finance, would have their funds frozen for years and lose a substantial portion of their supposedly 'safe' investment. MFS's satellite funds, including MFS Diversified and Living and Leisure, would come close to collapse, losing around 90 per cent of their market value.

Almost more than any other company, MFS would symbolise the sheer foolishness of the debt-funded infrastructure and funds management boom—an era that would come to a very quick and painful end.

CHAPTER 4

Village Roadshow

How the Kirbys became their own leading men

*One of Village Roadshow's greatest assets does not appear on
the balance sheet. It is our deep understanding of one of the
fundamentals of our industry, the art of showmanship.*
Village Roadshow, annual report 1999

ROC'S LEGACY (1954–1988)

Roc Kirby was a true giant of the Australian screen. Not in the sense
of Errol Flynn or Clark Gable, but rather the actual screen. Kirby
built Village Roadshow from a single drive-in theatre in regional
Victoria into one of the world's largest cinema groups, with interests
in film exhibition, production, radio and theme parks.

Publicly listed on the ASX since 1988, Village has been controlled
by Roc Kirby's two sons Robert and John Kirby and Graham Burke,
who started with Village as a 14 year old at a Kirby cinema in Ballarat.
(Even as CEO of Village, Burke certainly wasn't the typical corporate

executive, with long flowing hair and owl-like glasses.) While Village's time as a listed entity has been remarkably turbulent, one constant has remained, especially over the past decade — the amount of money the Kirbys and Burke have taken from the business and the appalling returns received by minority shareholders.

Roc Kirby's father owned a chain of theatres across Victoria. Shortly before the adoption of television, Roc gambled that the new technology would not harm cinema sales and developed a drive-in movie theatre in the suburb of Croydon in Melbourne's east. Village would soon expand to more than 40 drive-in cinemas in the 1960s. Soon after, Village would make the transition to indoor cinemas and also film distribution. During the 1970s, under Roc Kirby's visionary leadership, the company went into the film production business. (This business would significantly expand in the late 1990s after the company entered into a joint venture with Warner Bros.)

In the late 1980s the company started acquiring theme parks in Queensland's growing Gold Coast region (including Wet 'n' Wild, Movie World and Sea World), before purchasing the Triple M radio network. (In one of its few successful recent investments Village would later successfully merge Triple M with popular Fox FM and 2Day FM to form the Austereo Radio Network.) Village would later spin off Austereo into a separate listed entity, but retain a majority holding in the business. At the same time, Village was rapidly increasing the number of 'multiplex' cinemas it operated and commenced a daring international expansion. That expansion, like most other Village risks of the past two decades, would fail dismally.

After conducting a 'back-door' listing onto the stock exchange in 1988, Roc Kirby handed control of the company to his two sons, Robert and John, and the man described as Roc's surrogate son — long-time employee Graham Burke. Through their privately owned vehicle, Village Roadshow Corporation, the troika would retain a majority ownership of Village.

After a stellar run, Village would rapidly fall out of favour with investors in the late 1990s. Amid a sea of related-party transactions, burgeoning executive remuneration and opaque financial statements, shareholders would flee. As one analyst observed, 'whilst [Village] has some excellent businesses and it has had outstanding success at the box office with two *Matrix* movies released to date, it continues to have a black cloud hovering. We have never quite known the whole story and perhaps we never will'.[1]

HEADING ABROAD (1998–2002)

Village began to attract widespread investor interest in the mid 1990s, when the company undertook a dramatic international expansion and completed the buyout of the Austereo radio network. By 1998, it ran cinemas in Germany, Hong Kong, Greece, Italy, India, Thailand and Korea, and was investigating expanding into the Czech Republic, France and Switzerland. In 1998 alone, Village increased its number of screens by 27 per cent.

At the same time, Village embarked on a risky expansion into film production through a joint venture with Warner Bros. The venture would produce hits such as the *Matrix* trilogy and *Analyse This*, as well as a series of box office flops including *The Adventures of Pluto Nash*, *Ghost Ship* and *Dreamcatcher*. If Village was seeking to use its expertise in cinema to become a leading independent movie producer, it should have stuck to its day job.

Despite lofty hopes, Village's international cinema expansion was also destined to fail. In 1999, the company announced that profit fell from $70 million to $27.2 million—largely due to an 'abnormal loss' of $48.2 million. The failure related to $58 million of 'losses on rationalization of business interests' (specifically Warner Bros. studio stores and video game business Village Nine Leisure) and $12 million squandered on resort assets (such as Laguna Quays and Daydream Island Resort).

Sadly for Village shareholders, losses on non-core investments would be far from abnormal in the next decade.

The company's share price, which had been on a constant upwards trajectory throughout the 1990s, rapidly changed course. An investor who bought $1000 worth of Village shares in 1990 would have seen this stake grow to $13 344 in 1996—only to fall back to $8877 by 1999.

But the worst was yet to come.

In 1999, Village started telling shareholders how much its executives were being paid. The timing was perhaps unfortunate given that the company had also just announced a series of write-downs on ill-advised investments. Despite poor earnings and a flailing share price (Village shares had slumped from around $5.00 in early 1997 to $2.50 by 1999), Village senior management had been very well rewarded. Village's remuneration committee (which happened to include managing director Graham Burke) paid John Kirby $2.3 million, while Robert Kirby and Burke collected $2.2 million (each receiving a performance bonus of $700600).* In addition, Village Roadshow Corporation, the Kirby's vehicle for ownership of 51 per cent of Village, was paid more than $10 million in dividends.

Further, Village paid the relatively hefty sum of $1.01 million to a company called Chanel Press Pty Ltd for 'stationery and printing services'. Perhaps coincidentally, Robert and John Kirby were directors (and part owners) of Chanel Press. A further $1.3 million was paid for other 'stationery and printing services' to another company called Southport Printing—also controlled by the Kirbys and Graham Burke.† Burke also received a trust distribution of $1.3 million from the Roadshow Unit Trust.

In total, the Kirbys and Graham Burke received $10.3 million in combined salary, bonuses and other payments from Village in 1999 — this compared with the company's entire profit of $27 million.

In salary terms, the highest paid employee was not a Kirby or Graham Burke, but executive director and former Ernst & Young partner Peter Ziegler, who was paid more than $3.1 million. Ziegler's relationship with Burke and the Kirbys would soon break down, in very dramatic fashion.

In 2000, Village's performance improved, with the company reporting net profit of $65 million, largely spurred by a solid performance from the company's Austereo radio division; however, return on equity remained at 7.3 per cent, an exceedingly poor return for a listed entity. Keen to improve returns and share in the abundant

---

* Village's nomination committee included Robert and John Kirby. The nomination committee was responsible for 'monitoring the composition of the Board in light of corporate governance best practice, making recommendations to the full Board'; in reality, this meant the Kirbys hand-picked the directors who would ostensibly serve to represent the interests of minority shareholders. Those very same directors would then sit in judgement of the Kirbys' salaries as part of the remuneration committee.

† Village's annual reports claimed that 'as detailed in the Corporate Governance Statement, all purchases of major consumables are obtained by a periodic competitive tendering process'. However, some may question the efficacy of the tendering process given the frequency with which tenders appear to have been granted to companies associated with the Kirbys and Burke; that is, if there was a tendering process at all, given the purchase of stationery may not have even been deemed to be a 'major consumable'.

dotcom riches, in 2000 Village sought to establish an internet presence through the development of SCAPE, in a joint venture with the Ten Network.

Village claimed that SCAPE would possess a 'competitive advantage based on a focused strategy with guaranteed access to highly sought after content...a proven management team [and] an established physical presence providing genuine contact with customers'. This was not to be.

Less than two years later, Village wrote off the entire value of its investment in SCAPE. In its 2001 annual report, Village noted that 'unfortunately, the take up of our on-line service failed to meet expectations...so we promptly closed the business to limit further losses'. In around 18 months of operation, SCAPE would cost its owners more than $44 million.

The Kirbys and Burke again were well rewarded in 2000, with Robert Kirby and Burke receiving $2.2 million and John Kirby collecting $2.3 million. Robert Kirby's remuneration also included a termination payment of $682 749, which represented accrued long-service leave. Kirby's alleged 'termination' did not last too long; he was re-appointed an executive director of Village a short time later, in July 2001. At the time of his apparent retirement, Village noted in its annual report that the company was 'anxious to retain [Robert Kirby's] vast knowledge and experience, and as a result, entered into a two year consulting agreement (with a two year option to extend at the company's discretion) with Kirby Corporation Pty Ltd, of which RG Kirby is the sole director. That agreement provides for a retainer of $750 000 p.a. and reimbursement of out-of-pocket expenses for the period of the contract'.

Upon his 'termination' Robert Kirby was also granted an option to acquire 12.5 per cent of Village Online Investments Pty Ltd for $6 250 000. The option was valued by Ernst & Young. One could question exactly how independent the opinion provided by Ernst & Young was, given that the firm was the long-running auditor of Village and recently departed director Peter Ziegler was a former partner of EY.

It also appears that there was no shortage of pens at Village's head office, with the company continuing its stationery splurge, paying more than $2.2 million to companies associated with the

Kirbys and Burke for stationery and administrative expenses. Burke also collected a $1.77 million trust distribution.

While Robert Kirby briefly stepped away from executive duties, John Kirby and Burke continued to be very well paid courtesy of Village shareholders. In 2001, weak product led to Village's exhibition division recording a loss. Coupled with various write-offs of failed investments, this resulted in profit sliding by 27 per cent. Village also announced that it had sold (for a loss) its exhibition operations in Germany, Austria, France, Switzerland, Hungary and Malaysia — however, those missteps didn't prevent the company from seeking to expand into Italy and Taiwan.

The loss wasn't the only problem troubling Village in 2001 — it also fell victim to an elaborate fraud, costing the company more than $3 million, after the CFO of its US subsidiary, Ross Andrew Henry, used more than $20 million of Village's funds to invest in a fraudulent scheme. Henry was later jailed after entering into a plea bargain with US authorities. In an even more bizarre twist, Village was later sued by one of the alleged perpetrators of the fraud, causing a company spokesman to note that 'Village Roadshow is not just the victim of a well-orchestrated fraud, it is also being sued by the bandleader for good measure'.[2]

Village's poor financial performance didn't prevent Kirby and Burke from collecting their standard multi-million salaries, while Burke also received six million options. Those options were not considered valuable enough to report as income to Burke, with Village claiming in its 2001 annual report that 'in view of the future ordinary share exercise prices set and length of time before they may be exercised, it is considered that these options are of negligible or nil value to Mr. Burke when granted and accordingly no account of them has been taken in the above table of emoluments for the year ended 30 June 2001'.

Village's reasoning appears to take little notice of options pricing models (such as Black Scholes) which are regularly used by other corporations. What's more, an exercise price of $3.00 did not appear especially fanciful given that Village shares were trading at above that level little more than one year earlier. If Village shares were to ever return to their 1996 levels, Burke's options would have been in-the-money by more than $15 million.

However, a return to previous peaks was becoming increasingly unlikely, with Village's profit dipping again in 2002 as the company wrote off even more dud investments (including $40 million in an Argentinean cinema business; the loss was because the company neglected, or forgot, to hedge its currency exposure). Village also restructured executive remuneration, upon the advice of external 'experts'—a sure-fire way to give executives a pay rise.

The pain for shareholders continued in 2003, with Village losing $26 million, largely due to its disastrous overseas cinema investments and $93 million from its 'continuing operations'. Disturbingly, the company also announced a net operating cash outflow for the year of $65 million (the previous year Village had operating cash flows of $189 million). This, along with the need to finance the two costly *Matrix* sequels, led to Village suspending its dividend payment to conserve cash. The decision to cut the dividend resulted in $60 million being erased from Village's market capitalisation in one day, and its share price falling by 35 per cent in the following weeks. (Shareholders tend to not like it when companies remove their dividend, often a signal that all is not well.)

Lesson #1: Cutting dividends is risky business

Many investors are wary of companies that reduce or remove dividends —and rightfully so. A company should increase its payout ratio (which is the proportion of earnings that it pays to shareholders as dividends) if it is unable to invest retained earnings more profitably than shareholders. It should retain earnings if its returns exceed what shareholders would expect elsewhere.

However, if a company removes its dividends for other reasons, this is often a signal that it is unable to obtain funding from other sources (such as banks or new investors). Not only does removing a dividend harm cash flows received by shareholders but companies will tend to use dividend reduction as a 'last resort'. Most directors and executives are fully aware that removing dividends usually causes the company's share price to fall substantially.

Fortunately for the Kirbys and Graham Burke, they were again well compensated for failure—collecting a combined $5.1 million, including a $290 000 performance bonus each. It seems that the trio's performance bonuses were not based on shareholder returns— Village noted in its annual report that $1000 invested in the company in 1994 would be worth only $516 a decade later, making it among the worst performing companies on the ASX.

A PREFERENCE FOR TROUBLE (2003)

With its share price crumbling, Village bore witness to a remarkable corporate entanglement in late 2003 as the company sought to buy back its preference shares for 25¢ cash, with the balance of $1 being applied as a convertible note. Preference shareholders were, somewhat understandably, not particularly impressed with the offer. (Village had two classes of shareholders—ordinary and preference shareholders. Preference shareholders would traditionally receive priority in terms of dividend payments, while ordinary shares have more substantial voting rights. One Village preference shareholder noted that: 'Preference shares, more than ordinary shares, are structured like debt, so think about it in terms of someone just deciding to stop paying the interest on their debt obligations'.)

Earlier that year, Village infuriated preference shareholders by removing the dividend on its preferred shares. This would be the first time in more than 50 years that a company with strong retained profits would suspend dividend payments on preference shares.[3] The excuse proffered by Village was that it required the money to fund production of the *Matrix* sequels and *Catwoman: the Movie*. The decision appeared to shock shareholders—only months earlier, a spokesperson for major Village preference shareholder Hunter Hall stated that 'we expect to be paid our dividend and we are very confident they have the funds to pay the dividend and we can't believe they would be foolish enough not to pay it'.[4] As it turns out, one should never underestimate the foolishness of Village management.

A two-week ASIC investigation regarding the legality of suspending dividends on preferences shares allowed the move, with the watchdog noting that 'ASIC considers that in future, issuers of preference share prospectuses should comprehensively disclose any risk of suspension of dividends'.[5] This, however, did little to placate furious preference shareholders.

In an apparent attempt to avoid litigation, Village management put their heads together and came up with a proposal to buy back its preference shares. However, if avoiding costly court action was Village's intention, its actions proved to be a dismal failure.

The price offered by Village to preference shareholders pursuant to the proposed buyback (of 25¢ and $1.00 of notes) was low, especially since the shares once traded at $4.00, and slipped down to 74¢ largely due to the decision to remove the dividend. Further, the ability of Village to fund the $362 million buyback was also questioned, given that a few weeks earlier the company suspended dividends on the grounds that it needed the cash to pursue its expensive film production business.

Interestingly, one consequence of Village's decision to remove the dividend was that it reduced the value of the preference shares. This was very convenient for Village management as it allowed the company to buy back those shares for a far cheaper price.* This in turn benefited Village's ordinary shareholders by reducing the number of shares on issue and effectively increasing the company's 'earnings per share'.

Unsurprisingly, the Kirbys' shareholding in Village was almost solely in ordinary, rather than preference, shares.[6] In this regard, Robert Kirby noted that as a result of the buyback, 'considerable value moves to the ordinary shareholders'.[7]

The independent expert hired by Village to assess the fairness of the transaction concluded that while the buyback was 'in the best interests of holders of the preference shares', it attributed a value on Village shares at between $2.17 and $2.75 per share—far above the buyout offer price. The report concluded that, notwithstanding the preference shares being far more valuable than what Village were offering, the 'underlying value is of only limited relevance; holders of preference shares can only access underlying value if there is a takeover offer for [Village]'.[8]

---

* Another potential benefit which would accrue to the Kirbys as a result of the buyback was that it avoided the possibility of a 'triggering event' occurring, which would allow the preference shares on issue to be converted to ordinary shares. If such a 'triggering event' were to occur, the Kirbys' ownership in Village would be diluted from 50 per cent to around 25 per cent, removing their gerrymander of Village decision making.

The Kirbys effectively had a gun to the head of preference shareholders, who were left with the choice of either approving the buyback and receiving below market value for their shares, or holding onto their shares and not receiving any dividends. Faced with that dilemma, the vast majority of preference shareholders voted in favour of the scheme.

It appeared that Village had neatly solved its capital structure problems. However, Village's joy would be short-lived.

THE GERMANS ARE COMING

Before the buyback could be finalised, it needed to be approved by the Victorian Supreme Court. Such approval is, in most cases, a formality (it is very rare for anyone to object to a scheme of arrangement that has been approved by shareholders). For Village, however, nothing is usual.

The company would not have been expecting an expensive legal challenge using top-tier Australian corporate law firms from a mysterious German shareholder (which ostensibly owned only 1000 ordinary and 1000 preference shares purchased only four days prior to the scheme meeting) called 'Boswell Filmgesellschaft'. Little was known about Boswell, other than that its managing director Hans Brockmann was involved in financing several films, including *The Usual Suspects* and *Sirens*. Upon Boswell's objections, the Supreme Court disallowed the buyback based on a technical legal argument concerning voting eligibility.*

A second attempt to conduct the buyback was thwarted in January 2004 after only 70 per cent of votes were cast in favour of the buyout†, led by opposition from an anonymous shareholder (believed to be related in some way to Boswell) who amassed 8 per cent of Village's ordinary shares and 15 per cent of preference shares.[9] (Village would later successfully apply for ASIC to sell the 15 per cent stake after its Swiss nominee banks refused to divulge the true owners of the holding.)

---

* The Supreme Court held that the vote was invalid on the grounds that Village had not provided sufficient notice to shareholders who owned *both* ordinary and preference shares that they were allowed to vote *against* the buyback resolution.

† For the scheme of arrangement to be approved, 50 per cent of shareholders and 75 per cent of votes needed to be cast in favour of the resolution.

After months of legal wrangling (with Village unsuccessfully appealing to the Victorian Supreme Court), it eventually gave up on its stingy buyback proposal and proceeded to buy back more than $200 million of its preference shares 'on market' over the following year (the on-market buyback would continue over the next five years). The entire incident, which represented an attempt by the Kirbys to further entrench their control of Village (and cost the company more than $4 million in legal fees) and wrest value away from preference shareholders, certainly did little to enamour Village management—already loathed by some institutions—to its major equityholders.

And Village never answered the question as to how it was able to conduct a $200 million buyback, and pay the Kirbys and Burke upwards of $10 million annually, but did not have enough cash to pay preference shareholders their promised dividends.

SOME OF MY BEST FRIENDS ARE JEWS

While struggling with the preference share imbroglio, the Kirbys and Burke were struck with another legal problem in September 2003 when Village received a shock $148 million claim from former executive director Peter Ziegler.[10]

Ziegler, a former university lecturer, qualified lawyer and tax partner at Ernst & Young had been employed by Village since 1993 and was an executive director between March 1998 and December 1999. Ziegler's primary role was initially to reduce the company's tax bill, but he later became responsible for securing non-recourse financing for Village's film production unit—a task which he successfully completed, earning him a $5.2 million 'success fee' in 2000.*

As part of his legal claim, Ziegler sought 7.5 per cent of the assets and future earnings of Village's film production business, as well as a termination payment of more than $75 million. Village alleged, among other things, that Ziegler was not owed a termination

---

* Non-recourse finance means that the borrower (in this case Village) was not responsible directly for repayment of the loan, rather the borrowings are effectively 'ring fenced' in a separate vehicle. Ziegler convinced insurance companies that a portfolio of films would allay risks of debt repayment as a means to secure the non-recourse funds.

payment because his contract ended naturally, as opposed to the contract being terminated prior to its conclusion.

After 71 days of Supreme Court hearings, Ziegler's claim would ultimately fail on technical legal grounds, with the court holding that his agreement with Village was not enforceable as it had not been approved by shareholders (the former lawyer would end up owing Village more than $12 million after the company successfully counter-claimed for misleading and deceptive conduct[11]).

However, it was not the verdict but rather the oral evidence given by Ziegler during the case which would shock the tightly knit Australian corporate community. Ziegler, who departed to head up Kerry Packer's private firm CPH Capital, claimed that as the relationship began to sour, Burke made an anti-Semitic remark to Village executives in 2000, stating 'that f—king Jew isn't going to be getting $500 million of our money. He never expected it and we don't intend to give it to him'.[12] Ziegler would later confirm that the comments were not directed at him, but rather at Bruce Berman, the Jewish head of Village Roadshow Pictures. Ziegler testified at the Supreme Court case that Burke stated, 'Peter, it is not you, it is Berman, and we are happy for you to have a couple of hundred million dollars for having created this opportunity for us'.[13] In 2005 Ziegler resigned from CPH Capital to focus on the legal action against Village.

(Berman's contract with Village entitled him to 15 per cent of the group's adjusted film production profits, later reduced to 2.5 per cent and a maximum of US$750000 annually. In 1998, Village had told shareholders that 'the appointment of Bruce Berman, formerly Worldwide President of Production at Warner Bros. as Chairman and CEO of VRP not only strengthens our independent production capacity but gives new life to our partnership with Warner Bros. Warner and VRP plan to co-produce 20 films over the next five years'.)

Burke would later point out in a letter to *The Age* newspaper that he was not anti-Semitic and that most people he dealt with in Hollywood were Jewish (it is also noted that Village employed Jewish people in an array of senior roles). It appeared therefore that Burke really didn't mind dealing with Jews, but as the Berman and Ziegler incidents would show, he just wasn't especially happy to pay them.

While in the Kirbys' inner sanctum (Robert Kirby allegedly told Ziegler once that he had made an 'extraordinary contribution...in creating the opportunity for Village to play in the big league of film production without risk or substantial investment'[14]), Ziegler was a beneficiary of Village's largesse towards favoured executives.

Between 1996 and 2003, Ziegler collected $25 million, making him one of the highest paid executives in the country (for instance, Ziegler was paid significantly more than former Telstra CEO Ziggy Switkowski).* Exactly why the Kirbys and Burke agreed to pay Ziegler so much remains a mystery, but it appears that the lure of Hollywood film production and Ziegler's financing talents initially captivated Burke. John Kirby once told *BRW* that lucrative remuneration arrangements were in 'the nature of the [film] industry...and you have to pay a lot for talent',[15] and would later tell shareholders at the company's 2000 annual general meeting that 'Village Roadshow is in an industry where it is necessary to be a high paying company. It always has been, and is essential to create the foundations the company has today. Actually, there wouldn't be such a company as Village Roadshow, but for the founder's tradition of sharing profits and equity with its executives [and] Peter Ziegler who has always been a consultant to the group has uniquely crafted and put in place nearly $1b low risk funding mechanisms which have enabled the group to build a valuable asset for shareholders and considerable future income streams. Also fees paid to Peter represent considerably less than what would be commanded by an investment banking team and, therefore, his efforts represent real value'.

The Ziegler incident provided a telling insight into the mindset of Burke and the Kirbys. For those allowed into the Kirby–Burke inner sanctum, the rewards (which were subsidised by Village's minority shareholders) were plentiful. But should one fall foul of the Village cabal, retribution would be swift and brutal. As Peter Ziegler would no doubt attest.

In its closing submissions to the Victorian Supreme Court (which were not agreed with by the court), Village counsel claimed that 'Ziegler's conduct while at VRL and during this proceeding demonstrates that he is an individual whose driving motivation is

---

* In 2004, Ziegler sold his Toorak mansion and paid $11.75 million to purchase Russell Crowe's villa Berthong, located in Sydney's Elizabeth Bay. See W Frew, 'Ziegler to Vacate Packer Job', *The Sydney Morning Herald*, 25 March 2004.

the accumulation of significant quantities of money. In the single minded pursuit of this ambition he has demonstrated a willingness to cross normal moral lines, including deceiving people who trusted him, manipulating his work colleagues, setting out to avoid the requirements of the Corporations Law and being dishonest with the ATO. For Ziegler telling untruths in the witness box is just another necessary part of the fulfillment of his ambitions'.

THE KIRBYS KEEP ON CASHING IN (2004–08)

Through the preference share (and later, ordinary share) buyback, the Village troika strengthened their grip on the company. By not selling any shares into the buyback, the Kirbys' voting stake in the company would increase to around 63 per cent.[16] With unfettered control, the Kirbys were able to continue to pay themselves, and long-time surrogate Graham Burke, some of the most extraordinary salaries in Australia.

In 2004, the Kirbys and Burke took home remuneration of more than $5 million, as well as related-party transactions valued in excess of $1.8 million. Burke, who still remained on Village's remuneration committee, was the company's highest paid director, although Bruce Berman, the man Burke once called a 'f—king Jew', earned even more total pay, taking home $2.78 million.

Village's 2004 annual report noted that Burke's contract 'provides for the grant of 6 million options over ordinary shares and a loan of up to $2 million on terms and conditions to be agreed by the Remuneration Committee of the Company'. Burke himself made up one-third of Village's remuneration committee. During the year, Village also paid Burke a further $5.1 million to acquire his holding in the Roadshow Unit Trust and half of Burke's stake in 'New Zealand Management Fee Rights'.

Shareholders witnessed a further drop in earnings in 2005, with profit slipping to $40.7 million, down from $75 million five years earlier. It appeared that everything Burke and the Kirbys touched turned out badly for shareholders (it was once claimed that Village's performance in the past decade was akin to putting a lighted match to a big pile of money). With the exception of Austereo, virtually none of Village's investments ever seemed to work.

In their 2006 annual report, Burke and Kirby conceded that Village's botched international expansion 'proved traumatically disappointing and drove our share price into a slump'. Such trauma, however, didn't prevent Village's remuneration committee, led by Burke, paying more than $6 million to the Kirbys and Burke.

Lesson #2: International expansion for dummies

With few exceptions, Australian companies have enormous difficulty exporting their business model overseas, often resulting in steep losses for shareholders. Investors should be very wary of companies that announce grand overseas expansion plans. If the expansion succeeds, executives are feted and generally receive a significant pay rise. If the venture fails, shareholders are forced to accept huge write-downs while executives are farewelled in typically golden fashion.

The long list of overseas failures includes ABC Learning Centres (US and UK), Centro (US), Harvey Norman (Ireland), AMP (UK), GPT (Europe) and Brambles (Europe). The most notable exception is property developer Westfield (as well as the late Richard Pratt's privately owned cardboard and recycling company Visy).

During 2005 Village undertook an especially unusual transaction, even by Village's standards, when it acquired 3 000 000 shares in property developer Becton, for the sum of $1.5 million. The purchase was a strange one—why would Village, an entertainment and leisure company, seek to acquire shares in a developer of, among other things, retirement homes? It is noted that William Conn was a director of both Becton and Village. Regardless, the investment would later resemble most of Village's other decisions, with Becton shares falling from $2 to only 4¢ in 2009, not long after Village sold out of its entire holding.

The year 2006 would provide further disappointment, as non-cash items once again hurt Village's bottom line. After yet another restructure, Village reported a loss of $35.1 million—continuing the trend of the Kirbys' apparent poor investment sense leading to substantial shareholder losses. In June 2006, Village paid an unnamed buyer $33.5 million to effectively take its UK cinemas off its hands. (Village was required to pay a third party to acquire the cinemas due to the significant cost incurred in breaking the long-term leases to which it had previously agreed.) Village's much vaunted overseas expansion, which led to it acquiring cinema assets in more than 20 countries, had been slowly whittled back to only four countries — with massive losses incurred along the way.

In 2006, Village's return on equity slumped to only 5.7 per cent, meaning that shareholders in Village received a return barely exceeding the government bond rate, despite the abundance of risk attached to their investment. Village's film production unit, the source of much of recent angst, reported a $32.3 million loss, despite strong box office results from its release of *Charlie and the Chocolate Factory*. However, the poor performance did not appear to concern Village directors, who met only seven times during the year.

The Kirbys and Burke collected a combined $7 million in remuneration, while Graham Burke fared best, receiving more than $3 million (including a $1 million cash bonus). Also, despite Village's production unit recording a significant loss, its head, Bruce Berman, was paid a cash bonus of $1.1 million.

If you're wondering how Village was able to justify the payment of bonuses in 2006, the answer perhaps lay in the benchmark chosen by Village's remuneration committee; that is, Village paid short-term bonuses largely based upon the company's cash flow return on investment (effectively calculated as EBITDA as a percentage of capital employed), as well as one-off 'transactional bonuses'.

In 2006, Village paid Graham Burke and various other senior managers a substantial bonus due after the successful financial restructuring of Village's film production interests with the Crescent Entertainment parties and the effective creation of Village Roadshow Pictures Group. Some may have considered such an accomplishment within the normal confines of an executive's role, and that bonuses should have been forgone given the company's lacklustre earnings performance.

The use of cash flow return on investment was convenient for Village executives. That was because Village's businesses tended to generate large amounts of cash (with that cash flow often squandered on ham-fisted investments such as overseas cinemas, internet forays or film production). When an investment is eventually written off, the actual write-down is considered a non-cash event and therefore is not relevant in determining a company's EBITDA and it would not alter the 'cash flow return on investment'.

For example, in 2006 Village wrote off $39 million from its film production business and $17.8 million from cinemas in Austria and the UK; these losses would have been ignored in calculating executive bonuses, even though the loss borne by shareholders was the direct result of poor performance by those very same executives.

AN UNHAPPY ENDING (2007–09)

Perhaps amusingly, Village headed its 2007 report to shareholders with the claim that the company was 'stronger financially and a more focused enterprise with an increased emphasis on corporate governance'. Perhaps Village was commenting from a relative standpoint, given the company's traditional view on corporate governance appeared to be borrowed from Kim Jong-il. While Village appointed two new independent directors, its board still consisted of a majority of executives and Graham Burke remained a steadfast fixture on the company's remuneration committee.

There was, however, some long-awaited joy for Village share-holders after the company paid a special dividend of 34¢ per share; coupled with a buyback program and higher earnings, Village even reported an increase in its return on equity to 9.75 per cent. However, its net profit of $45 million was still far less than the earnings generated by the smaller Village back in 2000.

Despite the apparent turnaround in corporate governance attitude, shareholders were not easily impressed. In a non-binding resolution relating to the company's remuneration report, excluding votes submitted by the Kirbys and Burke, only 6.9 million shares supported the resolution, compared with 12.9 million shares against. This represented an 'against' vote of more than 65 per cent, an extraordinarily high figure—almost two-thirds of independent Village shareholders thought that the Kirbys and Burke were paying themselves too much.

It was, however, Village Roadshow Pictures chief Bruce Berman who again scooped the pool, collecting a $1.3 million cash bonus and total remuneration of $3.55 million, the vast majority in cash—this was despite Village's production unit reporting a $55 million before-tax loss. (The following year, the production unit would be deconsolidated by Village, resulting in an after-tax profit of $194.7 million.*)

Speaking to Village's annual general meeting, chairman John Kirby managed to once again display the company's uncanny knack for making investments at precisely the wrong time. As the company continued with its hostile bid for the Sydney Attractions Group (which owned assets including Sydney Aquarium and Wildlife World), Kirby noted that Village saw 'theme parks as our primary vehicle for growth'. Less than a year later, worldwide leisure travel would be rocked by the onset of the global financial crisis. Village would write down its investment in Sydney Attractions as attendances fell by almost 10 per cent and its US theme parks would lose $3.1 million.

With the collapse of Lehman Brothers and the onset of the financial crisis, investors suddenly lost all tolerance for risk—this led to Village's share price returning to its previous nadir, falling from $3.13 in January to less than 96¢ by November. While part of the fall was due to dividends paid to shareholders of 26.5¢ per share, the level of debt on and off Village's balance sheet (of almost $1.4 billion) was of significant concern to investors.

As Village's share price was dropping, Kirby, Kirby and Burke's remuneration continued to rise in 2008, with the trio each receiving more than $3 million total pay, inclusive of a cash bonus of $916088. Fortunately for the triumvirate, Village had altered the benchmarks underlying its payment of short-term bonuses. Previously, short-term bonuses were based upon 'cash flow return on investment' and share price performance. In 2007–08, Village's share price slumped by almost 33 per cent. But the company no longer used share price performance as a benchmark for the payment of bonuses, instead using earnings-per-share growth, which just happened to increase in 2008 (conveniently coming off a low base).

In 2008 Village shareholders not associated with the Kirbys and Burke were even more overwhelming in their condemnation of

---

* In February 2008 Village's film production business merged with Concord Music Group to form the Village Roadshow Entertainment Group (VREG). VREG would be 39.9 per cent owned by Village, allowing the company to remove the film production activities from its financial statements. Other owners of VREG included private equity firms Clarity Partners (48 per cent) and Tailwind Capital (12.1 per cent). Former Village Film boss Greg Basser continued managing the entity after the merger. Village received US$47.1 million (and priority payment of US$38.1 million in distributions) as consideration for the sale of its stake in the venture.

the salary packages paid to the lucky trio. In total, 70 per cent of independent Village shareholders rejected the company's remuneration report—a near record protest vote.

Not unexpectedly, Village's problems continued through 2009, with its spun-off film production business forced to delay payments of US$120 million owed for its share of financing for several films. Village Roadshow Entertainment Group, which was 40 per cent owned by Village, had spent the best part of a year battling lenders to renegotiate a US$1.4 billion line of credit. Financial problems also caused Village to once more reduce its dividend payment after ill-fated interest rate and currency derivative deals in late 2008.

The year 2009 culminated Village's decade of woe. Profit was again drastically hit by extraordinary losses, including a $59 million charge relating to recent acquisitions and $21 million in derivative losses. Proving that Village management were slow learners, its US cinema business delivered an $18 million loss. Perhaps ironically, Village chairman John Kirby told shareholders in the 2009 annual report that, notwithstanding the fact that Village never seemed to really make much money for shareholders, its 'management team remain focused on free cash flow generation and managing margins to drive strong returns'.

Between 1998 and 2009, Village shareholders witnessed more heartbreak than a jilted Hollywood leading lady. With poor international investments, a risky and flawed move into film production and inconsistent performance from its traditional exhibition business, shareholders could only look on in horror as Village's share price slumped from $6.00 to around $1.20 a decade later.

In 2009, Village's market capitalisation (including both ordinary and preference shares) was approximately $260 million. Since 1998, Robert and John Kirby and Graham Burke had been paid remuneration and related-party dealings of more than $86 million. Despite the monies paid, the managerial expertise supplied was dubious—for Village shareholders, the past decade amounted to a horror story worthy of a big-screen blockbuster.

CHAPTER 5

Toll and Asciano

For whom the cash tolls

*You better get your finger out and get some legal advice because
we're coming to get you mate, you are so f—ked up here.*
Alleged voicemail from Mark Rowsthorn to the former
CEO of Pacific National Stephen O'Donnell

FEW CORPORATE divorces have been quite as lucrative as the
acrimonious split between Toll Holdings and Asciano. A difference
of opinion between Paul Little and Mark Rowsthorn would lead
to substantial losses for shareholders and mask a series of generous
arrangements for executives.

THE BUYOUT (1986)

The story of Toll Holdings represents one of Australia's finest business
tomes. Toll was originally founded in Newcastle in 1888 by Albert
Toll to haul coal by horse and cart. In the 1960s Toll would become
a part of the Peko Wallsend mining group. While Peko was caught
up in the takeover frenzy of the mid 1980s, its logistics business was

purchased in 1986 for a pittance by former Mayne Nickless logistics executives Paul Little and Peter Rowsthorn, in a management buyout. Rowsthorn became the privately held company's initial chairman while Little assumed the role of managing director (a role he still occupies). In 1987 Peko Wallsend would be acquired by North Broken Hill, which itself would be taken over by Anglo-Australian miner Rio Tinto.

Little and Rowsthorn paid only $1.5 million to acquire Toll — the price would prove to be a bargain. Through shrewd management and careful acquisitions, Little would guide Toll from turnover of $16 million to $118 million at the time of its sharemarket float in 1993. By 2006, Toll's annual revenue had grown to more than $8.6 billion while its market value approached $13.1 billion — making it one of the most valuable companies in Australia. Before Toll spun off its infrastructure assets into Asciano, it was the 23rd most valuable company on the ASX by market capitalisation. In 2006 Toll employed more than 30 000 people.

After listing, Toll continued to acquire rivals, spending $145 million to purchase TNT Logistics in 1997 and $120 million on the acquisition of Finemore Holdings in 2001. In 2002, Toll had teamed up with Patrick to acquire the government-owned National Rail freight business, while four years later, amid much acrimony, Toll completed the $6.2 billion hostile takeover of ports operator (and its partner in the Pacific Rail business) Patrick Corporation in 2006.*

THE TAKEOVER OF THE DECADE (2005–06)

The year-long takeover battle between Little's Toll and Corrigan's Patrick Corporation would at one stage almost descend into high farce, with executives from both companies launching repeated public attacks towards each other. It may have been humorous had Little and Corrigan not been running multi-billion-dollar businesses and been partners in the $1.5 billion Pacific Rail enterprise.

At one stage, Patrick boss Chris Corrigan would note that being criticised by Little was much like 'being called stupid by the

---

* In its acquisition of Patrick, at the time the fourth largest in Australian corporate history, Toll also acquired a 62.8 per cent stake in airline Virgin Blue. Toll made its initial bid for Patrick shortly after the company announced a profit downgrade, partly due to its failure to hedge Virgin Blue's fuel exposure.

village idiot'.[1] Corrigan would later claim that Toll shares were little more than 'funny bits of paper',[2] shortly before accepting those bits of paper as consideration for his Patrick shares.* At one Pacific Rail board meeting Corrigan stated that 'I note that Mr Little referred to me on a number of occasions yesterday publicly as Corrigan ... if that is suitable for public reference, I now propose to adopt that protocol for our private meetings. I shall refer to the chairman as Little'.[3]

The feeling appeared mutual. During the height of the takeover battle, the Toll boss would become so enraged with a decision by business magazine *BRW* to place Corrigan on the front cover that he would personally call the publication's editor and berate him.[4]

Despite the animosity, Little must have forgiven Corrigan not long after—in Toll's 2006 annual report it was noted that Corrigan received a $10 million 'termination payment' from the merged entity. The golden handshake appeared particularly generous given that Corrigan was not exactly destitute—he had just received more than $150 million after selling his Patrick shares to Toll.

While Patrick would ultimately accept Toll's increased bid (despite some unsuccessful last-minute jockeying by Macquarie Bank to get a slice of the action), it was this acquisition that would raise the ire of Graeme Samuel, chairman of the Australian Competition and Consumer Commission (ACCC). Samuel was concerned that a merger between Patrick and Toll would result in a substantial lessening of competition in east–west rail freight, shipping services across Bass Strait to Tasmania, automotive distribution and integrated logistics services markets. (Corrigan appeared to hold a similar view, noting that expected revenue synergies derived by the merged entity amounted to 'profits you extract from lack of competition'.)

BREAKING UP IS HARD TO DO (2006–07)

The acquisition of Patrick, Toll's 47th since the management buyout two decades earlier, would prove a step too far for Little. The ACCC

---

* The very acrimonious takeover fight would also draw in Toll's financial adviser Citigroup. The US bank would be charged with (but ultimately exonerated of) insider trading and breaching fiduciary duties to Toll. The proceedings related to the actions of a Citigroup proprietary trader, Andrew Manchee, who had purchased one million Patrick shares the day before the hostile bid was announced. ASIC also accused Citi of a breach of its fiduciary duty to Toll because the buying created an unacceptable conflict.

demanded Toll divest half of its Pacific National rail business (and several other smaller assets) to a separate company with a different board and management.

In its 2006 annual report, Toll noted that the newly merged company would deliver a net profit of $243 million, up from $199 million the previous year. However, the Toll and Patrick union would not last long, with the company required to sell assets to comply with regulatory requirements.

In fact, Toll would go much further in splitting up its business than even the ACCC sought. Instead of selling a 50 per cent stake in its rail business, Toll shocked shareholders by announcing in December 2006 that it would completely separate its logistics business from its infrastructure and port assets.

While the structure of the transaction allowed Toll shareholders to retain their ownership of all of the rail business (existing Toll shareholders were issued with shares in Asciano, named after Mark Rowsthorn's favourite Tuscan holiday spot), it was widely believed that the scale of the spin-off was spurred by internal bickering between Little and Mark Rowsthorn.* Mark Rowsthorn was Toll's executive director of operations (and effectively Little's deputy)—Mark also happened to be the son of former Toll chairman Peter Rowsthorn, Little's original partner in the management buyout in 1986. (Asciano's website claimed that Mark Rowsthorn was, along with his father and Little, a 'co-founder' of Toll Holdings. This claim appeared ambitious given the younger Rowsthorn was only 31 at the time of the Toll LBO in 1986 and he didn't become a director of the company until 1988, two years later.)

It seemed like Toll spent months undertaking a bitter, hostile and expensive takeover battle with Patrick, with the primary rationale of combining infrastructure and logistics, obtaining critical mass and

---

* In an interview in 2008 Paul Little denied that he and Rowsthorn had a falling out, but noted that 'Mark clearly was ambitious and wanted an opportunity to demonstrate his management skills and we always knew that and at some stage that was something that needed to be addressed. That was more of a succession issue…Graeme Samuel made that a condition of approving the Patrick acquisition so we had little choice but to comply'. This claim did not appear to be correct, given that the ACCC merely required that Toll divest 50 per cent of its stake in Pacific Rail. (See A Kohler and R Gottliebsen, 'KGB Interrogation: Paul Little', *Business Spectator*, 21 July 2008.) Another indication of the strained relationship between Little and Rowsthorn would occur when Rowsthorn outed Paul Little as having cried after the ACCC initially refused Toll's bid for Patrick, presumably not the kind of publicity a corporate hardman like Little would have been especially happy to receive. (See S Washington, 'The Scramble for Brambles', *The Sydney Morning Herald*, 22 September 2007.)

gaining a competitive advantage in rail and ports to complement its freight forwarding business.[5] Less than a year later, Toll would sacrifice all of those aims and spin off the majority of the assets it obtained from Patrick (other than Virgin Blue) into a separate company.

When questioned about the spate of transactions, the best rationale Paul Little could come up with for the expensive Patrick takeover and subsequent Asciano spin-off was that Toll was able to retain a defence business (that business accounted for less than 5 per cent of the company's turnover). Given that was the best explanation Little could come up with, it could be suggested that the several hundred million dollars Toll and Patrick spent in transaction costs was not money well spent.

Little and Mark Rowsthorn would divide the spoils into 'new Toll' (to be managed by Little), which owned the Australian, New Zealand and Asian logistics businesses, as well as the company's 62.8 per cent stake in airline Virgin Blue, and the separate infrastructure company Asciano (to be run by Rowsthorn). Asciano held 100 per cent of Pacific National as well as Toll's port operation and stevedoring businesses. Asciano would endeavour to grow its business by acquiring investments in ports, airports, rail, toll roads and other similar assets.

While it didn't realise it at the time, Asciano's growth prospects would be severely curtailed because the company would also be saddled with almost $5 billion of debt. The heavy gearing meant that even prior to the onset of the global financial crisis, pro-forma forecasts estimated that Asciano would face an interest bill of $312 million in 2007, rising to $325 million in 2008. Forecast net profit after tax would be $17 million in 2007, increasing to $71 million the following year. The debt burden meant that Asciano had little margin for error. By contrast, Toll would have debt of $2.2 billion, cushioned by almost $1.5 billion in cash.

Lesson #1: Always prepare for the worst

During 'boom' times, companies (usually encouraged by investment bankers) will be tempted to utilise more leverage to improve returns on equity. That is because during periods of credit expansion, despite classical finance suggesting otherwise, the expense of debt will appear far less costly than raising equity.

The problem is debt remains a fixed obligation (interest payments are contractually owed, whereas dividends are discretionary)—when the boom ends and risk premiums readjust, highly leveraged companies can quickly descend into insolvency if the value of their assets falls.

The dilemma is exacerbated if a company has short-term debt which needs to be refinanced. Investors should look closely at the level of short-term interest-bearing debt that a company needs to refinance in the coming years. If a company's 'current liabilities' are similar to or greater than its 'current assets', and its operating cash flow is negative or falling, there are probably better places to invest your savings.

Under the terms of the spin-off, the two companies were required to maintain separate directors and management. Importantly, Little was forced to divest his interest in Asciano, while the Rowsthorn family would have to sell its stake in the 'new Toll'. Immediately prior to the spin-off, Little's stake in Toll was worth around $700 million, while the Rowsthorn's shareholding was valued by the market at more than $600 million.

Toll and Rowsthorn were, for the time being, Australia's transport kings. Little would live at Coonac, one of Melbourne's finest properties, located in leafy Toorak (around the corner from Australia's other trucking magnate, Lindsay Fox). Rowsthorn would have the luxury of purchasing a once-prime Melbourne CBD block, across the road from the redeveloped Southern Cross Station, and allow it to simply sit there, practically dormant and undeveloped.

For Toll shareholders the restructure did not come cheap, with total costs exceeding $80 million (as will be explained, a fair proportion of that managed to find its way into the hands of Toll's executives). For Asciano's owners, however, that cost would be little more than the tip of the iceberg of what they were about to experience.

ASCIANO GOES FOR BROKE (2007–08)

The spin-off of Asciano was, at first, a roaring success for Toll shareholders (shareholders would receive one Asciano stapled security and one 'new Toll' share for each 'old Toll' share they owned). After its first day of trade, Asciano securities closed at $10.76, while Toll shares would reach $13.26. The companies shared a combined market worth of $15.3 billion. Prior to the proposed restructure, Toll had a market capitalisation of around $11 billion. At first glance, the spin-off would appear a boon for shareholders.

However, looks can be deceiving.

While Asciano's high debt burden should have curtailed Rows-thorn's expansion plans, someone clearly forgot to tell the scion. Perhaps in an attempt to prove his managerial mettle, Rowsthorn (who had been appointed a director of Toll at the tender age of 33) would gain a reputation for being somewhat of a corporate hardman (other, less generous, types would refer to the younger Rowsthorn as a 'bully'). Unlike his brother, the much-loved comedian Peter Rowsthorn (who was most famous for his role as Brett in the comedy series *Kath and Kim*), Mark Rowsthorn had developed somewhat of a reputation across the corporate world.

This was not helped by an infamous confrontation with the former CEO of Pacific National, Stephen O'Donnell. In 2005, O'Donnell quit his position as boss of the then joint venture after he was allegedly bullied and intimidated by Rowsthorn, culminating in a voicemail in which Rowsthorn is alleged to have told O'Donnell he had 'better get your finger out and get some legal advice because we're coming to get you mate, you are so f—ked up here'.[6]

Rowsthorn's bluster appeared to extend past his treatment of executives. As Asciano's security price rocketed, so too did Rowsthorn's growth ambitions. In August 2007, only months after Asciano was spun off from Toll, the company purchased a 1.2 per cent stake in pallet and information storage company Brambles. (At the same time, Toll acquired a 0.5 per cent interest, although both Little and Rowsthorn would furiously deny that they were acting in concert, a believable claim given the alleged animosity between the two former colleagues.) When Asciano acquired its stake, Brambles was valued by the market at more than $18 billion—three times the size of its would-be suitor.

Within months, Asciano would spend more than $700 million to increase its holding in Brambles to 4.1 per cent. Rowsthorn's aggressive entry onto the Brambles register appeared mystifying—there seemed to be few synergistic benefits from a merger between Asciano (a ports and rail operator) and Brambles (which owned a pallet and information business).

The most likely explanation for Asciano's newfound fondness for Brambles is that it wished to thwart Toll, which announced that it had also acquired a small stake in Brambles. Toll appeared to have far more to gain in terms of strategic and operations benefits from a merger with Brambles. In response, Asciano executives claimed that the company had been developing a 'strong understanding of Brambles assets over a long period of time'.[7] Those assertions appeared somewhat ambitious given that Asciano had only come into existence as an entity eight weeks prior to commencing its accumulation of Brambles stock.

Whatever the reason, Rowsthorn's dalliance on the Brambles share registry would end in disaster. By December, with Asciano's shares dropping by more than 30 per cent, Rowsthorn announced that Asciano would exit its stake in the pallet company. According to estimates, maintaining its holding in Brambles was costing Asciano around $30 million annually in interest payments.

Lesson #2: Beware the corporate raider

With the exception of smaller, earnings-accretive 'bolt-on' acquisitions, statistical studies indicate that in most takeovers the benefits accrue almost solely to the target company. The other major beneficiaries of such corporate actions are financial advisers (such as investment banks, lawyers and accountants), who are paid based on completed transactions, and managers of the acquirer (who are often paid more because they ultimately manage a larger company).

Investors in an acquirer rarely have any say in takeovers. Unless a management team has a strong record for operational excellence and honesty, owning highly acquisitive companies is rarely a path to investment success.

Despite its growing cost, Rowsthorn remained philosophical about Asciano's Brambles stake, telling the media that 'originally we always promoted this transaction as a friendly one...we met with Brambles and they were of a different view. And after some consideration we decided to make the decision we have'.[8] Rowsthorn also claimed that Asciano had recovered its holding costs and was in the process of implementing 'a strategy designed to maximise the value for us'.[9] After announcing that Asciano had lost $71 million for the December half (well below forecasts), Rowsthorn enthusiastically proclaimed that he was 'reasonably confident that [Asciano] would get out of [its Brambles foray] with a profit'.[10]

Rowsthorn's optimism did not extend to investors, who were rapidly shunning Asciano's highly leveraged structure. As a result of the global financial crisis, any company laden with debt was being punished by investors. Already Centro, MFS and ABC Learning Centres had collapsed—and now it seemed that even Asciano's brand-name assets would not spare it from the fallout.

By March, not long after announcing its December financial results, Asciano securities had fallen from their June 2007 peak of $11.64 to only $3.33—a drop of more than 70 per cent.* While securityholders were giving Asciano an important message, Rowsthorn didn't appear to be listening, telling investors that the entity's total debt of $4.9 billion was an 'appropriate level'.

Lesson #3: Even for fundamental investors, the trend is your friend

There are two types of investing strategies: fundamental analysis (which involves analysing a company's performance to determine whether the company is under- or overvalued) and technical analysis (also known as 'charting', which provides that a trader should only consider share price history in making buying and selling decisions).

While most of the great investors (such as Warren Buffett, Peter Lynch, Charlie Munger, Jim Rogers and Benjamin Graham) rely on fundamental analysis to discover mispriced securities, even fundamental investors need to consider a company's price history—if a company's share price has fallen substantially but its assets and profitability still appear strong, that is most likely because the company has not 'come clean' about its actual plight to investors. Some companies whose share price plummets recover—most don't.

---

* The loss of value would have been especially painful to the Rowsthorn family, which had witnessed the value of their Asciano securities fall from more than $770 million to only $230 million. Even worse, Mark Rowsthorn had spent a further $50 million buying additional Asciano securities for $10.65 months earlier.

It came as somewhat of a surprise that one month later Asciano revealed that it had disposed of its entire stake in Brambles, at an average price of $10.11 per share (well below its purchase price of more than $12 per share). Asciano claimed that the share sale would help retire debt, which its CEO had noted was not a problem a few weeks earlier. Rowsthorn reassured investors that 'importantly, the sale [of Brambles] allows Asciano to focus on our core businesses and on enhancing security holder value'[11]—but it was starting to appear that enhancing securityholder value was very much a non-core promise of Asciano management.

Aside from ill-advised corporate forays and enormous debt levels, Asciano was also facing the problem that its core rail and ports businesses were being harmed by the worldwide recession and dampening economic trade. In its first six months of existence, Asciano would be forced to take a $140 million write-down as a result of restructuring and redundancy costs on its grain haulage operations. However, the losses, and looming $4.5 billion debt, didn't curb Rowsthorn's enthusiasm for growth. By mid 2008, with its security price recovering slightly to $4.50, Asciano announced plans to spend more than a billion dollars on capital expenditure and entering the Queensland coal rail business.

The mini revival of Asciano's security price coincided with (or perhaps, given the Australian market's inability to keep a secret, was caused by) a takeover bid emanating from two private equity firms, TPG and Global Infrastructure Partners (GIP). While GIP had a low profile in Australia (it was owned by General Electric and investment bank Credit Suisse), TPG, one of the world's most powerful private equity firms, was a name already well known to Australians.

Run by quietly spoken Harvard graduate and former lawyer David Bonderman, TPG's Australian operations were managed in Australia by Ben Gray, the son of the former Tasmanian premier Robin Gray. In late 2006, TPG would team up with the Myer family and pay $1.4 billion to acquire the iconic Myer department store. Later that year, TPG would be a participant in the failed bid for Qantas and an unwilling partner in Wesfarmers's acquisition of Coles Group. (TPG, in total, had more than US$50 billion in funds under management, and had owned a wide array of businesses, including Continental Airlines, Burger King, MGM and Univision.)

In August 2008, not long before the collapses of Lehman Brothers and AIG would rock debt markets, TPG and GIP made an indicative, non-binding offer to purchase Asciano for $4.40 per security—the offer represented a small premium to the prevailing security price. Including debt, the offer valued Asciano (on an enterprise basis) at $7.6 billion. (TPG was familiar with Asciano's rail assets—it was an under-bidder in 2002 when the federal government sold its rail network to Patrick and Toll.)

The bid would receive short consideration by Asciano management—putting it kindly. Asciano would not even allow TPG to conduct due diligence, effectively closing the door to any potential formal offer. (Private equity firms prefer to conduct 'friendly' mergers, usually with the benefit of extensive research into their target. By refusing to cooperate with TPG and GIP, Asciano prevented its securityholders from being able to consider any potential takeover bid.) Asciano was supported in its rejection of the bid by most analysts and even its old foe the Maritime Union of Australia, which dubbed a potential private equity purchase as a 'recipe for job cuts, union busting and asset stripping'.[12]*

Asciano's steadfast refusal to deal with its private equity suitors would, however, be made more difficult by its announcement only days later of a terrible profit result. While Asciano reported an increase in revenue of 5 per cent to $2.9 billion, it would record a net loss of around $200 million. The loss was due to restructuring costs of $122 million, expenses related to the demerger from Toll of $12 million and crippling interest costs of more than $386 million.

Asciano also claimed that it lost $103 million from its Brambles frolic. However, the fine print of the entity's finance statements actually revealed that it really made a capital loss of $102 million and incurred financing costs (less dividends) of $7.1 million. In total, Asciano lost $109 million from its brief holding in Brambles.

---

* One analyst from Citigroup dubbed the offer by TPG an 'April Fool's Day prank'. Three months later, that same Citigroup analyst, Sanjay Magotra, would downgrade his share price target on Asciano from $6.08 to only 82¢, noting that 'shareholders can only handle so much disappointment... talk of balance sheet recapitalisation started last year and Asciano has still not much to show for it'. Citigroup stood by Magotra's report, with Equity Research boss Bruce Rolph stating that 'we are not talking about some young upstart; the guy is one of the most experienced infrastructure analysts in the country. We stand by the integrity of the research'. Proving that perhaps honesty isn't always the best policy for analysts, two weeks after his highly critical report on Asciano, Magotra was no longer Citigroup's Head of Infrastructure Research.

Astonishingly, despite the loss (which would lead to the entity being forced to contemplate a $1 billion asset sale to reduce debt), Asciano management, led by Rowsthorn, were paid like management giants. While other executives who presided over such a catastrophic waste of securityholders' funds would expect to be looking for other jobs, the Asciano management team actually received performance bonuses that year.

PAYING FOR UNDERPERFORMANCE: ROWSTHORN CLEANS UP (NOVEMBER 2008)

Asciano's 2008 remuneration report made for interesting reading. While ever-increasing executive salaries have become the norm across the United States, United Kingdom and Australia, generally in the Antipodes there has been a reticence by directors to make substantial payments to executives whose companies have performed poorly. There however appears to have been no such hesitation on the part of Asciano's three non-executive directors (the fourth board member was Rowsthorn).

Asciano's poor performance was not solely due to difficult operating conditions—while credit markets were tightening, in fact, Asciano had managed to increase revenue and keep a relatively tight leash on costs. Rather, its performance was weighed down by hubris-inspired managerial incompetence. Not only was Asciano's investment in Brambles illogical, but it was expensive.

Despite the Brambles debacle, Asciano's board saw fit to pay Mark Rowsthorn a base salary of $1.8 million plus a short-term cash incentive bonus of $1.3 million (Rowsthorn would also collect options worth more than $500 000). While other Asciano executives also received bonus payments, they would pale in comparison to the largesse lavished upon Rowsthorn.

In total, Rowsthorn received 70 per cent of his potential bonus. The payment was the direct result of the Asciano board's inability to devise a remuneration structure which properly aligned executive pay and long-term (or even short-term) shareholder returns. According to its 2008 annual report, Asciano paid bonuses based on the business achieving a 'threshold level of...earning before interest, tax, depreciation and amortization...and [which] are leveraged based upon individual performance against pre-agreed key performance indicators'. To translate—Asciano bosses were paid based on the cash performance of the business, before capital expenditure and financing costs were considered.

Fortunately for Rowsthorn (and other executives), the cash flow performance of Asciano was pretty reasonable in 2008. And that had very little to do with anything management did—the assets were long-established infrastructure oligopolies such as ports and railways. It would be difficult even for the most incompetent of managers to not generate a cash profit from those blue-chip assets.

Where Rowsthorn did err, and err very badly, was in the botched investment in Brambles. (Remember: a CEO's primary role is to allocate capital. Some CEOs play little or no role in a company's operations.) It was this investment, coupled with Asciano's already substantial debt load, that largely contributed to its security price falling by almost 95 per cent between June 2007 and November 2008. However, the Brambles loss was considered by Asciano to be a 'significant item' and was therefore excluded from the company's EBITDA calculation. This was very convenient for Rowsthorn, who was paid a bonus based on EBITDA on a pre–significant items basis. (The exclusion of 'interest' payments from a bonus calculation was also curious—given that financing costs were so substantial for Asciano.)

In summary, the one thing that Asciano management could control (and made an absolute mess of) was not considered in the calculation of those very executives' bonuses. Rowsthorn was effectively paid a $1.2 million performance bonus despite directly causing the loss of $109 million of wealth. It must have been with a wry smile that Asciano chairman Tim Poole would tell securityholders at the 2008 annual general meeting that 'it's important to recognise that what we try to put in place in terms of hurdles are [the] things in control of the relevant executives'.*

---

* Amid the turmoil at Asciano, in 2008 the *Australian Financial Review* would name Asciano's chairman Tim Poole as Australia's 'Young Director of the Year'. The honour appeared somewhat ill timed, given that Poole, a former executive of infrastructure manager Hastings Fund Management, could count his Asciano chairmanship as his main role. Perhaps the *Financial Review* was not able to come across any other young directors to award the prize to, given that Asciano's security price fell at one stage by 95 per cent in its first 15 months since listing.

In an attempt to quell mounting securityholder backlash, Rows-thorn would take the near unprecedented step of forgoing $750 000 from his 2009 short-term bonus (and actually ended up forfeiting slightly more). The action would lead to securityholders narrowly approving the group's remuneration report, although a substantial 41 per cent of independent securityholders still rejected the report.

However, as will be revealed later, that act of generosity would appear to be another non-core promise.

In another move which raised the ire of securityholders, Rows-thorn was awarded 2.1 million options with an exercise price of $4.24—this was lower than the offer which was rejected as being 'inadequate' by the Asciano board only two months before. It appears that the Asciano board had a vastly different impression of the entity's value when it was receiving takeover approaches than when it was paying its CEO. (It was also questionable whether Rowsthorn needed equity incentives at all given he already had an 11 per cent equity stake in the business.)

LITTLE'S BIG WINDFALL
(REVEALED: NOVEMBER 2008)

While Rowsthorn was being paid extraordinary amounts of cash to run Asciano, his former boss at Toll was proving that he was no slouch in the remuneration department either.

Despite not suffering the same catastrophic fate as the debt-laden Asciano, the 'new' Toll's first year was not a pleasant one, especially by Toll's own lofty standards. High oil prices (US crude at one point reached US$147 per barrel) did few favours for a logistics and airline business whose major input cost is fuel. During the 2008 financial year, Toll's share price fell by more than 50 per cent (from $15.00 to $6.34 per share), while the value of its Virgin Blue stake was written down by $1.3 billion (Toll would later spin off Virgin Blue to shareholders via an in-specie transfer of shares). Toll did, however, manage to increase revenue by 15 per cent and net profit rose by 24 per cent to $258 million (before the Virgin Blue write-down was considered).

While analysts and media were focusing on the Virgin loss, Toll directors attempted to quietly disclose to shareholders one of the most outrageous examples of executive largesse seen in Australia.

Toll's management team, led by executive directors Paul Little and Neil Chatfield, were already very well paid, and justifiably so, given the value they had created for shareholders since Toll's 1993 ASX listing. In 2007, Little received cash remuneration of $3.9 million, followed by $3.3 million in 2008, despite Toll reporting a $690 million loss. In 2007, Chatfield was paid $4.5 million cash, including a $3.7 million short-term performance bonus. While the handsome fixed and base payments were defensible, less so was a surprise entry for 'deferred compensation' of $8.9 million (Little) and $5.2 million (Chatfield).

Toll's 2008 remuneration report would provide no further details regarding the substantial and mysterious 'deferred compensation' payments, however further investigation by corporate governance adviser RiskMetrics revealed the hidden underbelly of Toll's exceedingly generous remuneration practices.

The story of the 'deferred compensation' dated back to 2006 when Toll shareholders approved options granted to Little and Chatfield.* The grants included 2 million options to Little and 1.2 million options to Chatfield. The options contained reasonably challenging earnings-per-share hurdles which needed to be satisfied before the executives were able to exercise their options.†

However, not long after the options were approved by shareholders, Toll management began working on a plan to spin off its port and rail assets into a separate entity (which would become Asciano). As a result, Toll never actually granted the options to its executives.

At the time of the demerger, Toll needed to do something about the options which had been approved by shareholders, especially for Little and Chatfield who would become senior executives of 'new Toll' after the demerger. Pursuant to that, Toll converted the first tranche of options (484 000 for Little and 284 000 for Chatfield) into what became the 'deferred compensation payment'. (Toll would pay such compensation to almost 400 Toll executives, however a substantial amount of the payments would accrue to the executive directors.) Dubbing the payments 'deferred' was not exactly accurate — the payments were actually cash sums paid to the Toll executives.

---

* Because Little and Chatfield were directors of Toll, any grants of equity required shareholder approval pursuant to the ASX Listing Rules.

† For full vesting to occur, Toll would need to achieve compound growth in earnings per share of 15 per cent per annum.

Based on advice provided by KPMG, Toll deemed that the options approved (but not yet granted and certainly not yet vested) were worth $18.30 each.[13] At the time its 2008 remuneration report was released, Toll shares were trading at around $6.00 each.

If that amount paid by Toll for the options seemed generous, that's because it was. Very generous.

While beyond the scope of this book, options are generally priced using complex mathematical models such as the Black Scholes formula (named after the Nobel Prize–winning economists who developed it) or the Monte Carlo method. The models determine a theoretical value for the options based on a number of variables, such as the exercise price, duration, volatility and performance hurdles which need to be satisfied before the options are able to vest.

Using the Monte Carlo method, KPMG (which was hired by Toll to provide an independent assessment of the value of the options) determined that the options had a 'present value' of $11.87 per share (this value was based on Toll's historical earnings-per-share growth, an assumed volatility level and the combined share price of Toll and Asciano at the time of the demerger of around $25). The 'present value' of the options would then be 'grossed up' by 46.5 per cent—this was because the executives were being paid cash for the options (and were not able to receive favourable, deferred, tax treatment).

However, there were several major errors with KPMG's determinations: first, Toll's earnings-per-share growth would soon drop dramatically (meaning that it would be unlikely that the options would vest in full, if at all); and second, the combined share prices of Toll and Asciano would fall to less than $7.00 a year later. (There was also a third and fourth problem; that is, the tax rate on options is not zero, so grossing the value of the options upwards by 46.5 per cent was excessive, and also the volatility assumption was believed to be exceedingly generous.)

In short, after Toll's share price slumped, the options would become virtually worthless—and even had Toll's share price not fallen, the options would most likely not have vested due to Toll's earnings-per-share dropping from $2.03 in 2007 to negative $1.07 in 2008.

Based on all that, Toll effectively paid its founder and managing director Paul Little $8.8 million and CFO Neil Chatfield $5.2 million for options that were almost certainly worthless. Toll could have allotted the executives Toll shares (instead of cash), or granted fresh options with similar performance hurdles (this would have seen the value of the incentives fall in accordance with Toll's diminishing share price). Instead, Toll's remuneration committee (which included Paul Little) and its board felt it best to hand over millions of dollars of shareholders' cash to the executives for options which were worth nothing.* It could also be said that Little didn't exactly need the cash; even with Toll's share price falling from its 2007 highs, Little's personal wealth was estimated by *BRW* to be $718 million in 2009.

Conspiracy theorists suggested that KPMG (which came up with the generous options value) was an inappropriate choice to determine the independent valuation of the options. Those theorists may have a valid point—few would deem KPMG to be particularly independent from Toll given their relationship. KPMG were the long-time auditors of Toll (and the firm would also audit Asciano following the demerger).

In fact, Toll was one of KPMG's most important clients—in 2007 Toll paid the firm (which was already embroiled in controversies at Allco, MFS, City Pacific and Westpoint) $2.4 million for audit work and more than $9.7 million for non-audit services. In 2008, KPMG would receive $2.6 million in audit fees and a further $3.7 million for taxation, assurance and due diligence services. Even the most independent of minds would notice $12 million in fees.

Ultimately, more than 49 per cent of independent Toll shareholders voted against the company's 2008 remuneration report—an especially high figure given the outstanding shareholder returns that Toll's management team had delivered over the previous 16 years. Perhaps Toll shareholders had enough of being treated like a money-box for their executives.

PLEASE SIR, MAY I HAVE SOME MORE? (ASCIANO, 2009)

While Toll was grappling with secret payouts for worthless options to executives, the Asciano board had a whole different set of problems.

---

* In 2008, Little attended all six meetings of Toll's remuneration committee, however it is common practice for executives to excuse themselves from committee meetings when their own interests are being considered.

A year earlier, Asciano's securityholders almost voted down the entity's remuneration report due to the size of Mark Rowsthorn's short-term bonus and the generous terms of options granted. Things didn't improve during 2009—courtesy of a moribund economy and Asciano's crippling debt burden, the company recorded a wider $244 million loss. There was bad news across the board, with revenue dropping by 4 per cent while earnings before interest and tax were 9.5 per cent lower. Significant items, such as impairment of goodwill ($142 million) and restructuring costs ($34 million), would lead to the net loss widening by 34.1 per cent. (Rowsthorn also provided a dire forecast of Asciano's future prospects, noting that 'there remain few, if any, signs of an imminent recovery in the domestic and international economies'.[14])

Poor financial performance aside, Asciano chairman Tim Poole —the former Young Director of the Year—would trumpet to securityholders in Asciano's 2008 annual report that 'during the 2009 financial year…Asciano has undertaken a full review of the structure and operation of the Asciano Short Term Incentive Plan, including strengthening individual performance hurdles…and further strengthen[ing] our commitment to ensuring our executive remuneration strategy is aligned with wider people strategies'.

Remarkably, despite Asciano's performance worsening in 2009 and the company making a note of telling shareholders it had rectified its maligned remuneration policy, CEO Mark Rowsthorn still received a performance bonus of $741 678 and a fixed salary of $1.8 million. Asciano stated that Rowsthorn had voluntarily forfeited $764 772 of his short-term bonus; if he hadn't, the CEO would have collected a bonus payment of $1.5 million—an *increase* on the prior year. Asciano securityholders would be somewhat fearful should the company ever actually deliver a profit given the amount it would presumably be required to pay its executives.

Instead of strengthening the alignment between executives and securityholders, the gulf widened. And 2009 was a year which Asciano shareholders would prefer to forget—Asciano's security price fell from $3.52 to $1.30, the company slashed dividends to zero and undertook a highly dilutive equity raising at only $1.10 per security not long after rejecting a $4.40 bid.

In June 2009, after spending a year unsuccessfully trying to sell assets, Asciano raised $2.35 billion by way of a private placement, entitlement offer and share purchase plan. As part of the capital raising, Rowsthorn was entitled to participate in a personal $151 million placement (as well as in the one-for-one entitlement offer which was available to all shareholders). The deal appeared to substantially benefit Rowsthorn, who was able to avoid diluting his holding, unlike retail shareholders who were unable to participate in the discounted capital raising (the new shares were issued at $1.10 each, a 40 per cent discount to Asciano's prevailing security price). Asciano securityholders would have found it difficult to reject Rowsthorn's deal as it would have meant that the entire raising would fall over, casting serious doubt over Asciano's viability.*

Shortly after the capital raising, Asciano told shareholders that Rowsthorn's short-term cash bonus was based upon 'achievement of target EBITDA', safety improvements and debt reduction — rather than share price, dividends, earnings-per-share or net profit. The use of EBITDA was once again fortuitous for Rowsthorn given that the debt-laden Asciano incurred higher interest payments, depreciation, write-downs and restructuring costs in 2009, all of which are ignored in the calculation of EBITDA.

Those pesky items were, of course, of great relevance to securityholders, who aren't paid dividends based on an accounting make-believe world where interest payments and asset write-downs apparently don't exist. (Asciano noted that from 2010 it would pay short-term bonuses based on EBIT, rather than EBITDA. In 2009, perhaps coincidentally, EBITDA happened to be the only metric which Asciano managed to improve.)

In the space of two years since listing, retail shareholders had seen the value of their equity plummet, Asciano record two substantial losses, an extraordinary loss of $109 million relating to an ill-advised Brambles adventure, their equity diluted by a substantial capital

---

* Ultimately, Rowsthorn would not participate in his private placement after being unable to finance the purchase. Rowsthorn was, however, able to participate in Asciano's 'one-for-one entitlement offer'. This was because Asciano's financial adviser, UBS, undertook a book-build on his behalf to sell 40 million of Rowsthorn's existing holding at a price of $1.25 each. The investment bank then provided Rowsthorn with a 'collar' loan to allow him to acquire his full allotment of 76.2 million securities at the discounted price. The deal with UBS effectively allowed Rowsthorn to collect a paper profit of $10.2 million. UBS, whose assistance allowed Rowsthorn to reap the profit, would later share in approximately $50 million in advisory fees, paid by Asciano securityholders.

raising at only 10 per cent of the listing price, dividends slashed to zero—and their CEO receive two consecutive performance bonuses. Few CEOs can boast being paid a performance bonus in a year where their company's market value fell from $8 billion to less than $300 million. Even worse, Asciano's actual business is basically running a bunch of monopoly or duopoly assets, hardly requisite of high-level managerial expertise.

Perhaps the Asciano board felt a little sorry for Rowsthorn; after all, according to *BRW*, Rowsthorn's wealth slipped from $1.09 billion to $572 million during 2009. And what better way to cheer up the son of the Toll Holdings founder than boost his balance sheet with a big bonus.

SHAREHOLDERS PAY THE TOLL

Between 1986 and 2006 Toll delivered stunning share price growth, with its owners and managers sharing in the gains of Paul Little's shrewd acquisition strategies and skilful integration. However, the company's bitter hostile takeover of Patrick, and its subsequent spin-off of virtually all the assets it acquired (into Asciano), appeared to change things for the worse.

The successful Little–Rowsthorn family partnership which had ensued since 1986 would dramatically end. Asciano was laden with too much debt, almost causing its death in 2009, while Toll fell out of favour with investors who for the first time questioned Little's ability to grow the business in the face of worldwide financial turmoil.

While his company was crumbling (and much of its senior management team departing), Mark Rowsthorn was being paid like a king, receiving consecutive performance-based cash bonuses based on metrics that bore no resemblance to Asciano's appalling shareholder returns. Paul Little meanwhile would benefit from a secret options payout never fully revealed to shareholders.

CHAPTER 6

Allco

A fall from grace

Sydney developed a cluster of experts in financial structuring who have been pioneers in world financial markets ... with all those companies competing against each other, they enhance each other's success.
Tony Berg, former CEO of Allco's managed investment fund Record Investments, speaking about Allco and its competitors, Babcock & Brown and Macquarie Bank, in April 2005[1]

We goofed a couple of times.
David Coe at Allco's 2007 annual general meeting, four months prior to the company's collapse[2]

DAVID COE had reached the pinnacle of Australian society, not only through his lofty position on the annual Rich List, prepared by a well-known business magazine, but also through his ubiquity on some of Australia's best known charitable boards, including the Museum of Contemporary Art, National Gallery of Australia and Sydney Children's Hospital Foundation.

By 2009, however, Coe's once stellar reputation would lie shattered, strewn across the body of Allco and its indebted satellites, themselves collapsed among a sea of debt. Coe would fall victim to the twin evils of hubris and leverage, becoming embroiled in one of the most controversial transactions of the last decade, even by the loose standards that prevailed at the height of the bubble époque. Allco had become a poster-boy of the highly leveraged and overly complex nature of the corporate world which grew in the wake of the internet crash and years of low interest rates and high risk appetite.

THE RISE OF THE FINANCIAL ENGINEERS (1979–2001)

The David Coe story was a slow rise to the top of Sydney's social and financial scene. Coe, son of a suburban Sydney tiler, had grand plans for himself—after completing a law degree, Coe became a partner and tax specialist at blue-chip law firm Stephen Jaques and Stephen (which would later merge to form Mallesons Stephen Jaques).

Leveraging off his unique legal skills, in 1979 Coe created Allco with the help of funding from backer John Kinghorn. Initially, Allco provided equity and leveraged leases for plant and equipment primarily for the public sector, before specialising in aircraft leasing based on exploiting tax arbitrage opportunities. Allco would assist airlines in (legally) exploiting tax loopholes in different countries, allowing them to claim multiple deductions on aircraft lease costs. It was basically free money for airlines, which paid substantial fees to Allco for its expertise in arranging the deals.[3]

Allco initially consisted of Coe and a sole employee, David Lowe. Its business of large and complicated cross-border leasing provided a steadily increasing income to Coe, enabling him to pursue other business interests, including a founding stake in production and promotions company Sports and Entertainment Limited (SEL), with former IMG executives James Erskine, Tony Cochrane and Basil Scaffidi. Formed in 1997, within four years SEL would catapult its owners to the top of the list of *BRW*'s highest earning entertainers, with the company estimated to have generated income of $37 million in 2001. (While Allco would later collapse, SEL continues to provide a handy nest egg for Coe through its ownership of Cricket Australia's merchandising rights, Australian Rugby Union's licensing program and a quarter stake in V8 Supercars Australia, as well as managing the likes of Shane Warne and Michael Parkinson.)

After two decades running Allco, Coe made his first real leap into the public eye with the public float of Record Investments. By that time, Coe was already a wealthy man, accumulating a personal fortune in excess of $85 million.

GOING PUBLIC (2001–04)

After running Allco as a tightly held private company for more than 20 years, Coe finally spun off the investment company, Record Investments, on the ASX in 2001. Record was dubbed a 'pooled development fund', and according to its prospectus was 'formed with the objective of providing an alternative exposure to the financial services industry by investing in a range of businesses'. Record would invest in deals supplied by Allco such as equipment leasing, securitisation, funds management and other more exotic structured financial investments.

The underlying reason for the creation of Record was to provide Allco with additional capital to develop new annuity streams (previously, Allco generated most of its income from transaction-based fees). The plan was for Allco to find the deals and Record to supply the money to fund the deals. Record would be externally managed by Allco Management Limited, a subsidiary of Allco. Unlike the satellites managed by Macquarie, Babcock or MFS, Record had a strong, independent board, led by former Macquarie Bank and Boral CEO Tony Berg (the board would choose which of Allco's deals it would accept or knock back, with Record generally requiring an internal rate of return of more than 15 per cent).

Allco did not charge Record for management services (unlike Macquarie and Babcock which literally made billions from charging its hapless satellites for its management 'expertise'). Allco would even reimburse Record for its administrative costs, which in 2003 totalled $5 million. (By contrast, Macquarie Airports Fund—which was created by Macquarie Bank—paid Macquarie $546 million in fees between 2002 and 2009, and a further $345 million to Macquarie in

2009 to internalise management.) Record would receive a first and last 'right of refusal' over any transaction originated by Allco.*

The Record IPO raised $190 million from investors (by way of two instalments)—of which 10.6 per cent was owned by Coe and his associates via 'Allco Management Limited'. Allco obtained its ownership stake after being granted a free option over 11.1 million Record shares. (Coe would personally hold a further 1.5 million shares.)

Shortly after listing, Record launched its first satellite fund, known as Record Realty. Record Realty was a highly geared property fund which would invest in commercial property. (From humble beginnings, Record Reality would ultimately go the way of most of Allco's empire—collapsing with debts of $1.7 billion in 2009.)

During 2003, Record invested $14 million to acquire non-conforming home loans from a company called Mobius Financial Processing Pty Ltd, in what Record dubbed the 'first public securitisation'. In a few short years, Allco executives (and shareholders) would wish they had never heard the words 'Mobius' or 'securitisation'.

But those problems were still well out of sight in 2003, with Record's performance appearing impressive. During the year, it announced an after-tax profit of $17 million, up from $7 million in 2002, while revenue more than tripled to $37 million.

The trend continued in 2004 with profit leaping another 57 per cent, allowing the company to raise another $126 million from investors at $3.50 per share—a handsome 84 per cent premium to the listing price in a little more than three years. Investments rocketed to $413 million (up from $165 million). The vast majority of Allco's business was generated by its leasing division (including aircraft, rail, IT and medical equipment).

The success of Record was having a helpful effect on David Coe's wealth, with the Allco boss judged to be Australia's 155th richest person by *BRW* with an estimated wealth of $141 million in 2004. However, it would not be enough for the ambitious former lawyer.

---

* Fairfax scribe Michael West once described the act of 'asset origination' as 'concocting, then marketing, some structure which impresses people enough to write a cheque out'. See M West, 'Over and Out for Allco', *The Sydney Morning Herald*, 15 February 2008.

TAKING CONTROL (2005)

Its limited ownership of Record Investments was a clear annoyance to Allco, especially given the independence shown by Record's chairman Tony Berg.

The Record–Allco relationship bore a passing familiarity to another great Australian corporate fiasco — Elders IXL. Elders was an investment company run by colourful business identity (and former outspoken president of the Carlton Football Club) John Elliott. In the mid 1980s, before Elliott was declared bankrupt and prosecuted by the National Crime Authority for theft and fraud, Elders was (by sales) one of Australia's largest companies. However, Elliott (and his associates, including successful businessman Peter Scanlon) had a problem — like Allco's management team, Elders executives owned only a small equity interest in the company. They were making everyone else rich but were not enjoying the fruits of their labour, unlike Kerry Packer or Alan Bond, who owned much larger stakes in their companies.

Elliott, like Coe, was perhaps under the impression that it was his ingenuity and hard work that created Elders and, therefore, he should be receiving a greater proportion of the spoils. To achieve this end, Elliott (and his fellow senior executives) attempted a risky management buyout of Elders using a vehicle called Harlin Holdings (which was owned by Elliott and several other Elders executives). Sadly for Elliott, Harlin was prevented from fully taking over Elders due to a decision by the corporate regulator; left owning half of Elders and being unable to use its cash flow to pay off interest or sell assets to pay down debt, Harlin would collapse within a few short years.

By late 2004, Coe and the other Allco principals were getting edgy.* They had created enormous value (so it seemed) for Record shareholders, who had witnessed the group's market capitalisation increase from $190 million to almost $1 billion. However, while the Allco managers were doing all the hard work (between 80 and 90 per cent of Record's investments were originated by Allco), they were limited by their meagre 11 per cent equity interest in Record. Even worse, Allco didn't receive management or advisory fees like

---

* The Allco principals were a group of 10 senior executives of Allco: Coe, Nicholas Bain, Chris West, David Veal, Timothy West, Nigel Windsor, Justin Lewis, Jim Hope Murray, Robert Moran and Mark Worrall.

Macquarie Bank or Babcock & Brown, and even had to cover its own expenses. The horror, the horror.

To alleviate the problem of Coe (and his nine fellow Allco principals) not being rich enough, a two-pronged solution was devised. First, Record would issue 30 million shares directly to Allco principals at a price of $5.25 each. This would increase Allco management's stake in Record from around 9 per cent (the Allco principals had been slightly diluted) to 25 per cent. Record would amusingly entitle the deal, which at the time involved handing discounted Record shares to a related party, as an 'economic alignment transaction'. (At one stage after the proposed issue was announced but prior to shareholders voting on the issue of shares, Allco principals were sitting on a paper profit of more than $35 million.)

The reason Allco principals were able to negotiate what appeared to be a very favourable deal was because Record's 'first and last right' on Allco's deals would expire in a few years. If and when that happened, much of the value created for Record would fade away (Allco was responsible for the vast majority of Record's investments). Given the Allco principals' relatively low ownership stake, it may have been in Allco's interests to simply jettison Record and create a new vehicle when the exclusivity expired. (When the deal was eventually agreed, Record would extend its exclusive 'third party' right to Allco's deal flow until 2018.)

In addition to the share issue, chairman Tony Berg and non-executive director Michael Perry would resign from the Record board, with two new directors appointed and David Coe becoming chairman of the group. Most believe that the reason for Berg's resignation was a breakdown in his relationship with Coe, spurred by his willingness to act in the interests of Record minority shareholders.

Lesson #1: Watch out for departing directors

The most powerful tool in the arsenal of an independent, non-executive director is the power to resign. For a director to resign, he or she is usually strongly opposed to the direction that the company is headed. If a respected director departs a board for 'personal' or 'family' reasons (and retains other business roles), it is usually a sign that all is not well.

The potential conflict between Allco and Record was also not helped by one of the two new directors appointed, Christopher West, being an Allco principal as well. While Record would tell shareholders that 'the Board...will continue to comprise a majority of directors independent of the Allco group', that was not necessarily accurate. In its 2005 annual report, Record would list Coe, Gordon Fell and Christopher West as non-executive directors.* Only Irene Lee and Barbara Ward could be deemed truly independent from Allco, while CEO Mark Phillips was the sixth board member. It appears that Allco's definition of independent is not altogether different from that held by China unto Tibet.

But while Allco would successfully increase its stake in Record to almost 25 per cent and dominate the Record Investment board, Coe had even grander ideas. With Macquarie Bank and Babcock & Brown flying high, Coe would soon go one step further and seek to merge Allco and Record, creating his own infrastructure giant to conquer the world.

HITS AND MISSES (2004–05)

Before the Allco story continues, it is worth taking a step back and delving into the back-story of how Coe and his fellow Allco principals were able to fund their increased stake in Record.

While he was hardly destitute, Coe and his fellow Allco principals needed to raise several hundred million dollars to fund their increased equity stake in Record. They had one small problem — they didn't have the cash. To overcome this dilemma, Allco would turn to what it did best: complicated financial engineering.

From 2004, Allco was already spinning off various entities on the ASX, including private equity company Allco Equity Partners (more on AEP's exploits later) and Allco Max Securities and Mortgage Trust. However, it was through Allco Hybrid Investment Trust (known as Allco HIT) that the principals would fund their stake in Record Investments.

---

* Allco claimed that Fell was an independent director; however, Fell was a close associate of David Coe, with Fell owning 45 per cent of property fund manager Rubicon Asset Management and Coe holding a 19.9 per cent stake. Coe was also a non-executive director of Rubicon.

With the benefit of hindsight investors may look back upon Allco HIT (particularly the PoDs hybrid securities it issued) and Allco Max in the same way a fashionista would look back at Hypercolour T-shirts—with a combination of bemusement and deep regret.

Allco HIT raised money to allow the Allco Principals Trust to increase its stake in Record. The funds were raised through the listing of hybrid securities—most notably, $250 million of what were called PoDs (in one of the more ironic acronyms of all time, PoD stood for 'protection on downside').

The PoD issue is worthy of further discussion, if for no other reason than they represented a truly appalling investment. To explain, a hybrid is a financial instrument which has both debt and equity characteristics (in that sense it is part share and part bond)—in the case of PoDs, they provided the holder with a 9 per cent tax deferred annual return (the bond-type feature) and the ability to convert to units in the Allco Principals Trust or Allco itself (the share-type feature). Investors in such instruments expect to receive a better than average cash flow initially, and the possibility of enjoying capital gains down the track when the instrument converts to equity. (There was also the $100 million in assets—specifically, Record shares—which the Allco principals chipped in as collateral, supposedly shielding investors from potential capital loss.)

Hybrids are, however, dependent on two things: first is the ability of the issuer to make the regular payments, and second, the holder requires that the underlying equity (in this case, Allco shares) has value when the conversion is due to occur.

The money raised by the issue of the PoDs was used by Allco principals to fund their increased equity stake in Record Investments (the remainder of monies raised, around $63 million, would be used to co-invest with Record in other assets).

One of the major problems with PoDs was that they had limited recourse to certain approved investments or preference units in the Allco Principals Trust. The other drawback was the hefty fees charged by HIT, including a contribution fee, ongoing fees, administration fee and expense recovery fee. The fees appeared especially burdensome given PoD investors were effectively giving money to Allco principals to allow them to increase their holding in Record Investments. (Eventually, when the Allco mothership collapsed, the value of PoDs fell to nothing, as the hybrids were effectively secured by and would convert into Allco shares.)

Lesson #2: If it looks too good to be true, it usually is

Any fixed-interest investment that pays a high yield (in comparison to the prevailing 'risk-free rate', which is the rate of return an investor is able to receive by purchasing government bonds) should be treated with enormous caution. As the promised return grows, risk will often increase at a far greater rate. Remember: rational entities will pay as little interest as possible—if a company is forced to pay a high rate of return to unsophisticated investors it is most likely because sophisticated ones thought the risk was too great.

Despite the fees and risks, somehow the PoDs issue was fully subscribed.

While PoDs would act as a moneybox for the Allco principals, the equally imbecilic Allco Max Trust would become a juicy source of funds across much of the Allco empire.

In 2005 Allco Max sought to raise $200 million to lend to structured finance transactions originated by Allco and its related entities. Senior debt issued by Max would be rated AAA by Standard & Poor's. Admittedly, that was not too impressive an achievement. Back in 2005, the ratings agencies were rating pools of American mortgages which had been granted to unemployed, illiterate, former bankrupts AAA.

The Max Trust would make money by 'credit arbitrage'. That, however, was not an especially accurate description of what Allco Max really did. Students of finance would be well aware that an arbitrage is a 'riskless profit'. To give an example, say a company such as BHP Billiton has shares which are traded on two different markets (for example, Sydney and London, which for BHP Billiton is actually the case). If both markets were identical (which is not actually the case) and BHP Billiton's share price was higher in London than it was in Sydney, an investor should be able to simultaneously sell one BHP Billiton share in London and buy one BHP Billiton share in Sydney and theoretically crystallise an immediate, riskless profit. (In reality, there are legitimate reasons why company's trade for different prices in different jurisdictions, but that is not relevant to the example.)

However, arbitrage is not really what Allco Max did. In fact, Max's business model carried enormous risks. Allco Max raised funds from investors (and obtained additional debt using its AAA credit rating) and lent to what were supposedly 'high-quality, investment-grade counterparties'. Because these counterparties had low credit ratings (BBB− or below), Max would earn an interest rate margin, a bit like a bank would on a mortgage.

The problem was, the 'high-quality, investment-grade counterparties' were not really high quality after all (which is probably why their credit rating was only slightly above 'junk' levels). In fact, there was no arbitrage because, as it turned out, there was an abundance of risk, especially since the counterparties were invariably related to Allco.* (Allco Max also noted that while the counterparties were required to be investment grade when the debt was purchased, there was no guarantee that the investee's credit rating would not be lowered subsequently.)

To make matters even worse, the trust would be very highly geared, at a ratio of 7:1. That meant for every one dollar of equity it raised, the trust would borrow seven dollars. Such leverage was needed to generate satisfactory returns given the interest rate margin earned by Max was fairly thin and its manager (which happened to be another Allco entity) also needed to take its fairly substantial fees. The difficulty with maintaining such high gearing levels is that there is minimal protection for equityholders should the value of underlying assets fall.

There was also a major structural problem with the entire concept underlying the Allco Max Trust. That is, Allco Max was set up to lend funds to Allco to conduct transactions. At the same time, Allco Max was managed by an entity called Allco Managed Investments Limited (or AMIL for short). AMIL was owned by Allco itself.

---

* If only investors in Allco Max were as shrewd as legendary *Australian Financial Review* scribe Trevor Sykes; they may have avoided losing their investment in Allco Max when it collapsed in 2008. In August 2005, Sykes warned in his Pierpont column that Allco Max's disclosure document 'has obviously been written in the belief that the wood ducks will throw money at any instrument bearing the Allco name ... since receiving his copy in the mail, Pierpont has been trying to think of a single reason for investing'. See T Sykes, 'Wanted: More Wood Ducks for Allco', *Australian Financial Review*, 26 August 2005.

Therefore, investors were handing over cash to a fund managed by Allco to invest in transactions originated by Allco.

> **Lesson #3: Business is business, charity is charity, business is not charity**
>
> If an entity has the choice between looking after itself and looking after investors, investors will always lose out. Never place your savings in an investment which is managed by someone whose interest is opposed to yours.

Directors of AMIL included several senior Allco executives and 'Aussie' Bob Mansfield, who was a non-executive director of Allco. Those directors would have faced a difficult task figuring out exactly who they were working for. On one hand, the directors were obligated to provide the maximum return to Allco Max investors by obtaining a higher interest rate on funds invested. On the other hand, those same directors had a duty to maximise profits for Allco (and pay a low interest rate on funds borrowed).

It doesn't take much to realise that those aims were somewhat contradictory.

Allco did kindly note in its Max prospectus that it expected future unitholders would receive a quarterly distribution of a variable margin above the bank rate; however, Allco was not able to forecast a specific return. Further, not only would Allco use funds raised by Max Trust to further its asset origination business, but it would also charge investors a 3.25 per cent underwriting fee, 1 per cent capital raising fee, 0.5 per cent administration fees, sliding issuer fees, 20 per cent outperformance fees, a managed portfolio management fee and expense reimbursement fee for their trouble. The fees were so substantial, it appeared that Allco was a bit like a driver who runs over a pedestrian crossing the road and then sends him the panel-beating bill.

In short, Allco Max was a fee-laden trust which would invest in pet Allco projects for an unspecified return, all the while being managed by Allco executives. What is most surprising is that the trust was able to last for three years before collapsing.

Proving the adage about fools being quickly parted from their money, the trust was oversubscribed.

ALLCO TAKES RECORD (2005–06)

With its increased equity stake, Allco was now in the driving seat at Record, the company it created four years earlier. With David Coe assuming the executive chairman's role, Record's rapid growth continued in 2005, profit more than doubled to $53.4 million while investments increased from $413 million to $799 million. Like its contemporaries Babcock & Brown and Macquarie Bank, Allco benefited from historically low interest rates and strong demand for infrastructure assets and financial structuring.

During 2005, Record established a 'strategic relationship' with property fund manager Rubicon. Rubicon was created by Dr Gordon Fell, a Rhodes Scholar and chairman of Opera Australia. Fell would reappear in the Allco story in the years to come in a scene worthy of Bellini's finest masterpiece.

By October 2005, Record's share price had risen to $8.05 per share—meaning that in only six months, Allco had generated a 'paper profit' of more than $80 million on its newly purchased holding in Record. However, even that wouldn't be enough for the Allco principals, who were in the throes of an even better idea—merging Allco and Record to create a 'fully integrated global financial services business'. Record's highly regarded managing director Mark Phillips would be pushed aside as the merger talks got underway, despite his employment agreement having several years remaining.

Under the terms of the merger, Record shareholders would own 52 per cent of the new entity (to be called Allco Finance Group), outside Allco shareholders would hold around 30 per cent and the stake of the Allco principals and Coe would be approximately 17 per cent of the merged entity.* The market appeared to approve of the deal—upon its announcement, Record shares leapt to $10.25, representing a gain of more than 500 per cent since its float five years earlier (and a 60 per cent increase since the merger was first suggested). David Coe was a major beneficiary, with his stake in the

---

* Following a series of transactions, Coe's interest in Allco would fall to 7.1 per cent following the merger as Coe would no longer have a 'relevant interest' in the Allco Principals Trust.

merged entity valued at more than $210 million. (Coe's long-term associates Nick Bain, David Veal and Chris West would see their stakes grow to be worth more than $100 million.)

Part of the rationale for the merger was to correct the governance inadequacies that existed between Record and Allco (Record was one of several listed vehicles managed by Allco and relied on Allco for the vast majority of its deal flow). In theory, the deal made good sense, fully aligning the interests of Allco and Record and removing the unnecessary opacity which pervaded the relationship.

However, as with all things Allco, theory and practice were quite far removed. While recommending the deal to Record shareholders as being 'fair and reasonable', the independent expert, Grant Samuel, noted that the merged entity would provide lower dividends, reduced net tangible assets (Allco's tangible assets were a paltry $25 million) and higher earnings volatility. Further, Record would lose 'control' over its destiny, although given it previously relied on Allco for deal flow, it was never fully independent anyway. Essentially, Record switched its actual business for a stake in its manager (by issuing 86 million Record shares to Allco in exchange for shares in various Allco entities).

In June 2006, Record shareholders almost unanimously approved the merger with Allco. Six months later, Allco announced itself to the world as a key member of the consortium which would try to take over an Australian icon.

FLYING THE FRIENDLY SKIES—ALLCO MOVES ON QANTAS (DECEMBER 2006)

One of the satellites spun out of the Allco mothership was a company called Allco Equity Partners (AEP). Floated in 2004 (with backing from the Liberman family, AMP and Allco), AEP was a publicly owned cashbox which would be run much like a private equity firm. Allco would retain a relatively small ownership interest in AEP, and the company was headed by Peter Yates, the former boss of Kerry Packer's Publishing & Broadcasting Limited. (AEP's external management company would be owned by Allco, the Libermans, Yates and Liberman group CEO Greg Woolley.)

The notion of 'private equity' had been around for about 30 years—initially called 'boot-strap' acquisitions, early iterations of private equity involved an investment bank or firm (of which Bear Sterns partner Jerome Kohlberg was an early pioneer) purchasing a (usually private or family owned) business, often in order to allow 'asset-rich' vendors to 'cash out' their ownership stake. The deals would be 'friendly', with the former owners often continuing to manage the business and retaining a smaller equity stake.

The bank or firm would use swathes of debt and a sliver of equity to fund the acquisition, often selling off parts of the acquired business to reduce leverage. During the private ownership stage, the privately owned business would not make substantial accounting or tax profits because it would be paying off a large interest bill (the other reason for this was the private equity vehicle would also pay very little, if any, income tax). Eventually, the company would be sold again (through a trade sale or initial public offering) and the private equity firm would hopefully make a capital gain. (Private equity would benefit substantially from the fact that interest payments on debt are tax deductible, whereas dividend payments to shareholders are paid out of 'after-tax' profits.)

In the mid 1970s, Jerome Kohlberg teamed up with his protégé Henry Kravis and Kravis's cousin George Roberts to form KKR. KKR would be an early pioneer of leveraged buyouts, and in 1989 undertook the biggest takeover in history—the leveraged buyout of tobacco and food manufacturer RJR Nabisco. KKR's success would breed a host of imitators—the most successful would be: Blackstone (which was founded by former Lehman Brothers executives Stephen Schwarzman and Pete Peterson); Carlyle (founded by lawyer David Rubenstein who once employed former president George HW Bush); and Texas Pacific Group, whose first major success was the leveraged buyout and turnaround of US-based carrier Continental Airlines.

While the large buyout firms would usually remain privately run (although Blackstone would eventually list on the New York Stock Exchange in 2007), as the private equity boom reignited in the mid 2000s, a new breed of buyout shop would eventually emerge—the publicly listed 'cashbox' company. In Australia, Allco's larger competitors Babcock & Brown and Macquarie Bank both created cashbox companies that would raise money from shareholders and invest in listed and unlisted equity. The returns, like those of the true private equity firms, would be bolstered by generous use of leverage.

Ultimately, most publicly owned cashbox companies would prove to be dismal failures. While operating a private equity firm may appear easy, with the generous tax treatment of debt compared with equity, in truth the use of leverage significantly amplifies the risk involved. The best private equity firms are able to profit from improving efficiency and profitability at their investee businesses—this was not a skill necessarily possessed by the likes of Babcock or Allco, which specialised in technical areas such as cross-border leasing but lacked the experience in operating real businesses. The use of debt would increase risks. Warren Buffett made the percipient analogy that utilising enormous amounts of debt encourages discipline in the same sense that mounting a dagger on a steering wheel encourages a driver to take more care. The only problem is, when the car encountered a small pothole or piece of ice, the driver would end up gasping.

But in 2004 debt was certainly not a concern for investors, with daggers appearing on many companies' balance sheets. When Allco floated Allco Equity Partners, the $550 million issue drew an extraordinary $1 billion in applications, suggesting investors would have probably purchased shares in a company that installed condom vending machines in the Vatican so long as it was called 'Allco Prophylactic'.

In 2005, AEP made its first investment—the botched takeover of debt collector Baycorp Advantage. Despite attempting an unusual proportional takeover (AEP did not have the requisite balance sheet strength to mount a full takeover), it managed to convince only one institution to sell its shares, ending up with a 17.3 per cent stake in Baycorp. AEP would later make an unsuccessful approach to embattled paint manufacturer Wattyl, before eventually acquiring Signature Security Group for $140 million in January 2006. Its inability to close deals wasn't impressing investors, with AEP's share price never recovering to its $6.00 float price. In late 2006, AEP traded at around $4.00, a 33 per cent discount to what investors had paid two years earlier and a substantial discount to the company's tangible asset backing.

Both of AEP's failed takeover bids were hostile in nature; that is, they did not have the backing of the target board. While it is not unheard of for private equity firms to launch hostile takeover bids (the aforementioned US$31.4 billion RJR Nabisco acquisition by KKR was eventually very hostile, providing much fodder for the entertaining tome *Barbarians at the Gate*), generally private equity firms prefer to conduct extensive due diligence before completing an acquisition, which by implication requires a friendly relationship with incumbent management (private equity firms also tend to prefer to retain existing management after the company is purchased).

The following year AEP finally made its move into the big league when it served as Allco's funding vehicle for what was one of the most controversial takeover plays seen in Australia: a private equity bid for Qantas—Australia's national airline.

The Qantas bid represented the apex of the private equity and financial engineering/infrastructure boom in Australia. The bid team consisted of private equity firm Texas Pacific Group (which had previously undertaken a successful leveraged buyout of Continental Airlines), Macquarie Bank, Onex, Allco Finance Group and AEP.*

The consortium was chaired by 'Aussie' Bob Mansfield, a non-executive director of Allco and the former head of McDonald's Australia and Optus. The Qantas bid represented Allco's true shot at the big time. Having recently completed its merger with Record, Allco had just announced another strong profit rise for the 2006 financial year, up 57 per cent to $97 million, while its market capitalisation surpassed $3 billion. Allco's share price would finish the financial year at $12.35—a 110 per cent rise.

It would not all be rosy for Allco though, with the company being caught out 'cooking the books' in relation to its 2006 financial reports. Companies generally release a preliminary financial report shortly after the end of the financial year, and their final annual report in around October.

In August 2006, Allco released its preliminary financial results which indicated that the company lost $13.7 million from 'investments with associates' and stated that its accounts receivable had increased by $50.6 million (generally, higher accounts receivable and mysterious

---

* Texas Pacific Group's involvement in the consortium was surprising given TPG boss David Bonderman had been quoted by trade magazine *Airline Business* only months earlier stating that 'the [aviation] industry is probably at its peak. It has been the same phenomena every six–eight years since the Wright Brothers. The massive aircraft orders that Airbus and Boeing booked last year is the almost perfect predictor to the top of the cycle. In two years' time you are going to see everyone canceling those airplanes'; Bonderman's predictions would prove eerily prescient.

losses are not a good thing). By the time the company's annual report was released a month later, Allco had changed its mind and instead reported a profit from 'investments with associates' of $13.7 million and noted that its accounts receivables balance had increased by only $23.1 million.

Allco didn't think it necessary to inform investors of the changes and dubbed the error a 'bookkeeping glitch', claiming that it had 'nothing to do with profit and nothing to do with anything that was in any way material for the business'. Allco's financial results for 2006 were audited by leading firm PricewaterhouseCoopers (PwC). During the year, PwC was paid around $340 000 to audit Allco but also performed non-audit services worth more than $1.4 million.[4]

Still, Allco now had the firepower to mix with the big boys and it would be damned if it wasn't going to use it.

The Macquarie-led consortium, which would be called 'Airline Partners Australia' (or APA) initially offered $5.50 for each Qantas share, but after brief negotiations with the Qantas board, led by Margaret Jackson, the consortium increased its bid to $5.60 per share, valuing Qantas at more than $11 billion.

Allco's involvement in the bidding team proved pivotal; because Texas Pacific and Onex were based overseas, Allco's equity participation was necessary to ensure that Qantas remained majority 'Australian owned'. This was necessary because of the *Qantas Sale Act 1992*. The bid was structured such that AEP would hold a 27 per cent economic stake in the airline (to fund its stake, AEP would raise $700 million from shareholders). Allco Finance Group would hold 11 per cent in the new Qantas and provide its expertise in leasing and structured finance to the consortium. Because AEP would remain publicly listed, perversely it would become the only way investors could obtain exposure to the privately owned Qantas.

The APA bid very much resembled a traditional private equity play—the consortium teamed with Qantas's existing management (Qantas bosses, including CEO Geoff Dixon and CFO Peter Gregg, would receive a substantial equity stake, worth more than $100 million, in the privately owned vehicle). Dixon and other Qantas executives would have received an even more immediate windfall, sharing in a $91 million payout for incentive shares, even if the required performance hurdles had not been met due to 'change of ownership' provisions in their existing contracts.* The consortium also planned to utilise a large amount of debt to fund the purchase.

In hindsight, APA's bid for Qantas was the equivalent of someone ringing a bell to signify the end of the decade-long boom. While share indices would continue their inexorable march upwards for another year, the APA bid was a highly priced, debt-funded monstrosity, which if successful would have most likely required a government bailout of Australia's national airline and resulted in billions of dollars of lost equity and debt. The deal also represented what could have been private equity's finest moment—at a time when the mere mention of 'leveraged buyout' struck fear into the hearts of even the most hardened non-executive director.

The APA plan involved borrowing more than $10.7 billion from a bevy of lenders including Morgan Stanley, Citigroup, Deutsche Bank, Goldman Sachs, Royal Bank of Scotland and Greenwich Capital Markets—a veritable who's who of the global financial crisis. But back in 2006, bankers were falling over themselves to lend to highly leveraged private equity plays—so much so that APA's financing package gave the consortium the ability 'to make interest payments in kind, in lieu of cash'. Such 'covenant lite' borrowing was similar to what had emerged during the last private equity boom in the 1980s, where financiers such as Michael Milken would devise structures that involved borrowers not making interest payments, having the notional interest cost being added to the value of the loan. The loans APA had negotiated were little different to 'junk bonds', or to use a more recent analogy, resembled sub-prime loans for the big kids.

The consortium would use the swathes of debt to undertake a capital spending program (of $10 billion) and make capital reductions of up to $4.5 billion in its first year of ownership.

However, fate would intervene. While the deal was approved by Australia's Foreign Investment Review Board, it also required 70 per cent of Qantas's shareholders to accept the offer. Only hours before the takeover deadline the consortium was still waiting on final acceptances. (APA had earlier reduced its 'minimum acceptance'

---

* Geoff Dixon would have personally received $8 million if the APA takeover went ahead, on top of long-term incentives worth upwards of $60 million. See S Washington, M Davis and S Rochford, 'Revealed: Millions for Qantas Chiefs', *The Sydney Morning Herald*, 21 February 2007.

requirement to only 50 per cent to extend the bid period by two weeks, after several large Australian institutional investors refused to accept the offer.) One US-based hedge fund, run by billionaire Samuel Heyman which owned 4.9 per cent of Qantas, had not yet accepted the offer. Without Heyman's acceptance, the bid would fall agonisingly short.

As the deadline passed Heyman's acceptance had still not been received—as a result, APA only managed to secure acceptances from 45.66 per cent of Qantas shareholders—below its minimum 50 per cent threshold level to extend the bid period. The take-over—like virtually everything AEP had attempted in its short, listed life—would end in what appeared to be an embarrassing failure. (It would later be revealed that the reason Heyman failed to accept the bid was that he slept in.)

In a bizarre twist, APA's inability to reach 50 per cent ownership of Qantas would end up being the saviour of AEP and the airline itself. Not long after the bid was withdrawn, the financial world was enveloped in a global crisis which drastically curtailed business and leisure travel, turning what would have been a marginal takeover proposition into an unmitigated disaster.

Between 2007 and 2008, Qantas's cash flow dropped from $1.4 billion to only $378 million; this would have made servicing the company's $10 billion debt burden virtually impossible. (Based on the amount of debt APA had planned to use, interest payments would have been almost $1 billion.)[5]

Despite Allco Equity Partners being spared from near certain oblivion after escaping from the Qantas mess (it would have invested $1.3 billion in equity under the terms of the deal), two years later AEP shares would trade as low as $1.39 per share, well below its tangible asset backing. While AEP shareholders had lost more than two-thirds of their initial investment, the company would remain the most successful of all the Allco entities—at least it survived.

RAMMING IT HOME (AUGUST 2007)

Not long after the Qantas debacle, another friend of Allco hit the headlines for all the wrong reasons. John Kinghorn, the man who funded David Coe's initial Allco foray way back in 1979 (and was a partner of Coe's in the Australian Krispy Kreme master franchise), had for the previous 16 years been building his RAMS Home Loans into the leading non-bank provider of residential home loans in Australia.

The growth of RAMS, Wizard and Aussie Home Loans had been extraordinary, with the large banks losing a substantial market share to the more dynamic non-bank lenders.

In 1991, Kinghorn would provide wholesale funding to borrowers before creating the RAMS Home Loan brand in 1995. By 2007, RAMS's loan book had grown to $13 billion, and Kinghorn used the burgeoning stock market to float his business, selling $650 million worth of shares while retaining a 20 per cent interest in the publicly traded company.

RAMS was a family affair—joining Kinghorn on the RAMS board were: Greg Jones, the co-founder of RAMS and a partner in Kinghorn's e-Lect IT business (Jones collected $10 million cash himself in the RAMS float); John McGuigan (who was another of Kinghorn's partners in Krispy Kreme's Australian business); and David Coe (who managed to split his time at Allco with Krispy Kreme and RAMS commitments). RAMS's executive general manager would be Geoff Kinghorn, John's son.

RAMS's prospectus predicted strong growth, with earnings forecasts suggesting that profit would increase by 34 per cent in 2008. However, in a warning not well heeded by investors, the prospectus also noted that 'a major liquidity event could cause RAMS to replace some or all of the short-term portion of its funding with longer term funding at a cost which might be higher than the present cost of its short term debt'.

In a remarkable piece of timing, within weeks of RAMS listing on the ASX, two Bear Sterns Hedge Funds collapsed, causing the first ripples of what would become the sub-prime crisis and virtually closing the market for low-quality securitised debt—very much the kind being peddled by RAMS.

Three weeks after listing, RAMS shares dropped by more than 60 per cent in one session after the company announced that it had been unable to sell $6 billion worth of 'extendable commercial paper' in international credit markets. In less than a month, RAMS shares fell from $2.50 to only 57¢. Three months later, Westpac paid

$140 million for RAMS's brand name and distribution business (which had been valued at more than $800 million in its float), and contributed a further $500 million to enable RAMS to continue its lending business. RAMS would then be wound down, retaining its legacy business.

RAMS's performance as a listed entity inspired the *New York Times* to dub it 'the worst initial public offering of the decade'—an impressive effort given that the past decade had seen initial public offerings of the calibre of Webvan and Pets.com.[6] (Fortunately for Kinghorn, RAMS's performance had little bearing on his wealth—he was able to pocket millions from the exquisitely timed float.)

The following year, with RAMS existing as little more than a shell (having been consumed by Westpac), the RAMS board, which still consisted of Kinghorn's long-time friends and associates Jones, McGuigan and Coe, authorised the repayment of a $28.5 million loan to Kinghorn a full two years before it was due. The repayment was especially generous given that RAMS's entire market capitalisation at the time was only $35 million. It appeared that the only beneficiary of that decision was Kinghorn himself.

Some would make the observation that David Coe, one of three RAMS directors who had authorised the payment, had plenty of reason to be grateful to Kinghorn. Months earlier, the RAMS founder and long-time Coe backer invested $95 million in Allco to help stave off Coe's Allco Principals Trust having its stock sold by its margin lender. (Kinghorn had acquired a 6.8 per cent stake in Allco and also purchased a 10 per cent stake in Record Realty.)

CROSSING THE RUBICON (DECEMBER 2007)

While RAMS was collapsing, the House of Allco was encountering a few problems of its own.

In October 2007, not long after the sub-prime meltdown began in the United States, ratings agency Standard & Poor's dubbed Mobius Financial Services, which was wholly owned by Allco, as Australia's worst performed sub-prime lender, with $680 million of its portfolio deemed to be in technical default.[7] A month earlier, Allco had been forced to place $4 million in two of Mobius's securities funds to prevent investor losses. (That figure would later balloon, with more than 26 per cent of Mobius's loans in arrears by 2008.)

However, Allco investors would have been none the wiser; in its 2007 annual report, Allco told shareholders that 'throughout the year, the quality of [Mobius's] loan book improved [while] the recent issues associated with U.S. sub-prime mortgages do not affect Mobius. The Mobius platform does not offer the affordability products/features prevalent in U.S. sub-prime portfolios, which are a large factor in losses in those portfolios'. Similarly, on 2 August 2007 Allco announced to the market that 'Allco Finance Group (Allco) confirms it has no direct exposure to US sub-prime assets, and therefore remains largely unaffected by current issues in this sector'.

The claim may have been true in a technical sense, but neglected to mention that Mobius's 2005 loan fund called 'NCM 03' had the somewhat dubious honour of being the worst performed of all Australian mortgage-backed securities. Within six months, Allco would announce the closure of the Mobius business.

However, those problems were yet to materialise, and during 2007, the first full year after the merger of Record and Allco, the company delivered what appeared to be another stellar profit result, with earnings increasing by 41 per cent to $211 million. However, the headline profit figure may have diverted attention away from a far more crucial number: Allco's liabilities. During 2007, Allco's interest-bearing loans and borrowings leapt from $630 million to more than $6.1 billion. Meanwhile, its reported intangible assets (specifically, 'goodwill' emanating from the merger between Allco and Record) increased from zero to $1.1 billion. However, shareholders would be comforted by the fact that Allco (and its new auditors KPMG) noted that only $193 million of its borrowings were 'current'—meaning due and payable within 12 months.

While Allco's balance sheet was revealing some disturbing truths about the company, David Coe and long-time associate Gordon Fell were plotting one more transaction. Fell, a Rhodes Scholar and former boss of Ord Minnett, had been a director of Allco since 2001. During that time, he had been building up his Rubicon Funds Management business.

Rubicon had shared a reasonably close relationship with Allco. Allco owned 20 per cent of Rubicon, while David Coe was a non-executive director and 19.9 per cent shareholder. Similarly, Fell was a director of Allco. In 2004, Allco lent Rubicon $150 million — that debt, which would later balloon to $176 million, would never be repaid.

Rubicon made money by charging management fees to three satellite funds — Rubicon America Trust, Rubicon Europe Trust and Rubicon Japan Trust. Allco's explanatory memorandum claimed that Rubicon had 'proven capabilities in asset origination, principal investment and the creation, syndication and management of specialist real estate funds'.[8] In a similar manner to Babcock & Brown and MFS, Rubicon would 'originate investment opportunities' (a fancy term for buying stuff) and generate fee revenue by selling those assets to its own managed funds. The group would also receive income from providing advisory services to its managed funds. Rubicon also managed a number of smaller, unlisted hedge funds.

Assets owned by Rubicon America Trust and Rubicon Europe Trust predominantly consisted of commercial properties, while the Japanese Trust owned a more balanced mix of commercial and retail assets. Rubicon only started acquiring assets on a large scale in 2005, not long before the height of the commercial property bubble. That the entity would ultimately collapse should not have been too much of a shock — in history, few entrepreneurs have had success with a 'buy-high, sell-low' business model.

In October 2007, Allco agreed to acquire the 79.4 per cent of Rubicon that it did not already own from Fell, Coe and Matthew Cooper (another Rubicon executive). The deal enriched the three directors; Fell collected almost $30 million in cash, while Coe would reap more than $12 million in cash alone, not to mention Allco shares which at the time were worth more than $170 million. (In the previous six years, Fell, Coe and Cooper had also collected hundreds of millions in management fees from Rubicon, including $77.9 million in 2007 alone. A 'nice little earner' as they might say on Martin Place.)

Because of the close relationship between Allco and Rubicon, and the fact that the transaction basically involved paying David Coe (Allco's founder and executive chairman) a lump-sum cash payment, the deal required approval by non-related Allco shareholders. The transaction would also need to be cleared by Allco's 'related-party committee' (the presence of such a committee was only necessary because Allco's board was horrendously un-independent).

Allco's related-party committee included 'Aussie' Bob Mansfield (fresh from the debacle as chairman of the Qantas bid vehicle), former Ansett and TNT executive Barbara Ward and Sir Rod Eddington (former British Airways boss and director of Rio Tinto). The independent directors of Allco and the independent expert both recommended that shareholders approve the deal.

The major reasons given in favour of the acquisition were significant revenue synergies, provision of a broader range of growth opportunities for Allco, increased funds management income and the ability for Rubicon to strongly grow real estate assets under management. The fact that the global real estate market had commenced its descent and the US sub-prime property crisis had already begun appeared to be of little concern to the Allco directors. It shouldn't have taken too much insight to work out that if the global property market slumped, Rubicon's business would be in a spot of bother, given that it earned most of its revenue from non-recurrent fees charged to managed funds and its future growth was dependent on undertaking a large number of property transactions.

The independent expert, Grant Samuel, while on balance recommending in favour of the deal, conceded that 'the purchase price is, however, less clear as a result of the significant proportion of Rubicon's earnings that are generated by transaction advisory fees from acquisitions and capital raisings'.[9]

Lesson #4: Independent experts may not really be independent but sometimes they can be expert

Most corporate transactions are appraised by an 'independent expert'. The expert will make a judgement as to the approximate value of the target company and whether the transaction is fair and reasonable. In the past decade, there have been a mere handful of instances where an expert has contradicted the views of the company paying its fees. Some of the worst cases of experts getting it wrong include Grant Samuel's dismissal of AMP's offer for GIO and Lonergan Edwards's rejection of the Foster's bid for Southcorp.

While investors would gain little benefit from the ultimate finding of an expert's report, often the expert will express his or her real opinion on the transaction in the 'risks' section. If the expert spends a great deal of time discussing risks or problems with the deal, that can be a better indication of its (un)fairness than what was actually noted in the executive summary.

On 12 December 2007, Allco shareholders voted to approve the purchase of Rubicon (only 20 per cent of Allco shareholders voted against the deal), implying that they were incredibly lazy or very stupid. For while the Rubicon purchase appeared marginal at the time, it would soon become much worse.

A few weeks after Allco agreed to buy Rubicon (the deal was completed on New Year's Eve) the Rubicon managed funds closed their books for the year. Remember — Rubicon itself was simply a management company, it did not own any hard assets but would generate profits for its owners (who were now Allco shareholders) by charging management fees to its satellite funds.

By February, Allco shareholders would come to realise that Coe and Fell timed the sale of Rubicon to Allco perfectly; perhaps a little too perfectly. Coe and Fell admittedly had a few advantages over other Allco holders — they were both on the board of Rubicon so they should have known exactly how the company was performing.

The auditor of Rubicon America Trust, PwC, told unitholders in their report for the year ending 31 December 2007 there was 'significant uncertainty regarding continuation as a going concern [and that] the consolidated entity's current liabilities exceeded its current assets by $144 309 000. This condition … cast[s] significant doubt about the trust's and consolidated entity's ability to continue as a going concern'. In 2007, Rubicon America Trust (RAT) had paid Rubicon $13.8 million in fees. PwC provided similar views on Rubicon Europe Trust and also Rubicon Japan.

The position of the aptly named RAT was not helped by the generous use of leverage and questionable acquisitions. For example, a chunk of RAT's assets consisted of risky 'mezzanine loans' over US property (which were purchased from related parties) — many of those loans were on loan-to-valuation ratios that exceeded 85 per cent and would soon be worthless, as US property slumped and the sub-prime crisis took hold. While many investors thought the Rubicon trusts were literally safe as houses, it turned out they were more toxic than a nuclear waste site.

The three trusts, which according to their auditor were all on the brink of collapse, had paid the Rubicon mothership fees of $29.9 million during 2007. Without those management fees, Rubicon would have made a loss of $17 million instead of its reported profit of $12.9 million (the three trusts consisted of more than 92 per cent of Rubicon's funds under management).

When Allco acquired Rubicon, Fell, the former Rhodes Scholar, was Rubicon's chief executive—he was also a director of Rubicon America, Rubicon Japan and Rubicon Europe. It would seem inconceivable that PwC would not have discussed its concerns with the directors of the Rubicon trusts, which included Fell. Given that Fell was also a director of Allco, he presumably had a fiduciary duty to inform Allco shareholders of the precarious nature of the Rubicon managed funds.

Fell (and Coe, who was also a director of Rubicon) appeared to do no such thing—in fact, the explanatory memorandum sent to Allco shareholders claimed that 'Allco is confident that the Rubicon business is capable of generating significant sustainable growth in real estate assets under management. Allco believes that Rubicon, as a standalone business, has the ability to achieve future asset origination levels of at least $1.5 billion per annum'.[10] It would appear difficult for Allco directors, including Fell and Coe, to justify such optimistic claims, especially since Rubicon's trusts were on the verge of collapse (the trusts would lose more than $1.5 billion in 2008).

Fell, however, had good reason to conceal Rubicon's problems from Allco. As part of the Rubicon sale to Allco, Fell collected $28.6 million in cash. In a quirk of timing, a couple of days later Fell's wife Vivian would purchase the $28.7 million harbour-side mansion *Routala*, in Sydney's exclusive Point Piper. In a moment of perverse irony perhaps, Fell would later claim that the acquisition of *Routala* was the pinnacle of his stellar business career.

While Fell and Coe would retain their cash payouts from the Rubicon deal, the independent directors who approved the purchase did not get away scot-free. The fallout from the Rubicon purchase and Allco's subsequent collapse would lead to Rod Eddington withdrawing his nomination as chairman of ANZ Bank and suffering a substantial backlash from Australian shareholders of Rio Tinto; meanwhile, Barbara Ward would receive a near record 42 per cent 'against' vote when she sought election to the Qantas board in 2008.

The purchase of Rubicon would soon prove to be the beginning of the end for Allco — only months later, David Coe's Byzantine structure of 66 entities would come crashing down. No-one would be spared.

THE DEATH SPIRAL (JANUARY 2008)

While the controversial related-party purchase of Rubicon would further weaken Allco, much like HIH's purchase of debt-laden FAI, the empire built by David Coe would almost certainly have collapsed anyway; the Rubicon fiasco simply served to speed things up.

Allco's share price had been steadily falling as institutional investors punished highly leveraged, opaque financial engineers — of which Allco was very much a poster-boy. After reaching $13.24 in February 2007, Allco shares gradually slumped to around $6.00 in January 2008. However, the real shock was about to come.

On 21 January 2008, an article in the *Australian Financial Review* questioned Allco's survival; within hours, panicked investors fled from the stock, with Allco's share price slumping almost 40 per cent to $3.10.

Two days later the Allco Principals Trust, which was owned by David Coe and several other Allco executives, would be forced to sell half of its 45.8 million share holding in Allco (and almost all of its stake in Allco HIT) after receiving margin calls from lenders such as Tricom.* (On 25 January, board member Barbara Ward resigned from Allco, without providing any reason, although one suspects 'jumping from a sinking ship' would have been a reasonably accurate description of her rationale.)

Allco's complex and interlinked structure would lead to absolute calamity. As mentioned earlier, Allco had spun off several satellites, including Allco Max and Allco HIT. The primary purpose of those satellites was to provide funds to the Allco mothership and to the

---

* Tricom would soon be faced with serious problems of its own, encountering the near unprecedented situation of being unable to settle on trades the previous week after short-selling hedge funds failed to deliver Allco stock in time to the broker.

Allco principals to allow them to fund their share purchases in Allco. The problem was, when Allco's share price went down, so too did the value of the collateral which supported the HIT and Max investments.

That dilemma was exacerbated by the fact that not only did the principals use investor monies to fund their stake in Allco, but they supercharged their purchases by using margin loans as well (one of APT's four margin lenders, NAB, confessed to lending $110 million to the principals to fund their position—the majority of that loan would later be written off by the bank after the value of the collateral fell to nothing).

Allco HIT's unit price would slide 90 per cent from its highs. Readers would remember Allco HIT was the entity responsible for the infamous PoD hybrid notes. The issue of those notes allowed the Allco principals to increase their stake in Record Investments and they were secured by Allco shares (which were slumping in value). The PoDs would ultimately only partially live up to their name, offering very little protection but a great deal of downside.

For the next month, Allco shares would wobble sideways as the market awaited the company's results for the half-year ending 31 December 2007. Twice Allco's financial results would be delayed with directors loathe to sign off on the company's reports. Directors were perhaps concerned that the statements were misleading, potentially exposing them to personal litigation by shareholders.

On 25 February Allco finally released its financial statements, and revealed a gruesome truth: its lenders had the ability to 'review' the company's debt facilities should Allco's market capitalisation fall below $2 billion. This threshold was breached way back in December when Allco's share price slipped below $5.80 (and again on 9 January 2008).

Allco boss David Clarke (who had replaced Coe as CEO in 2007) claimed that shareholders were not told of the breach in December because the company had no obligation to tell shareholders that its bankers had the right to effectively place the company in receivership. Clarke's view (and that of Allco's highly paid lawyers) appeared to contradict corporations laws and ASX Listing Rules, which require companies to continuously disclose to shareholders (subject to con-fidentiality) any information which would influence shareholders to buy or sell shares.

It is not a stretch to suggest that the possibility of Allco being wound up would be considered material by investors. This view was reinforced by Allco's share price, which promptly slumped by 70 per cent when the 'review clause' was revealed.

Aside from the market capitalisation clause, which was more of a symptom of the disease than a cause, Allco's problems largely resembled those encountered by fellow financial engineers MFS and Babcock & Brown—specifically, too much debt, myriad related-party transactions and poor disclosure. While Allco's 2007 financial statements revealed that the company had embarked on a $6 billion debt binge, investors were under the mistaken belief that only $193 million of those borrowings were due within 12 months.*

As it would turn out, that wasn't entirely accurate.

> **Lesson #5: Financial statements might lie, but share prices usually don't**
>
> If a company's share price has fallen substantially, that is usually an indicator that a company's financial statements belong in the 'fiction' section. Investors should always avoid trying to catch falling knives.

When Allco finally released its December 2007 results, the company noted in the fine print that its current liabilities (which was debt owing within 12 months) was actually $2.3 billion. Oh, and on 30 June 2007, it was really $2 billion, not $193 million. Whoops.

As US Senator Everett Dirksen once opined, 'a billion here and a billion there, and pretty soon you're talking about real money'.

Exactly how Allco managed to misclassify more than $1.8 billion worth of debt is a mystery that will probably never be solved (Allco would begrudgingly admit the error only after it was revealed by the *Sydney Morning Herald*). How its auditor, KPMG, missed it is another matter entirely (KPMG would have been busy though; it managed to charge Allco $3.1 million in non-audit fees during the year).

---

* Allco's December 2007 financial statements were also riddled with other signs that all was not well. While its headline profit figure was claimed to be $84 million (only a slight reduction from the previous year), that figure included gains of more than $150 million from the sale of assets, the vast majority of which were to other Allco entities. On a cash flow basis, Allco suffered a cash outflow on operations of $26 million. In that sense, Allco's reported profit would not have been out of place in a Disney-produced fairytale. In addition, Allco's assets would be augmented by $1.3 million in goodwill, largely from its merger with Record, which was more likely to be worthless.

As Allco's auditor, KPMG should have closely reviewed the company's loan documents to familiarise itself with the repayment terms and to ensure the company's accounts reflected those terms. Given KPMG was paid $3 million to audit Allco, checking current liabilities was the least shareholders would have expected.

Much like MFS, Allco's major problem was that it had gone on a spending spree just before the cost of debt skyrocketed. This meant that Allco was lumbered with a bunch of overpriced assets on its balance sheet, was unable to transfer them to related-party funds and was also unable to refinance the money it borrowed to purchase those assets.

Allco had also made hundreds of millions of dollars of 'loans' to related parties which would never be repaid. Allco's dire predicament led to its auditor, KPMG, providing the ominous warning that 'the group is dependent on the ongoing debt facilities provided by its financiers to continue to operate as a going concern'.[11]

OH WHAT A TANGLED WEB WE WEAVE...

The revelation that Allco needed to refinance a couple of billion dollars worth of debt pushed the company further towards the precipice. In early March 2008, David Coe resigned as executive chairman and Gordon Fell departed as an executive director of the group (Fell temporarily continued to run Allco's real estate business).

Allco's share price continued its death spiral, falling to only 21¢ in late March — almost 99 per cent below its peak. Whatever minimal equity the Allco principals retained in Allco was being washed away amid a sea of margin calls. Shortly margin lenders would appoint administrators to the Allco Principals Trust.

Among the creditors of Allco Principals Trust was Allco HIT, which was owed $45 million and was also managed by Allco. (Allco HIT would also appoint a receiver to Allco Principals, which was becoming quite the debtor of ill-repute.) Allco HIT must have had a great deal of confidence in Allco Principals when it handed over the $45 million, given its security for the loan was two US$1 shares in a Bermudan subsidiary of APT, which itself had stakes in various leased assets through a chain of subsidiary companies.[12]

As the Allco empire crumbed, other insidious deals came to light. It was revealed that the Alleasing Trust (which was two-thirds owned by the Allco principals) had received a 'letter of support' from Allco in November 2007 shortly before things started to unravel. The support would prove helpful, especially since the trust's liabilities exceeded its assets by $100 million. Allco also granted a loan to Alleasing for $123 million. Such assistance is not particularly surprising given Alleasing was managed by the Allco principals themselves.[13]

Similarly, Allco Max had purchased securitised loans from Allco's deeply troubled wholesale mortgage lender Mobius. As readers would remember, Mobius was dubbed Australia's worst performed sub-prime lender, having a default rate of double its somewhat dubious competitors. Allco Max's acquisition of Mobius's troubled loans would have been helpful to Allco, but less so to holders in Allco Max, which had seen the value of its securities fall by more than 80 per cent in less than a year. Given Allco was the manager of Allco Max, unitholders in the satellite would presumably not have been overly impressed. (Mobius itself had closed its doors in February 2008.)

But perhaps most insidious of all of Allco's plethora of related-party transactions was the revelation by Allco's administrators that on 18 December 2007, only weeks before Allco's share price collapsed (and the day on which the company briefly breached its 'market capitalisation' debt clause), Allco Finance Group had provided a $52 million loan (called a line of credit) to the Allco Principals Trust.

The loan was made to prevent the trust from receiving a dreaded margin call on its shareholding in Allco Finance Group (which the Allco directors contended would have prevented its bankers from being able to rely on the 'market review clause'). However, while the loan momentarily delayed the margin call, there was very little benefit to the minority Allco shareholders, especially since the Allco principals were 'margin called' out of their stake a month later and the $52 million line of credit would lead to Allco joining a long list of unsecured creditors.

In total, Allco's administrator alleged that more than $1.1 billion in related-party loans had been made across the empire which remained outstanding and were potentially 'uncommercial transactions'.

The Allco fallout would also claim completely innocent victims. A Perth-based mortgage company, Australian Finance Group, which happened to share the same initials as Allco, became the victim of abusive phone calls, vandalism and even a hoax anthrax threat from disgruntled Allco investors. In a strange case of mistaken identity, the chief of the unfortunately named finance company would note that 'some of the language that's been used has been pretty colourful'.[14]

In November of 2008, as the second wave of the credit crunch struck with gay abandon, David Clarke and the remaining Allco directors would throw in the towel and appoint administrators to the company and its myriad subsidiaries.

The house that Coe built was no more.

AFTER THE FALL (2008–09)

In the space of little more than a year, David Coe would morph from genius financier and patron of the arts to greedy financial engineer in charge of the complex maze of a near insolvent group.

However, even with Allco in smoking ruins, in late 2008 Coe proved he still knew how to strike a deal. In an Australian record, Coe reaped $47.5 million from the sale of his harbour-front property *Coolong*, in the exclusive Sydney suburb of Vaucluse, to an executive of Barclays investment bank (the price eclipsed the previous highest selling price of $32.2 million for the sale of the late Rene Rivkin's Point Piper mansion).[15]

Coe also retained his quarter share in successful sports and entertainment management company SEL, as well as his stake in the Krispy Kreme donut business. Despite causing him to lose almost $100 million investing in Allco before the death, Coe also remained firm friends with RAMS founder John Kinghorn—in 2009, Kinghorn would buy Coe a $5 million luxury super-yacht.

Coe's long-time associate and Rubicon founder Gordon Fell retired to his $28 million harbour-side mansion, protected from creditors (Fell would note that the five-bedroom, eight-bathroom estate was his 'wife's and not for sale'). Ordinary Allco employees did not fare as well as Coe and Fell—in July 2009, they were forced to take legal action to recover annual and long-service-leave entitlements.

In March 2009, Allco's administrators McGrath Nichol announced potential civil action against Coe and Fell over the related-party sale of Rubicon, which resulted in them collecting $52 million cash, and the loan by Allco to the Allco principals to stave off a margin call.

However, Australia's corporate watchdog ASIC refused to be drawn on whether charges would be laid over the Rubicon deal, the line of credit or Allco's $1.8 billion disclosure error. However, given the civil action laid against directors of Centro Property group in October 2009, which, like Allco, allegedly misled shareholders in its financial statements, it is highly unlikely that the Allco story is finished yet.

The last word belongs to Gordon Fell, the man who collected hundreds of millions of dollars from Rubicon, before cashing out shortly before its inevitable collapse. When asked by a journalist whether he would consider returning any of his ill-gotten proceeds to suffering unitholders, Fell's reply was as telling as it was succinct: 'Would you do that?'

CHAPTER 7

Babcock & Brown

How the house of cards of Australia's financial engineers came crashing down

Villains fare well in this world, saints in the next.
Old Polish proverb

You can't keep delivering growth out of revaluing assets and borrowing more money and distributing the cash. We expect over the long term our funds to perform in line with the underlying assets and that performance will be steady, it will be secure, it will be what it should be for infrastructure assets.
Babcock & Brown CEO Phil Green in August 2006, before the collapse of those funds would lead to the downfall of Babcock & Brown[1]

IF EXTREME capitalism were an Olympic sport, former Babcock & Brown CEO Phil Green would be a gold medallist.

In early 2004, not many Australians had heard of investment bank and fund manager Babcock & Brown. Four years later, few would not have been aware of the infrastructure fund manager which was dubbed Macquarie Bank's 'Mini-Me'. Babcock would grow to be worth more than $10 billion and spawn hundreds of millionaire bankers. In May 2005, shortly before the height of the infrastructure boom, Green shared the front cover of the *Australian Financial Review* with Macquarie's Allan Moss and Allco's David Coe, under the banner 'Masters of the Universe'. At one time, Babcock & Brown would maintain offices in more than 30 countries and employ over 1600 people.

And then, almost overnight, it was gone. Shareholders and employees would be left scratching their heads wondering how it all went so wrong.

Phil Green would be a master no more.

THE STUDENT BECOMES THE MASTER (1977–2000)

While many believe Babcock & Brown to be an Australian investment bank modelled on Macquarie, the business was actually formed in the United States back in 1977 by Jim Babcock and George Brown. Babcock was a former lawyer and Harvard graduate who bore an uncanny resemblance to American actor Ted Danson, while Brown was the lower profile partner who quietly retired in 1986. The group didn't even open up a Sydney office until 1982 (the Australian office was initially run by Neil Lewis, who would later become a director of the failed Allco Finance Group).

Much like Allco, Babcock would specialise in complex aircraft leasing for almost a decade before expanding its operations in the early 1990s. Also like Allco, Babcock achieved a great deal of early success arranging aircraft leases in the United States for US-based airlines.

As Babcock's leasing business grew, so too did its expertise, with the company branching out into other areas such as project finance advisory work and aircraft finance (Babcock would act for the issuer of the debt, such as an airline, rather than the buyer of the debt, who would usually be institutional investors). While growing its aircraft business in 1984, Babcock hired a young tax accountant and lawyer by the name of Phil Green from Arthur Andersen. Green had attended Sydney Boys High before undertaking law and commerce degrees at the University of New South Wales. Finishing university, Green worked at Arthur Andersen, then the premier global accounting firm. Babcock had first encountered Green three years earlier working on a leasing deal and eventually managed to entice the young lawyer to join his fledgling firm.

Green would be joined in Sydney by a host of energetic executives who would form Babcock's inner sanctum—until its eventual collapse. These executives included Daniel Brickman (who would later become Babcock's head of American operations), Peter Hofbauer (who led the bank's infrastructure team) and Eric Lucas (Babcock's property boss). Lucas would later move to head Babcock's Japanese joint venture with investment bank Nomura.

Babcock's aircraft leasing business remained the group's mainstay until the late 1990s, when the group—now dominated by Green—began to notice the early success that Macquarie Bank had achieved with its model of acquiring infrastructure assets and spinning off those assets to managed entities. In 1997, Babcock took control of the Australian Industry Development Corporation (which included financial stakes in fruit juice company Berri and textile manufacturer Bruck Textiles). At the same time, it expanded its real estate business. Babcock's 2004 prospectus would tout that it had completed deals as an equity investor, mezzanine lender, project developer, fund sponsor and lease portfolio manager. It seemed that anywhere you could make a quick buck, Babcock would be there.

Babcock's move away from pure advisory work had been furthered in 2000 after Germany's second largest bank Bayerische Hypo- und Vereinsbank (often referred to as 'Hypo') spent $164 million acquiring a 20 per cent cornerstone stake in Babcock. Hypo's support substantially increased the capital available to Babcock. (Ironically, eight years later it would be Hypo's decision to freeze a relatively paltry $70 million of Babcock's funds that would almost tip the overleveraged group into administration.)

By 2003, Babcock's revenue would be split relatively evenly between structured finance, infrastructure, real estate and leasing.

The following year Babcock successfully implemented its new-found principal–satellite model. The firm had acquired assets such as Australia's largest hotel owner Tourism Australia Holdings, and in 2002 it purchased the Dalrymple Bay coal terminal in Queensland. Soon after, Babcock would successfully spin Dalrymple Bay into a satellite fund called Prime Infrastructure Trust, which was managed by Babcock.

With its Australian business dominant, Babcock would shift its head office from San Francisco to Sydney.

Phil Green's takeover was complete.

THE BROTHERS GREEN: DEATH AND ENVY

While Phil Green was enjoying enormous success in the mid 1990s growing Babcock in Sydney, his brother Max was having a slighter tougher time down in Melbourne. The more boisterous of the two brothers, Max should have had little reason to be concerned about money. He was married to Louise Baron, daughter of millionaire rag trader turned property developer and former *BRW* Rich List member Nathan Baron. Baron had amassed a fortune of more than $100 million, consisting largely of property assets.

Max Green, however, had not been able to emulate the business success of his older brother. Max, also a tax lawyer, had a colourful career which had taken him from an American fashion jewellery company to a small Melbourne-based law firm, Gary Shugg. Shugg was accused of misappropriating client funds and the firm would collapse after Shugg was disbarred (Shugg blamed the theft on Max Green, however nothing was ever proven).[2]

After departing Shugg, Max Green took up a role at another small Melbourne firm called Coleman Aroni. Not long later, Phil Green allegedly told Max about a loophole in the Australian tax system which allowed investors to claim substantial tax benefits from the purchase of low-cost equipment. Max would use Phil's idea to create a devilish scheme. The ruse involved using a small amount of investor monies and borrowing from a Hong Kong company to invest in equipment to be leased to Melbourne's CityLink road project. Due to the use of debt and tax loopholes, investors should have been able to claim a substantial tax deduction. More than $40 million was invested in the scheme, mostly by wealthy clients of Green's firm.

Max Green was, however, not content with merely screwing the Australian taxpayer—he would also deceive his own clients with a massive fraud. Max Green never actually invested any of the money raised in real equipment; instead, he forged documents and transferred the funds through a swathe of secretive tax havens, including Bermuda, Liechtenstein and Isle of Man, with the funds eventually finding their way to South-East Asia for the purchase of exotic gemstones.

By 1998, Max Green's scheme had come unstuck. While in the Cambodian capital Phnom Penh, Max Green was murdered, bashed to death in a five-star Sofitel hotel room. Max Green's stolen millions would never be recovered. Brother Phil, however, would continue on his merry way in Sydney, building an empire and making a fortune.

BABCOCK GETS LISTED (2004)

Babcock listed on the ASX in October 2004. The $5.00 per share offer price valued the company at more than $1.5 billion. In true Babcock form, the float was structured to give the impression of great demand — many existing Babcock shareholders (which consisted of Babcock executives and Hypo) didn't sell their stake in the float. Also, just under half of the $550 million offered for sale was given to long-term Babcock associates, known as 'foundation investors', which included Richard Pratt's Thorney Investments, as well as the Packer, Lowy, Ivany and Liberman families.

After the IPO, Babcock remained 54 per cent owned by employees — Phil Green would personally hold 12 million Babcock shares and Jim Babcock retained more than 20 million shares. (Hypo would retain an 11.9 per cent stake while public shareholders owned the remaining 34 per cent.)

The offer for Babcock & Brown was well supported and the shares hit the boards at $8.27 — a dotcom era premium of 65 per cent to the issue price. Within a day, Phil Green's wealth (based solely on his Babcock stake, let alone his other interests) exceeded $100 million, while Jim Babcock's holding was worth more than $160 million. One broker even dubbed Babcock's float the 'IPO of the century'.

Investors must not have been paying particularly close attention. Babcock's prospectus made it quite clear investors in Babcock & Brown were only receiving shares in another company called Babcock & Brown International Pty Ltd (BBPIL). It was BBPIL which would have ownership of the cash flow–generating assets. It was also BBPIL where Babcock's lenders would have recourse. This was a fact that would be made painfully obvious to Babcock noteholders and shareholders years later.

BOOM (2005)

A public listing provided Babcock with not only valuable capital to expand its principal infrastructure business, but also a well-known brand name which would resonate with investors.

Within months of listing, Babcock share price hit $10, with the company announcing a string of new developments, including the Royal Melbourne Showgrounds (which never proceeded), a European rail leasing business and—hot on the heals of the Allco Equity Partners float—a cashbox fund called Babcock & Brown Capital.* Other major developments were in real estate, with Babcock creating the Japan Property Trust and undertaking what would become a catastrophic multi-billion dollar European joint venture with GPT (more on that fiasco later).

Babcock also proposed to restructure and re-brand its Prime Infrastructure satellite and Babcock & Brown Infrastructure to 'capitalize on the Babcock & Brown name globally'. Within a few years, Prime shareholders would rue ever hearing the words Babcock or Brown.

Another one of Babcock's more unusual investments was its sponsorship of hedge fund of funds manager Everest Babcock & Brown. Everest was founded by Jeremy Reid, a young Sydney entrepreneur who created the firm with money provided from his wealthy father-in-law Stephen Eckowitz. (In 2009, Eckowitz, who was once on the *BRW* Rich List with an estimated wealth of $300 million, faced ruin after creditors placed his private investment vehicle in liquidation.)

Hedge funds are an alterative investment class which seek to provide a steady return regardless of the prevailing economic circumstances. In that sense, hedge funds theoretically will underperform during boom periods but outperform during downturns. Due to their so-called expertise, hedge funds charge customers on a '2 and 20' basis (this was slang for a 2 per cent fee being paid for funds

---

* Respected fund manager John Sevior would accurately dub Babcock's cashbox fund as a 'pretty opportunistic exercise'.

under management and a 20 per cent fee based on outperformance of a specific benchmark). This principle drew the ire of many, including Warren Buffett, who dubbed hedge funds unnecessary 'hyper helpers' and noted that these expensive funds would rarely beat a passive index investment after fees are considered. A hedge fund of funds is an even more hyper helper that charges yet another layer of fees to invest in a hedge fund which already charged exorbitant fees (many hedge funds of funds were exposed after they invested clients' funds in Bernie Madoff's infamous Ponzi scheme, charging millions in commissions).

Everest was a hedge fund of fund manager, which charged fees to investors for access to hedge funds which ordinary people would theoretically be unable to invest in. Like most of Babcock's investments, Everest would be struck down by the global financial crisis, forced to write of hundreds of millions of dollars and remove Babcock from its name.*

> **Lesson #1: Consider the quality rather than just the quantity of a company's earnings**
>
> Analysts and business commentators will often report a company's headline earnings result. Few will consider whether that result is sustainable. A company that generates a substantial proportion of earnings from large non-core asset sales faces serious risks in falling markets.
>
> Another problem with companies that rely on horse-trading assets to generate earnings is that buying and selling large assets doesn't require any particular 'barriers to entry', other than the capital or debt to afford the purchase.
>
> Anyone can look like a business genius when the market is rising — assets appreciate without their owners having to lift a finger, but as Warren Buffett once noted, 'you only learn who has been swimming naked when the tide goes out'.

---

* In September 2008, when Everest changed its name from Everest Babcock & Brown to Everest Financial Group, it wryly noted to shareholders that 'following [a strategic] review, both the company and Babcock & Brown acknowledge that there is now limited strategic overlap between their respective businesses'. Probably true, but at that time about the only business Babcock had much of a strategic overlap with was that of an insolvency practitioner.

These problems were, however, years away. Babcock's 2004 financial results beat prospectus forecasts by 13 per cent as the company reported a profit of $148 million. However, as with Allco and MFS, a closer look at Babcock's profit components revealed that the result was not necessarily sustainable. During the year, the business generated sales of $562 million, however of that figure $365 million related to 'profit from sale of assets'.

Despite the short-term nature of its profits, Babcock executives were paid very handsomely. In its first remuneration report Babcock's 12 most senior executives took away $60 million cash—Phil Green collected $10.3 million, inclusive of a $7.7 million cash bonus. The remuneration doled out by Babcock followed the trail blazed by US–based investment banks, which tend to pay out half the firm's profits to employees on the basis that it was the ingenuity of those employees which created true value for shareholders (it is claimed that banks' 'most valuable assets go up and down in the elevators').

Such thinking was convenient for senior employees, but certainly not for shareholders. As would be revealed in years to come, remunerating employees in cash creates a short-term mindset geared at generating potentially unsustainable, debt-funded profits. Little did shareholders realise, they were paying Phil Green and his merry band of executives tens of millions of dollars to sow the seeds of their own destruction.

SPINNING OFF: BABCOCK ADOPTS THE MACQUARIE MODEL

While Babcock's leasing business would for the time being be the biggest contributor to Babcock's revenue base, the investment bank would soon follow its forerunner Macquarie Bank, and 'spin off' a growing number of fee-paying satellite funds.

The Macquarie model, while laden with complexity and legalities, was really devilishly simple. It involved purchasing an asset which provided relatively stable long-term cash flows and often substantial barriers to entry. In most cases, the asset purchased would be a regulated infrastructure property—roads, power utilities or airports were most suitable. As Macquarie would tell investors, the assets that fitted the model best would possess 'strong, stable cash flows that grow over time [and which] can support above-average distributions to investors'.[3]

The sponsor investment bank would purchase and warehouse the asset temporarily on its balance sheet, before selling the asset to a fund which it would separately establish and float. (As the model progressed and shareholders in the funds become disillusioned, the banks would gradually convert to more commonly using unlisted funds.)

The major benefit of the model for the bank was fees. Lots and lots of fees.

Babcock or Macquarie would charge a fee for the asset sale to the satellite. Once the satellite was established, it would pay management fees (often based on the vehicle's market capitalisation plus its debt, usually referred to as 'enterprise value') and performance fees (which would be around 20 per cent of any outperformance of a benchmark index). The real kicker, however, would be advisory fees paid to the bank for providing financial advice, debt facilities or underwriting services on behalf of the satellite.

There is an obvious flaw in the Macquarie model (for investors); that is, the manager is incentivised to conduct additional and costly transactions to reap additional fees for two reasons. First, it would be able to charge millions in advisory and debt arranging fees, and second, when the satellite acquired more assets it would also assume additional debt, and this would increase the level of management fees paid to the manager. In this regard, the goals of investors in the various funds and the banks managing them were diametrically opposed — Babcock and Macquarie would be encouraged to bid up the prices of assets as that would mean they would require additional debt and would be paid a higher management fee. Overpaying for assets is generally not in the best interests of the unitholder.

Even worse, in many cases the satellite would be locked in to retaining Macquarie or Babcock as an external manager due to binding management agreements. As corporate governance expert RiskMetrics would note, the satellites combined aspects of the governance structure for a publicly traded real estate investment trust with that of a traditional company, creating an unusual structure in which the 'stapled company' would have two boards and be externally managed (by Babcock or Macquarie executives). This would make it practically difficult, and possibly expensive, for investors to replace the external manager even if they were unhappy with the manager's performance.[4]

Lesson #2: Don't invest blind

Most management agreements entered into between Babcock/Macquarie and their various managed funds were never fully disclosed to investors. Most people wouldn't buy a house or a car without reading the terms and conditions of sale. Similarly, a management agreement creates a legal obligation (on the managed fund) to pay management, performance or advisory fees to a third party, or pay a specified sum should the fund change managers.

This represents a real-life liability to the managed fund or trust. It is wise to avoid investing money in a business when you don't know the full extent of its liabilities.

While some management agreements provided that Babcock or Macquarie may be replaced upon a shareholder vote, in reality that would be near impossible to achieve. The managers put in place other obstacles preventing their removal, including pre-emptive rights attaching to the assets owned by the fund, covenants in financing arrangements preventing replacement of the manager and long-term management contracts. For example, in the case of Macquarie Airports (MAp), even though the management agreement specifically provided for Macquarie's termination upon agreement of a simple majority of unitholders, in 2009 MAp shareholders would be forced to pay Macquarie $345 million to buy out its management rights.

The other flaw in the managed fund infrastructure model was the tendency for funds to pay high distributions to attract unitholders. The high yield was a major drawcard to investors—not only would they be purchasing what appeared to be a 'safe' asset, but they would get a lucrative income stream as well. The problem was, the income stream was illusory. In a sense, it not-so-slightly resembled a Ponzi scheme.* That is, the distributions being paid to investors in the funds were not paid from operating profits — rather, the funds would pay distributions from capital as well as retained earnings. This was somewhat politely referred to as 'financial engineering'. Babcock & Brown Wind were arguably the finest exponents of such chicanery — in 2006, the fund paid investors distributions of $48 million despite generating a profit of only $16 million.

Lesson #3: Don't judge a yield by its cover

Many infrastructure funds appeared to pay investors a 'yield' which approached 10 per cent (that is, the dividend per unit paid to unitholders was around one-tenth of the unit price). However, these yields were not 'real', rather they were manufactured.

In many cases, the funds would pay income not based on underlying earnings or even operating cash flows, but rather they paid investors using borrowed monies or capital from new investors.

Investors should be wary of manufactured yields — whenever a company pays more in dividends to owners than it actually generated in profits, the company is simply creating a future obligation that eventually needs to be repaid.

The funds were able to conduct such 'financial engineering' due to the ever-increasing demand for infrastructure assets, combined with the cost of debt in the early to mid 2000s being barely above the inflation rate. The funds then regularly 'revalued' their assets upwards and paid investors distributions based partially on the profit which was generated after the assets were revalued. Eventually, the cost of debt would increase and the funds would slash asset values, report massive losses and, in many cases, cease paying distributions.

---

* The term 'Ponzi scheme' originated from Italian immigrant to the United States Charles Ponzi. Ponzi had devised a scheme that promised investors a return of 50 per cent in 45 days by purchasing postal coupons in foreign countries and redeeming those coupons in the United States. The scheme was an utter fraud, with initial investors being repaid by capital contributed by new investors. When the flow of new capital dried up, the scheme collapsed and Ponzi would spend seven years in prison. Since then, any scheme that involved using new investor monies to pay dividends or income to earlier investors has been known as a 'Ponzi scheme'. Fund manager Bernard Madoff operated such a scheme for almost 30 years, fabricating gains of upward of US$60 billion, before eventually being detected in 2008. Madoff was jailed for 150 years in 2009 after pleading guilty to 11 felonies.

But we are getting ahead of ourselves—back to Babcock, and in 2002 there were no such clouds on the horizon. Babcock would create its first listed satellite in the form of the Prime Infrastructure Trust which housed the Dalrymple Bay coal terminal. This was followed in 2005 by the spin-off of its cashbox Babcock & Brown Capital (BCM). BCM would effectively act as a publicly owned private equity firm (in a similar manner to Allco Equity Partners) and proved to be a fee bonanza for Babcock. BCM would once again be well supported by the 'Friends of Phil', the cornucopia of wealthy investors, including the Packer and Liberman families, who profited heavily from the Babcock float.

Babcock would eventually create a swathe of listed managed funds, including Babcock & Brown Environmental, Babcock & Brown Wind Partners, Babcock & Brown Power, as well as several funds listed in London and Singapore. Most of Babcock's managed funds entered into 25-year exclusive management agreements with Babcock.

In each instance, the satellite funds would prove to be horrendous investments for unitholders but prove extremely lucrative for Babcock and its executives (remember, a large proportion of the fees paid by the satellite funds to the Babcock mothership would be handed straight back to Babcock's executives as performance bonuses). In fact, Babcock's funds would be such a debacle it is worth considering some of them individually in greater depth.

Babcock & Brown Infrastructure (BBI)

BBI was originally called Prime Infrastructure Trust, the vehicle created by Babcock to house the Dalrymple Bay coal terminal in Queensland. Listing in 2002, Prime acquired other infrastructure assets including wind farms and New Zealand's second largest electricity distributor, Powerco, for $1.7 billion in 2004.

In early 2005, Babcock proposed to restructure Prime to 'more closely align the interests of Babcock & Brown [with Prime] Securityholders'.[5] The benefits of this so-called alignment were clear to Babcock—mostly in the form of higher fees. (Before the transaction, Babcock owned 12 per cent of Prime, appointed two of its seven directors and was responsible for its deal flow.) The motivation for

Prime securityholders appeared to be somewhat vague—especially since it meant that Prime shareholders would lose the ability to act independently, be stripped of any takeover premium and be wedded to Babcock for 25 years.

Despite the downsides, Prime shareholders voted in favour of the deal, possibly based on the promise of 'new investment opportunities' and 'strong brand recognition'. In fairness, the prospect of 'strong brand recognition' was not mere puffery; in the years to come the Babcock name would become well known by the investment community—in a similar sense that a drunken Amy Winehouse stumbling down the street is also widely recognised.

As part of the deal, management would be fully 'externalised' to Babcock, and Prime would sign a 25-year management agreement. (Prime unitholders were not shown the fine print; for example, the cost of breaking the management agreements and terminating Babcock, even if its performance was horrible, was kept confidential.) Prime's directors wholeheartedly approved the deal. Prime chairwoman Elizabeth Nosworthy would be forced to vacate herself from the Prime boardroom during the deliberations. That is because Nosworthy was also a director of Babcock and the chairwoman of another Babcock investment company, Commander Communications.

Babcock would eventually deliver a spate of investment opportunities to BBI as promised. The only problem was many of those investments were money-losing duds which BBI unitholders paid a fortune to Babcock for the privilege.

At the time Babcock took over the management of Prime, Prime units were trading at around $1.50 each, valuing the entity at more than $1 billion. Four years later, BBI unitholders would be forced to accept a recapitalisation offer which valued the company at around 4¢ per share from Canadian infrastructure group Brookfield Asset Management to avoid near certain voluntary administration (ironically, BBI would be renamed Prime Infrastructure). The true horror of Babcock's management of BBI was not merely the billion or so of lost market value, but the sheer quantum of fees that Babcock audaciously charged to unitholders.

In 2005, BBI would tell unitholders that 'there has been no increase in the management or performance fees otherwise payable to

Babcock & Brown'.[6] This, however, appeared to be either a horrendous error or utter fabrication.

In 2004, prior to Prime being re-branded, it paid fees to Babcock of around $7.5 million. In 2005, after Babcock signed a 25-year management agreement, it paid management, performance and advisory fees of $69 million. A substantial proportion of the fees were advisory fees charged by Babcock relating to the acquisition of assets.

The fee gouge would continue in earnest. In 2006, with BBI's market capitalisation increasing to $2.3 billion, BBI told unitholders in its annual report that 'we are pleased to report that the restructuring of the corporate governance and management arrangements of BBI, which took place on 1 July 2005, has proved very successful'. BBI must have been couching their judgement from the point of view of Babcock & Brown. The restructuring certainly was very successful for the Babcock mothership and its wealthy executives.

During 2006, BBI paid fees of $91 million to Babcock (compared with earnings of only $82.7 million at the fund). Babcock was highly incentivised to continue to make acquisitions using BBI monies—the more infrastructure assets acquired, the more Babcock would reap in advisory fees and management fees. Remember, the base management fee payable to Babcock was not dependent on the profitability of BBI but rather its market value *plus* the value of its debt. The more debt and assets that were loaded into BBI, the more Babcock (and Babcock's executives) would be paid.

In 2007 Babcock's fee rake continued as it collected management and advisory fees of $73 million. However, 2008 would represent the high watermark for sheer audacity. While 2008 saw BBI report a net loss of $51 million and BBI's unit price slipped from $1.72 to 70¢, the fees paid to Babcock reached a new zenith. In total, Babcock extracted $116 million from BBI in 2008.

For 2009, BBI announced a loss of $977 million while its units dropped to 2¢. Meanwhile it desperately tried to sell 'crown jewel' assets such as the Dalrymple Bay coal terminal to stave off insolvency and repay its crippling $8 billion debt (unitholders eventually agreed to Brookfield's recapitalisation plan which virtually wiped out their equity in the business). Despite its dire predicament, which was largely caused by Babcock's incompetent management, BBI still felt it appropriate to pay Babcock fees of $33.9 million in 2009.

While Babcock told securityholders that fees would not change after it assumed management of Prime Infrastructure, the reality was very different. In the three years up to 2004 where Prime was an independent entity, it paid fees of $20.5 million (or an average of $7 million annually) to Babcock. Between 2005 and 2009, while BBI's market capitalisation crashed, the fund paid fees of $314 million (or approximately $63 million each year) to Babcock. (BBI would also make a $200 million loan to a wholly owned subsidiary of Babcock & Brown.)

Even worse, the fee gouge was not even being received by Babcock shareholders (who may have also been BBI unitholders and therefore could have recovered at least some of those fees, albeit indirectly); rather, it was largely being accumulated by Babcock & Brown management through their extraordinary cash bonuses.

Babcock & Brown Wind Partners (BBW)

Babcock timed its share market float of Babcock & Brown Wind Partners to perfection. In October 2005 the infrastructure boom was in full swing and alternative energy sources were being actively promoted through government regulation. A few months earlier wind farm and hydroelectricity company Pacific Hydro had been acquired in a hotly fought takeover battle by Industry Funds Management.

With investor sentiment strong, BBW hit the boards at $1.40 per share and rose to $1.68 in its first day of trade. As with most Babcock floats, the share price leapt partly because of the short supply of stock—much of the initial allocation was handed to long-time Babcock clients. This was not altogether different from the heady days of the dotcom boom in the United States, where money-losing companies would list at excessive premiums due to a small float of available scrip.

The improvement in BBW's unit price was not all good news though. A few months after listing, the fund told shareholders that it would be unable to meet prospectus profit forecasts due to a delay in acquisition of assets, poor wind conditions and higher than expected management fees. Ironically, unitholders would see profit reduced because of the 'increase in market capitalisation' of the fund (readers will recall that Babcock's funds paid management fees based on the entity's enterprise value, which was its market value and the book value of its debt, rather than earnings performance).

Therefore, despite reporting a net loss of $14 million and having surplus operating cash flow of only $16 million, BBW paid Babcock more than $33 million in fees in 2006. (To make matters worse, during the year BBW CEO Peter O'Connell quit the company, partly due to its poor performance and partly because of his decision to sell his entire holding of BBW units around the time the fund announced its profit downgrade but neglected to inform the ASX for several months.)

In 2007 BBW generated a maiden profit of $13.8 million (which would later be restated downwards to $6.3 million) and, in true financial engineering fashion, managed to increase distributions paid to unitholders by 22 per cent to $50 million. It is not outrageous to suggest paying unitholders a distribution which was more than 700 per cent higher than actual earnings is not likely to be an enduring business model, but then again that is not what Babcock was paid management and advisory fees of $13.6 million for.*

As with BBI, the fact that BBW's executives were paid by Babcock & Brown gave rise to a clear conflict—specifically, were BBW management acting in the interests of the fund, or in the interests of Babcock itself? As previously suggested, it was very much in the interests of Babcock for its funds to increase their asset and debt base, even at the expense of earnings per security. This was noted by BBW's CEO Miles George in 2009 when he stated, 'one of the inherent conflicts of that managed fund model is that the manager, which I was previously employed by, compensates the executives such as myself, in our case with Babcock & Brown shares, and that was clearly a conflict'.[7]

But conflicts were again forgotten when in 2008 BBW made a profit of $39 million (and handed out distributions of more than $74 million). Unsurprisingly, management fees rose again, jumping to $29.2 million.

---

* BBW at least paid distributions from operating cash flow, not borrowings. However, operating cash flow ignored non-cash items such as depreciation and amortisation which affect accounting profit. This means that, in effect, BBW would pay distributions in part by returning capital contributed by owners.

The BBW story would have a slightly happier ending than that of the other Babcock funds. In early 2009, BBW internalised management, changed its name to Infigen Energy and broke away from Babcock, at a cost of $40 million. Unlike most other Babcock entities, BBW's security price even managed to remain above its listing price. Perhaps Babcock didn't charge it high enough fees.

Babcock & Brown Power (BBP)

Even our worst-case result in Alinta is not a bad situation.
Babcock & Brown CEO Phil Green in March 2007, one year before Babcock's $7.7 billion acquisition of Alinta precipitated its collapse[8]

After a heavily oversubscribed float BBP listed on the ASX in December 2006 at $2.50 per unit. The fund described itself in its 2007 annual report as 'a specialist investment fund of scale dedicated to delivering long-term capital growth and an attractive cash yield through owning and operating power generation assets'. If subsequent performance is any guide, it is fair to suggest that BBP's claims were a tad over-ambitious.

BBP was created to purchase a collection of power assets which were previously owned by other Babcock entities. It acquired Victorian and New South Wales power assets from BBI and a swathe of generators from the Babcock mothership.

A few months after listing, in May 2007 BBP units reached $3.70. Eighteen months later, BBP shares slumped to 2¢ in what represented one of the most remarkably poor performances by an Australian listed company. It takes truly exceptional management to lose more than 99 per cent of a business's value in less than two years—particularly when that business is not a technology or bio-tech start-up, but rather an owner of boring electricity-generation assets.

BBP's problem, however, had nothing to do with the assets it owned but rather how much it paid for them, and the absurd fees it paid to the Babcock mothership.

BBP represented the high watermark for financial engineering and the 'Macquarie model'. BBP's 'Waterloo moment' was when Babcock teamed up with Singapore Power to complete the $8 billion takeover of Alinta (itself a highly engineered Western Australian power company). Babcock and SP Ausnet 'won' a bidding war against Macquarie Bank by paying a 48 per cent premium compared with Alinta's prevailing share price. Alinta shareholders ended up receiving cash and shares in various Babcock satellites, including BBP, BBI and BBW.* (The bulk of Alinta's assets would be bought by Singapore Power for cash.)

For its part, BBP would be forced to take on billions of Alinta's additional debt and issue 335 million shares to Alinta shareholders. After the Alinta deal, the market valued BBP at an extraordinary $2.4 billion, making it briefly the 112th most valuable publicly listed company in Australia.

However, this was where Babcock's management of BBP (and BBI and BBW for that matter) was so critical. Had the satellites been truly independent, they would have probably baulked at the prospect of a highly engineered, debt-funded acquisition of an already highly engineered company for a substantial premium. For Babcock itself, the transaction, like virtually all of its deals, was essentially a win–win. It would earn transaction fees of $33 million from BBP alone for 'advising' on the deal (as well as fees from BBI and BBW) and it would also reap increased management fees due to the additional debt which was being incurred by its satellites.

For the 2007 financial year (prior to the Alinta deal closing), despite only being around for seven months and losing $71 million, BBP paid the Babcock mothership fees of $58 million — including an 'incentive fee' of $23.4 million and IPO advisory fee of $13 million. (The incentive fee was based on BBP's share price rising by more than 40 per cent in its first seven months as a listed entity. The problem for BBP shareholders is that the incentive fee would not be repaid in the event that BBP's share price subsequently fell.)

It was later in 2007, after the Alinta deal was completed and as the sub-prime crisis started to heat up, that BBP's awful predicament finally started to sink in. The Alinta acquisition (and other various

---

* Macquarie Bank had earlier teamed up with Alinta's Chairman John Poynton and its CEO Bob Browning, as well as several other high-ranking Alinta executives, to attempt a management buyout of the power company. The leveraged buyout (LBO) was heavily criticised, with Poynton, Brown and Macquarie accused of a conflict of interest (Macquarie had previously served as Alinta's financial adviser). Ultimately Poynton and Brown departed from their roles at Alinta to pursue their ultimately unsuccessful LBO, while the company would dump Macquarie as an adviser and demand the return of all work that the bank had previously undertaken. Poynton later opined that 'in an effort to make it look like we weren't getting an inside run, we were kind of made pariahs. The rest of it is I guess history, you know, a lot of bad press, a lot of things written that you know I'd rather weren't or hadn't been'.

leveraged acquisitions) meant that BBP was burdened with a total debt load of more than $7 billion (up from around $1 billion at the end of the 2007 financial year).

During the bubble, the minor issue of billions of dollars worth of debt would be ignored, or perhaps even embraced by analysts and investors (in the interests of better utilising a firm's balance sheet). However, by 2008 debt was no longer king. While in February BBP boss Paul Simshauser and CFO James Brown told investors that discussions regarding its debt refinancing were 'well advanced' and it had received offers to have the $3.1 billion debt burden underwritten, as the year progressed things appeared grimmer.[9] By May, BBP conceded that it needed to refinance $3.4 billion of short-term debt and capital, and hurriedly tried to undertake a fire sale of its electricity-generation assets. BBP would later face civil legal action regarding misleading representations of debt levels to investors.

The problem was exacerbated when BBP revealed it would only be able to obtain $2.7 billion from its bankers — meaning it needed to find another $700 million from somewhere. Understandably, investors did not react favourably to this revelation, causing BBP's share price to drop by 60 per cent in a week. (BBP was eventually able to pay off short-term debt after selling its Uranquinty gas facility to Origin Energy for $700 million.)

If things weren't bad enough, in early June a gas explosion at Varanus Island in Western Australia would cause even more problems for BBP. The incident at a gas processing plant disrupted more than 30 per cent of the state's power supplies and hurt BBP, which owned the Alinta gas distribution business (the outage forced Alinta to obtain gas from other sources to fulfil its supply agreements at a higher cost, reducing BBP's earnings).

For 2008, BBP reported a $426 million loss while its debts would total more than $5.7 billion. BBP also wrote off more than $400 million from its Alinta acquisition, an amount equal to three times its current market worth. The loss and a simultaneous earnings downgrade precipitated the departure of CEO Paul Simshauser, who was promptly redeployed to another part of Babcock & Brown. (For some reason, Simshauser was still paid $1.4 million during 2008, including a performance bonus of $412 475, in what would appear to be one of the more underserved bonuses received even by the somewhat loose standards of corporate Australia.*)

Despite its horrendous predicament, BBP paid Babcock—the manager that caused most of its problems due to the Alinta acquisition —fees of $106 million in 2008. In total, within less than two short years, BBP's share price dropped by 99 per cent while Babcock & Brown managed to pillage upwards of $164 million from its rotting corpse. (BBP would also owe Babcock almost $400 million—a relic from the Alinta acquisition.)

In its 2009 annual report, BBP warned shareholders that there was uncertainty over the ability of the company to carry on as a 'going concern', although that didn't prevent it from paying fees of $8.6 million to Babcock during the year.

JOINT VENTURING OUT (2005)

While creating a fleet of fee-paying satellite funds (which would soon meet their impending doom), Babcock would also direct its Sadim touch elsewhere.

In 2005, Babcock partnered Australia's oldest property trust, GPT, in one of the more controversial and ultimately idiotic property ventures attempted by Australian companies. While the GPT joint venture was one of many debacles to befall Babcock in its brief life as a publicly owned company, it would also be near fatal for the venerable GPT, owner of blue-chip properties such as Sydney's Australia House and the MLC Centre and the ASX building in Melbourne's Collins Street.

GPT had for decades been externally managed by Lend Lease, one of Australia's great property companies. Floated in 1971 by Lend Lease, GPT owned a suite of high-quality commercial properties.

However, with externally managed funds losing favour with shareholders, Lend Lease proposed to internalise GPT by paying GPT unitholders $3.72 per unit. Lend Lease would then incorporate GPT with its own Bovis and Delfin business in order to save upwards of $60 million annually in administrative costs.

---

* BBP claimed that Simshauser's bonus related to the 2007 calendar year, rather than the 2008 financial year; however, unitholders would have been forgiven for expecting that an executive who presides over a multi-billion loss is not deserving of any bonus—regardless of which period it is related to. See S Rochfort, 'BBP Defends High-Powered Bonuses', *The Sydney Morning Herald*, 27 September 2008.

The Lend Lease proposal was opposed by rival Westfield, which had its own ideas. Under an alternative plan, Westfield purchased three retail assets from GPT, which would use those funds to form a $1 billion joint venture with Babcock. Westfield boss Frank Lowy, one of Australia's richest men, used Westfield's 6 per cent voting stake to defeat the Lend Lease deal, with GPT falling into the warm embrace of Babcock.*

The joint venture was shrewdly structured by Babcock, which contributed only $100 million and a collection of what would turn out to be badly overpriced European residential properties located largely in Germany (described rather uncharitably by one commentator as a bunch of 'European slums'.[10]) GPT meanwhile contributed around $1.2 billion, mostly in preferred capital (and a further $750 million in late 2006).

By 2008, the joint venture would grow to own more than $7 billion in assets geared to almost 70 per cent. In one fell swoop, by hopping into bed with Phil Green and Babcock, GPT morphed from boring manager of commercial and tourism properties to high-risk financier (even independent expert, Grant Samuel, muttered that the deal favoured Babcock and selling the centres to Westfield was not a great idea). For GPT, the Babcock deal represented the financial equivalent of a man leaving his wife for a 22-year-old stripper.

Four years later the sub-prime property crash would turn the joint venture into a truly great money-losing fiasco—GPT would write off more than $700 million from the value of its share in venture from its balance sheet (and retain $1.2 billion in residual book value which would need to also be written down). While a downturn in the property sector also played a role, the joint venture was the primary reason for GPT's unit price slumping from more than $4.00 in December 2007 to 22¢ in March 2008.†

---

* The ability for Westfield to vote its 6.5 per cent stake against the GPT–Lend Lease deal represented a monumental blunder by the ASX and ASIC. Westfield was grossly conflicted—it stood to benefit financially should the Babcock deal succeed and lose out if the Lend Lease internalisation went ahead. Westfield should have been separated into a separate 'class'. Had this occurred, GPT unit-holders would have avoided an enormous amount of financial pain.

† In March 2008, Babcock chief Phil Green claimed that 'we have a high level of confidence that we will outperform...that as we sell assets we will deliver GPT profit over their original cost. And we've seen nothing in the market, particularly in Europe, to suggest otherwise and I suggest that will become evident over the next little while'. GPT would later write off virtually all of its investment in the joint venture. See 'KGB Interrogation: Phil Green', *Business Spectator*, 21 March 2008.

The GPT–Babcock joint venture ended up owning various over-valued assets, including European shopping centres purchased at the height of the boom and hundreds of millions worth of mezzanine finance with loan-to-valuation ratios in excess of 90 per cent. The joint venture's failure eventually forced GPT to conduct an emergency dilatory $1.6 billion capital raising in late 2008 at only 60¢ — more than 80 per cent less than Lend Lease's offer three years prior. The debacle eventually led to the departure of GPT's CEO Nic Lyons and that of multi-millionaire chairman Peter Joseph. (GPT would graciously waive a supposedly full recourse loan it had provided to Lyons. Lyons, who led the failed Babcock & Brown joint venture, ultimately had loans worth $8.29 million excused by GPT.) GPT would later be forced to tap the equity market once more in May 2009, raising another $1.7 billion at only 35¢ per unit.

GPT would be one of many victims of the Babcock machine, which before too long would turn on its own.

BABCOCK BOSSES' BIG BONUS BONANZA (2005–06)

The story of Babcock's listed satellites was merely a sideshow to the main stage — this was because the hundreds of millions of dollars in fees being paid by the likes of BBI and BBP were, to a large extent, ending up in the pockets of Babcock's management.

In 2005 the Babcock mothership was flying. By the end of the year its share price was $17.15 — a 300 per cent increase in 14 months. Cash was flowing in the door at a rate of knots from an ever-growing fleet of satellite funds paying ever-growing fees to the mothership.

Babcock, however, had earned a small but growing legion of doubters. In October, its share price plummeted 23 per cent in a few days after a report from a broker which specialised in infrastructure criticised Babcock's excessive remuneration practices, which resulted in the bank paying upwards of 55 per cent of revenue to its employees. The market was also questioning the wisdom of the 'Macquarie model', which was being voraciously copied by Babcock.

Those concerns were cast aside by Babcock — its 2005 financial results revealed that revenue had risen by 95 per cent while earnings beat prospectus forecasts by 85 per cent, rising to $180 million. Amid all the euphoria, Babcock managed to set aside $266 million for bonuses to staff—more than the firm's annual profit for the year. That was equal to more than $400 000 for every single Babcock employee (that is on top of the fixed salaries that Babcock staff received, which were equal to $233 000 per employee). Of course, the distribution was far from equal, with the lion's share being swept up by executives. It was perhaps no coincidence that executive directors Phil Green and Jim Babcock were both members of the company's remuneration committee.

In 2005, Phil Green received total remuneration of more than $12 million—of which $10.9 million was paid in cash. Babcock's head of real estate, Michael Maxwell, the man responsible for the GPT joint venture, would be paid more than $10 million, also mostly in cash. In total, Babcock's executive team received more than $80 million from shareholders, $72 million of which was paid in cash. The problem with paying executives cash based on short-term performance is that should profitability reverse, those bonus payments are not refundable. This encourages executives to take substantial risks with shareholders' capital—if things go well, the executives receive mountains of cash; if things go badly, the executives receive a juicy termination payment and the shareholders face substantial losses.

Lesson #4: Cash is not king

Investors will get the management they deserve. When considering investing in a company, look closely at how it pays its executives.

If senior management are paid substantial fixed cash or short-term bonuses (based on short-term metrics such as earnings per share or profit growth) then they will be encouraged to take more risks with shareholders' capital or reduce expenses such as staffing or research and development.

By contrast, if the executives are paid largely in equity which is 'locked up' for a number of years and vests based on challenging performance hurdles, they will be more incentivised to generate long-term growth and avoid risky investments.

Babcock's bonus payments were partially based on a comparative return-on-equity measure against a number of other investment banks. Those banks included Bear Sterns, Credit Suisse, Goldman Sachs, Lehman Brothers, Macquarie, Merrill Lynch and Morgan Stanley. Of those competitors, only Macquarie would remain an investment bank after the global financial crisis—the rest would elect to become 'holding banks', merge or collapse.

It wasn't only Babcock executives who were cashing in on the firm's success; non-executive directors also saw their remuneration almost double. Babcock's remuneration committee chair Elizabeth Nosworthy was paid $216 862, up from $122 855 the previous year. While Nosworthy was deemed by Babcock to be an 'independent director', it would have been somewhat difficult for the former corporate lawyer to be completely impartial; Nosworthy was dependent on Babcock in one way or another for most of her livelihood.

Nosworthy had previously been the chairwoman of Prime Infrastructure when it was managed and partially owned by Babcock (but before it became BBI). Nosworthy was also a director of GPT, which entered into that disastrous multi-billion joint venture with Babcock & Brown. In addition, Nosworthy was chair of Commander Communications, of which Babcock owned a 19.9 per cent stake between 2003 and 2005. Nosworthy had been a 'Babcock appointment' to the Commander board (along with other Babcock representatives Rob Topfer and Peter O'Connell). Given Nosworthy received almost $400 000 annually from her Babcock-related roles, investors may have been a little sceptical that she would have been overly willing to stand up for Babcock's minority shareholders when Phil Green sought a pay rise.*

While 2005 was lucrative, in 2006 Babcock consolidated its position as one of Australia's leading merchant banks. Its share price steadily rose, while earnings increased once more, boosted by a gravy train of acquisitions. The banks earnings were goosed by it charging a jaw-dropping advisory fee of more than $85 million to its listed cashbox Babcock & Brown Capital for it to undertake the acquisition

---

* Nosworthy would later achieve the dubious honour of being chairwoman of three collapsed ASX companies. Nosworthy was at the helm of Babcock & Brown, Commander Communications and Ventracor when they were placed in administration. Nosworthy was also a director of GPT while it lost almost 99 per cent of its market value. Nosworthy, who would be dubbed the 'Black Widow', was either a director of questionable competence or extremely unlucky.

of Irish telecommunications company, Eircom* as well as more than $30 million to BBI for advice regarding a Western Australian rail deal and ports acquisition.

In total, Babcock's revenue from 'corporate finance' activities (which largely consisted of financial advice provided to captive satellite funds who were unable to use other advisers) increased by 189 per cent to $266 million. Similarly, infrastructure revenue (which largely included fees paid by satellites such as BBI or BBW) almost doubled to $464 million. While total advisory fees charged to Babcock satellites leapt substantially, fees received from 'third parties'—that is, clients who were not Babcock entities—dropped significantly. In short, Babcock was making a lot more money, but that money was coming from its own funds. If those funds were to encounter problems the mothership's revenue stream would dry up. Fast.

But there were no such concerns for Babcock employees in 2006. Remuneration paid continued to increase, with Babcock's 1019 employees averaging fixed pay of $177358 while the average bonus doled out to Babcock staff was more than $455000. Again it was the executives who fared best—Green took home more than $17 million, including $14 million in cash and short-term incentives. Other big gainers were Green's lieutenants Rob Topfer, who was head of corporate finance, and Peter Hofbauer, Babcock's infrastructure chief. Topfer's remuneration jumped to $15 million while Hofbauer received $14.7 million. In total, Babcock's top 10 listed executives were paid $122 million, of which more than $100 million was fixed salary or short-term bonus payments.

GOING GANGBUSTERS—AND GOING BUST (2007–08)

The height of the financial engineering boom can probably be summed up with one word: Alinta. In early 2007, the already highly engineered Western Australian power company came under attack

---

* The purchase of Eircom would be a typical Babcock calamity. While BCM's 2007 annual report claimed that 'Ireland remains one of Europe's fastest growing economies with high population growth and new housing starts', in reality the Irish economy would soon fall into a deep recession, with BCM's share price falling by upwards of 90 per cent. Bizarrely, former Babcock executive Rob Topfer would in 2009 try to take over BCM (which was by then renamed Eircom) for €95 million. Only three years prior, BCM, of which Topfer was a director, had paid $8 billion for a controlling interest in Eircom.

from its own CEO, chairman and financial adviser. As described earlier in this chapter, Babcock would soon join the fee bonanza, outdoing Macquarie in a hotly fought takeover contest.

But the victory would come at a cost. While Babcock reaped millions of dollars in fees following the Alinta transaction, the debt burden assumed by Babcock's satellites would cripple them, destroy investor confidence and play a leading role in Babcock's eventual collapse.

However, in early 2007 doom was the last thing on Babcock shareholders' or executives' minds. In the wake of the Alinta acquisition, Australia's most respected broadsheet newspaper would scream 'Booming B&B Takes on the World' as Babcock shares approached $30 — a remarkable ascent given that the company had listed at $5 per share only two and a half years prior.

While the Alinta deal promised more untold riches, some were beginning to question the ethics of the Babcock empire, particularly the still popular Phil Green. It was revealed that Babcock's house broker Tricom, which was run by Phil Green's long-time associate Lance Rosenberg, had been accumulating a $500 million stake in Alinta at the same time as Babcock's offer. That stake would have a blocking effect should Macquarie Bank seek to make another offer for Alinta. At the time, Babcock had provided contractual undertakings that it would not acquire any additional Alinta shares.

Green and Rosenberg would deny that they were acting in concert — Green claimed that Tricom was acting independently of Babcock. Those claims may have been true, but appear to have been contradicted by the fact that Green and Rosenberg conducted joint conference calls with institutional investors regarding the bid. Further, Tricom also acted as the lead manager on the Babcock & Brown float in October 2004, co-manager in the Babcock & Brown Wind float in October 2005, joint lead manager in the Babcock & Brown Residential Land Partners float in June 2006 and co-lead manager in the Babcock & Brown Power float in December 2006.[11] Babcock and Tricom also had form in this regard — Tricom had built up a stake in New Zealand's Powerco before BBI's eventual acquisition.

In the end, Babcock won the battle for Alinta (and no-one would ever take action against Tricom for its purchases of Alinta scrip).

Babcock's success came at the expense of Alinta shareholders, who were lumped with a collection of scrip in various Babcock entities —rather than the somewhat more valuable cash being offered by Macquarie.

In June, Babcock shares hit $34.78. At that time, Babcock was valued by the market at more than $10 billion and Green's stake alone was worth $440 million. On top of that, Green's holdings in Babcock's various listed satellites were worth upwards of $70 million. It appeared that Green had, temporarily at least, succeeded where his brother Max had failed—achieving money and power.

Green and Babcock's time at the top of Sydney's financial and cultural world would be brief, although Babcock's implosion would take time.

The collapse of two Bear Sterns hedge funds and subsequent re-weighting of risk would lead to a sudden loss of investor faith in Babcock. Between June 2007 and January 2008, Babcock shares fell from $34 to $15—a drop of more than 55 per cent in a little over six months.

Crucially, investors were rapidly losing faith in Babcock's suite of managed funds, which had been the engine room of its rapid earnings growth. In November, BBI unitholders delivered a loud message to Babcock, when more than 30 per cent of them voted against its remuneration report. A further 20 per cent voted against the reappointment of Babcock executive Peter Hofbauer as executive chairman. The cause of the angst was the fact that senior BBI executives were paid partly in shares in Babcock & Brown, creating a horrendous conflict of interest.

The conflict arose because Babcock & Brown earned revenue from charging fees to its satellites (such as BBI). The more fees Babcock charged, the more profit it would make and the higher its share price would rise. Because BBI executives were being paid partially in Babcock (not BBI) shares, it was actually in their personal interests to pay higher fees to Babcock—of course it was in the interests of BBI unitholders to pay *lower* fees to Babcock. From BBI's perspective, it is hard to envisage a dumber way to remunerate its executives. (From a long-term perspective, gouging fees would turn out to be a pretty stupid idea as well, as Babcock depended on strong, well-supported satellite funds.)

However, while investors were rapidly losing faith in the financial engineers, Babcock was doing what it did best—making deals and milking fees.

In September, a Babcock-led consortium won the right to construct Melbourne's Children's Hospital. Weeks later, Babcock would float Babcock & Brown Air, an aircraft leasing business, on the New York Stock Exchange. In December, Babcock managed to raise $3.8 billion for an unlisted European infrastructure fund.

Babcock's 2007 annual report revealed little by way of concern, even with Babcock's share price down more than 20 per cent from its peak. In fact, Babcock managed to massage what appeared to be a beautiful set of numbers. Profit rose to $525 million (from $309 million) on the back of skyrocketing infrastructure revenues. Ever the optimist, Phil Green predicted a financial year profit of $750 million. The profit result buoyed Babcock, its share price rising from the canvas once more.

The profit result once again underpinned another round of even larger bonus payments. The company's total bonus pool leapt another 39 per cent to $573 million. In 2007, however, Babcock would finally take heed of investor concerns and pay the majority of its bonuses in shares, rather than cash. This led to Phil Green's remuneration of $22 million consisting of a more sombre $4.9 million cash. (Don't feel too sorry for Phil, though; his pay was equivalent to 400 times what was received annually by the average Australian worker.) In all, the company's key executives were paid a total of $156 million in 2007, of which $54 million was paid in cash and the remainder in Babcock equity.

While Babcock had ostensibly managed to avoid the carnage which had befallen MFS and Allco, there was still the pesky issue of debt. In total there was $50 billion of it (much of it non-recourse) across all the Babcock entities. The mothership alone had more than $13 billion in liabilities.

Further, while Babcock didn't have the complexity of Allco or the cross-shareholdings of MFS, it was massively dependent on advisory fees paid by its suite of satellites and 'principal investment' earnings (in 2007, Babcock's infrastructure satellites paid $147 million in financial advisory fees as well as $127 million in base fees). In short, Babcock's business model relied on a constant flow of transactions—without new deals, almost half of its revenue and all of its profit would vanish. (Only $25 million of Babcock's roughly $2 billion in revenue came from non-Babcock entities.)

Like a hard rocker waking up after a week-long bender, it would not be too long before reality started catching up with Babcock.

BABCOCK STARTS TO WOBBLE

The first real alarm bell rang in early March 2008 when Green sent an email to Babcock staff warning that there would be a two-week delay in the payment of bonuses. The move was somewhat surprising, as traditionally one would be safer standing in front of a tank rolling through Tiananmen Square than between an investment banker and a bonus payment. Green claimed that the delay was 'due to the fact the senior management, including myself, have needed to focus on dealing with issues caused by the current market conditions thereby delaying decisions on final bonus allocations'.[12]

Even though the bonus issue was quickly resolved, it would not take much for short-selling hedge funds to smell blood. Already fellow financial engineers Allco and MFS had collapsed — and despite Green's pleas that Babcock was different, its apparent heavy reliance on debt and fees from satellites bore a remarkable similarity to its recently deceased financial engineering brethren.

The second warning emanated from those very same short-selling hedge funds. One particularly enthusiastic hedge fund took it upon itself to circulate a document pointing out that Babcock had effectively used margin loans to fund its investment in satellites such as BBI and BBP (the information was publicly available, but was buried deep in the notes to Babcock's annual reports, unnoticed by most). When the satellites were flying high this wasn't a problem, however when the share prices of the funds dropped, the loan-to-valuation ratios skyrocketed. At one point, Babcock's stake in BBI had an LVR of 80 per cent. While Green would use Babcock's dwindling cash reserves to pay off the margin loans to head off the hedge funds, it was a second strike against Babcock that would not be forgotten.

The incident also tarnished the Babcock brand, despite the best efforts of Green to differentiate his company from the likes of Allco and MFS. As one commentator noted, Babcock had 'trumpeted itself as an "industrial group" and not one of those fancy pants financial engineers. But it has been borrowing money—huge amounts of it—using as collateral the inflated value of its stakes in some of the satellites it floated and managed'.[13]

The next strike was the revelation Babcock had allowed its bankers to insert a market review clause in its loan agreements—the clause provided that in the event that Babcock's market capitalisation slipped below $2.5 billion for a period of three months, its bankers would have the ability to demand repayment of debt facilities. Also around this time legendary US hedge fund investor Jim Chanos, famous for 'shorting' Enron prior to its collapse, launched a devastating critique of the Macquarie model (which had been closely followed by Babcock). Chanos's criticism followed a damning report by RiskMetrics which had accused Macquarie and Babcock of using excessive debt, paying distributions from capital rather than profits and cash flow, paying too much for assets, questionable related-party deals, conflicts of interests and atrocious corporate governance.

It seemed that investors were finally peering behind the curtain. What they saw wasn't pretty.

The earlier wobbles were merely a precursor to the real problems that would befall Babcock. By late May 2008, optimistic earnings forecasts were long forgotten with BBP's problems resonating through the group. As explained earlier, BBP was having difficulties refinancing $3.4 billion of borrowings, most of it picked up as part of the disastrous Alinta acquisition. Within weeks, the cataclysm would spread throughout the company—on 13 June, Babcock's share price plummeted 27.5 per cent in a single session, falling below $7.50, the critical level which allowed its financiers to 'review' the debt facilities.

Babcock had become a victim of its own hubris. A year earlier, the company's market capitalisation was more than $10 billion. It loaded up with debt, almost $50 billion worth, and continued to acquire assets (most notably Alinta), at the same time agreeing to a market value clause with bankers which would make it susceptible to sentiment (and short-sellers). In fact, Babcock was so popular with hedge funds trying to 'short' the stock that by mid 2008 it wouldn't be possible to bet on the company's downfall—no-one was willing to lend Babcock shares. (To 'short' a stock, hedge funds need to 'borrow' the stock, usually from a fund manager who has a long position, and then sell the borrowed stock. Eventually, the hedge fund would buy back the stock and return it to the stock lender. In Babcock's case, fund managers were unprepared to 'lend' Babcock stock.)

As Babcock's share price slumped so did the value of its satellites, which created a vicious cycle because Babcock also owned substantial stakes in BBI, BBW and BBP. Debt was now like a virus for Babcock; once one satellite was infected, it would flow through the entire group. Babcock's biggest problem, however, wasn't necessarily the debt review clause—ultimately, the banks would seek to maximise their position, and that is rarely achieved through a 'fire sale' of assets. The pitfall was that the dramatic drop in Babcock's share price and the dramas at BBP resulted in a widespread loss of confidence—for any bank or similar financial institution trust is critical to its ability to continue to do business.

The 'model' used by Babcock and Macquarie was especially based upon trust. Babcock's main business had turned into buying assets (usually by bidding more than anyone else was willing to pay), selling them to a related party and charging fees along the way (other businesses such as cross-border leasing had long taken a back seat to asset origination and fee gouging). If Babcock or investors lost faith in the satellites, they wouldn't be able to buy the assets from Babcock—this would reduce its fees and leave billions of dollars of overpriced assets on Babcock's balance sheet.

While Rome burned, the Babcock chiefs ploughed on. On 14 June, a day after its share price plummeted almost 28 per cent, triggering the market review clause, Babcock announced that its unlisted European infrastructure fund would spend $1.7 billion to acquire UK-based Angel Trains. Perhaps Babcock knew that without deals such as Angel Trains it would be dead anyway so it might as well go down punching.

In the space of one week Babcock's share price had fallen by more than 52 per cent to just $5.25.

While Babcock managed to negotiate away the market value review clause for a relatively low cost (Babcock's interest rate on its debt would increase by 50 basis points, or half of a per cent), this lucky break would only give Babcock minimal breathing space. But the wolves were still at the door.

Those wolves grew louder in August with revelations regarding the conduct of Babcock's European arm. A former Babcock executive accused three very senior Babcock employees, including executive director Martin Rey, of 'serious violations of corporate standards and inappropriate conduct'. Among the allegations were claims that 'there [was no] financial incentive to follow through on a deal just completed' with Babcock fostering an environment where 'senior people are rewarded for building ... up rosy projections to justify their rewards'. Later, it was alleged that 'deal makers [were] often allowed to set absurdly optimistic assumptions for models (or not disclose material facts)'.[14]

BABCOCK CRUMBLES

The next week the jig was finally up. Babcock came clean and told shareholders that profit would be between 25 and 40 per cent lower than expected. Analysts did not take the news well, with one noting that the revelation would 'do little to help rebuild management's already fragile credibility'.[15] Soon after, BBP announced a $400 million impairment charge relating to the Alinta acquisition. A week later, management was gone.

Phil Green and Jim Babcock, the men who had built Babcock into a $10 billion monolith, would resign as CEO and executive chairman. (Bizarrely, Green agreed to remain at Babcock as a non-executive director for a few weeks, before realising he was about as welcome in the Babcock boardroom as a mistress at Christmas lunch.) Babcock's share price continued to fall—down a remarkable 88 per cent in nine months.

While the company allegedly made a $175 million profit in the first half of the year, investors weren't fooled. On its balance sheet sat literally billions of dollars of infrastructure and real estate assets—the value which Babcock attributed to these assets in most cases was what it paid for them, not what they were currently worth in a depressed market. If Babcock had overpaid for these assets (which, even without the impact of the global financial crisis, was almost certainly the case) then its stated profit was a fairytale.

By November, Babcock's predicament would worsen, with its share price falling to 20¢ (more than 99 per cent below its peak).

Perhaps ironically, its problems were exacerbated by German bank Bayerische Hypo- und Vereinsbank freezing a $70 million deposit of Babcock's. Hypo was of course Babcock's biggest financial supporter in its early days, at one stage owning 20 per cent of the company before it listed on the ASX. Dieter Rampl, a long-time Babcock director, was chairman of UniCredit, the owner of Hypo. It appeared that the father had finally cut off his wayward son, before any more damage could be caused.

While staring into the abyss once more, miraculously Babcock (now led by former CEO Michael Larkin) would manage once more to stave off collapse, convincing bankers to accept a 'debt for equity swap' and a 'pay if you can' arrangement. The deal was a godsend for Babcock which had a limited ability to pay anything (at the time, secured debt was more than $3 billion, compared with the company's market capitalisation of $143 million). The banks figured the ailing company was worth more alive than dead, although this was possibly only because it wasn't worth anything dead.

By 2009, however, the Babcock story (as a publicly listed entity anyway) would finally draw to a close. Babcock's New Zealand–based unsecured noteholders (many of whom were retirees) would reject an offer of 0.1 cents in the dollar (the offer was much like a diner leaving a 5¢ tip in a restaurant).

The noteholders' vote would be the final straw—administrators would be appointed to Babcock & Brown on 13 March 2009. The company that once managed more than $72 billion worth of assets was—finally—dead.

BABCOCK NOTEHOLDERS GET SHAFTED (2009)

In most cases when an entity enters administration, equityholders (and often unsecured creditors such as noteholders) are left with nothing. That is because bankruptcy laws provide that secured creditors (along with a few other groups such as the administrators themselves and employees) are paid first. In a wind-up, the value of the company's assets are rarely substantial enough to cover the debts, for a couple of reasons. First, the business is often no longer a going concern, and second, buyers know that the seller (often a receiver appointed by the major debtor banks) simply wants to recover their client's money so the assets will often go cheap.

In the event of Babcock's administration, unsecured noteholders and shareholders had an even bigger problem—they didn't even have any direct rights to Babcock's assets (which included the right to receive revenues from management agreements and a collection of unsold infrastructure and real estate assets); rather, Babcock shareholders owned a company (Babcock) which owned 99 per cent of a company (Babcock & Brown International) which owned the assets.

To explain, the publicly listed Babcock & Brown's only asset was its ownership of and loans provided to Babcock & Brown International Limited (BBIL). It was BBIL which then owned all the relevant assets.

When Babcock raised money by issuing notes, the funds would find their way into the listed Babcock entity (Babcock & Brown). That listed entity would lend that money to BBIL. Crucially, it was BBIL which borrowed money from banks. Should anything ever happen to Babcock, those banks would have recourse to the assets but the Babcock shareholders would merely have recourse to Babcock's corporate shell.

When Babcock entered its 'pay if you can' agreement the prior year, it therefore had the effect of benefiting BBIL but not actually helping Babcock & Brown shareholders.[16] At that time, the major creditors of the Babcock mothership were noteholders, who were owed more than $600 million.

Even after Babcock & Brown was formally placed in administration, BBIL continued to trade as normal and charge hefty management fees to Babcock's decrepit satellites—the benefit would flow through to Babcock's secured creditors (namely, the banks). Babcock's chairwoman, Elizabeth Nosworthy, told noteholders that even if Babcock was placed in the hands of administrators, 'Babcock & Brown International Pty Ltd, the main operating and asset-owning entity of the Babcock & Brown Group, will continue to operate and continue with the program of asset sales'.

However, even that wasn't enough—by September 2009 even Babcock's secured lenders lost faith in BBIL's ability to recoup the billions owed, and sold the majority of secured Babcock debt to hedge funds for between 20¢ and 30¢ in the dollar. In all, Babcock's $3 billion of secured debt was estimated by the large Australian banks at being worth less than $900 million. Its unsecured debt and equity would be worth nothing at all.

The reason for the drop in value of Babcock's secured debt was its continued horrendous financial performance. While never formally lodging financial statements for 2009, it was revealed that Babcock managed to lose $5.4 billion in its last year of trading — a truly spectacular feat of sheer incompetence. It would be the third largest loss ever for an Australian company. Phil Green's prediction of $750 million profit would turn out to be somewhat optimistic.

THE SURVIVOR: PHIL GREEN LIVES ON

Despite Babcock's collapse, and the loss of billions of shareholder and creditor funds, Green's standard of living was not terribly affected. Green was able to retain ownership of his Point Piper mansion and a 50 per cent stake in a 30000 hectare property in the New South Wales Hunter Valley which had been purchased for $23 million in 2006. Green is also understood to still own a 5 per cent interest in a company called Tourism Asset Holdings Limited. Tourism Asset Holdings, Australia's largest owner of hotels, was purchased by a Babcock-led consortium in 2001 for $188 million and sold to a syndicate of investors, including Green, in 2003. In 2008, the company owned more than 6000 rooms across 40 hotels.

In 2009, Green joined forces with former Hoyts boss and Babcock investor Peter Ivany at the privately held company Roving Star. Another venture involved Green seeking to purchase distressed debt from General Motors's former finance arm.[17]

Green sold his remaining holdings in Babcock in October 2008; while receiving a pittance compared with its share price the prior year, he at least got something.

Similarly, Jim Babcock saw the writing on the wall shortly before Babcock's collapse and was able to offload around $100 million worth of shares before the company slid into administration. Babcock used some of the proceeds to build a US$14 million mansion in San Francisco.

Green and Babcock were not the only Babcock executives to have escaped from the wreckage with part of their loot intact. It is understood that several very senior Babcock executives, including Rob Topfer, Peter Hofbauer and Eric Lucas, were able to utilise 'cap and collar' arrangements to protect the value of their options. The trio also received cash pay of $27 million, $31 million and $33 million respectively during Babcock's four years as a public company.

Topfer and five other Babcock executives even attempted an audacious and unsuccessful takeover of Eircom in 2009, which was slightly ironic given that under Topfer's management Babcock & Brown Capital lost billions investing in the Irish telco which in turn paid tens of millions of dollars to Babcock for the privilege. Topfer's offer was rejected, largely on the grounds that it involved using Eircom's own cash to pay existing holders.

Babcock claimed in its 2005 annual report that 'the underlying philosophy is that when the company does well, both the employees and the shareholders should do well; and if the company does not do so well, both the employees and the shareholders should share in that pain'—the second part of that statement proved remarkably inaccurate. While Babcock shareholders would be left with nothing, its executives had been paid cash of more than $280 million over four years. During that time, Babcock's market value would race from $1.5 billion to $10 billion to zero.

For Green and the Babcock directors, the story is far from over. In September 2009, Babcock's liquidator raised funds from creditors to conduct public examinations of Green and Jim Babcock. The liquidators also alleged that the company may have been insolvent as early as November 2008, five months before it was placed in administration. Under the Corporations Act, directors can be held liable for debts incurred while a company was trading insolvent, and face personal civil actions.

There have also been allegations raised by Babcock & Brown's administrator, Deloitte, that Green may have also breached his duties as a director of Babcock when he authorised a $40 million loan to Babcock's broker, Tricom, in 2008. The loan allowed Babcock stock to be reclaimed by Babcock employees and prevented Tricom's collapse. It was alleged that the largest beneficiary of the loan was

Green himself. Babcock's administrator would also note that the loan appeared to be of little benefit, financial or otherwise, to Babcock.[18]

Since it listed on the ASX, Babcock was a company mired in vices—greed, gluttony, sloth—but for all its foibles its inevitable doom could be best described by its remuneration practices. In 2006 and 2007, the company paid around 50 per cent of its earnings to fund paying employees—this policy served to encourage the massive risk-taking culture which pervaded Babcock and would lead to its ultimate downfall.

CHAPTER 8

Timbercorp and Great Southern Plantations

Australia's rural tax rort comes up a cropper

> *Prospectus-based plantation forestry has made a major contribution to the national plantations strategy, with significant economic, environmental and social benefits. I expect that contribution to continue and expand.*
>
> Letter to the *Australian Financial Review* from former federal minister Wilson Tuckey on 16 June 2000

TIMBERCORP AND Great Southern Plantations stood like goliaths in Australia's agricultural sector. At their peak both would boast a market value in excess of $1 billion dollars, a remarkable achievement for an industry which essentially grew out of a tax-minimisation scheme.

While the founders of Timbercorp and Great Southern became rich men, thousands of investors and shareholders lost out, as would many farmers who were effectively priced out of the market and Australian taxpayers who underwrote what was described as one of the greatest rorts ever to be perpetrated on the Australian public.[1]

It would eventually be revealed that many of the schemes run by Great Southern and Timbercorp quite simply did not make any money. When you added up the sales from selling woodchips or mangoes or olives, in many cases they would be less than the cost of managing and harvesting the crops or trees. However, this was certainly not the story being told by the promoters. In 2002, Great Southern told investors that forecast returns from its woodlot projects were between 5 and 15 per cent annually.

For years before its collapse, to ensure that investors received their promised returns Great Southern used company funds to pay inflated amounts for harvested product from its projects. Eventually, the music would stop and someone turned on the lights. It would be an ugly scene.

But before the house of cards came crashing down, the managed investment scheme (MIS) industry, led by Timbercorp and Great Southern, would raise more than $8 billion from 47000 investors. Due to the taxation advantages of MISs, investment monies which would otherwise have been directed to more worthwhile ventures ended up being invested in agribusiness ventures of dubious commercial merit. This would lead to the contention that decisions to invest in agribusiness schemes were often the result of tax deductibility rather than profitability.*

Not only that, but returns were further hurt by MIS companies paying a fortune to conflicted financial planners to sell investments to hopelessly unsophisticated investors based on experts' reports which were being paid for by the companies being reviewed.

In the end, the spivs would win, while the naive investors and faceless taxpayers would lose.

But are you really surprised?

EARLY STUMBLES (2000–02)

Tax deductibility has long been a foolish but often popular rationale for investment decisions. Managed agribusiness investment schemes[†]

---

* In a submission to the Senate Committee on agribusiness managed investment schemes, Dr Judith Arjani claimed that 'MIS eucalypt pulpwood growers invest 4.5 times more than non-MIS growers to do the same job of planting and managing trees over the rotation'. See Parliamentary Joint Committee on Corporations and Financial Services, 'Inquiry into Aspects of Agribusiness Managed Investment Schemes', September 2009.

† In this chapter, any references to managed investment schemes will be in relation to forestry or non-forestry agribusiness schemes. Managed investment schemes can include a wide array of investments including property trusts, investment pools or serviced strata schemes.

such as those operated by Timbercorp and Great Southern were not the first, nor will they represent the last, tax-effective opportunity which enticed investors (some would argue that negative gearing investment properties is a similar vice).

Timbercorp and Great Southern's businesses involved establishing, financing and managing forestry or horticultural projects. Investors in the projects (who would become known as 'owner-growers') advanced cash to Timbercorp and Great Southern who would effectively pool the funds to support the project. These owner-growers would then gain a right to what was growing on the land (in the case of trees) or the fruits of a horticulture crop (such as olives or macadamia nuts) under management agreements.

Each project would form a separate 'scheme', with the owner-growers receiving an initial tax deduction for the amount invested and then the proceeds of the sales after expenses and management fees were deducted. Because there is a substantial time lag between the initial investment (prior to growing) and the crop being harvested, investors are able to benefit from the 'deferral' of tax payable for a number of years.* (The somewhat favourable tax treatment of the schemes stems largely from a policy decision in 1997, called 'Plantation 2020', which sought to triple Australia's timber output to satisfy demand for paper in 2020. It was believed that without tax concessions, rural industries would be effectively starved of capital.)

The MIS managers acted as the 'responsible entity' (effectively the manager) of the schemes and traditionally employed third parties to run the projects.

Implicitly, the more schemes which Great Southern and Timbercorp managed the more profits they would make. However, the agribusiness companies would not be excused from the law of diminishing marginal returns—as they created new projects they would also require additional land. Inevitably, scarcity of high-quality land would cause land prices to rise. (This problem was exacerbated because in some cases the MIS companies did not have sufficient land at the time they provided product disclosure statements to

---

* Owner-growers would not avoid tax entirely, but rather, the tax would be deferred for several years, or in the case of eucalyptus trees, upwards of 10 years. There were two benefits for taxpayers from this deferral. First, by the time the revenue was earned and tax eventually payable, the taxpayer would likely be on a lower marginal rate of tax. Also, there is 'time value' in delaying the payment, so that instead of paying tax, the investor would be able to utilise those funds elsewhere to earn a rate of return.

potential investors. Should the scheme be fully or over-subscribed, the manager would quickly acquire additional property at expensive prices or make high lease payments.)

The other problem with the model is that it risked an oversupply of product if the demand was driven by associated fees to the promoter and tax advantages for the investors, rather than a genuine commercial need for almonds or mangoes.

In addition to owner-growers, Great Southern and Timbercorp were listed on the ASX, so they also had regular shareholders as well. In a sense, the structure was not altogether different from the 'Macquarie model', however instead of satellite companies owning the infrastructure paying fees to a mothership, the MIS companies received fees from investors in each agriculture project.

Timbercorp and Great Southern's revenues and earnings took off in 2000, shortly after the implementation of recommendations from the Ralph Review of business tax laws. The Ralph Review, which was headed by former CRA boss and Commonwealth Bank chair John Ralph, specified new rules regarding the ability of investors to claim tax deductions for investment in new businesses against income earned elsewhere. The review confirmed that investors were able to deduct 100 per cent of the monies invested to the extent that services were provided in that year.

Deductibility of expenses with regard to MISs had long been accepted by Australian Taxation Office (ATO) policy, which allowed the schemes to be exempt from the normal rule which required losses to be incurred in the same period as gains. This was because there was a long lead time between the commencement of the activity and income from production (revenue wouldn't be earned from agribusiness schemes until the crop or plantation was eventually harvested and sold).

Normally, a business is only able to claim a tax deduction if there is a direct connection with earning revenue. For example, if you set up a business selling widgets and spend $10 000 designing a website but aren't actually able to sell any widgets, you can't claim a tax deduction for the site expenses until your widget business starts making money.

The law changes were a boon for the agribusiness MIS companies. In 2000, Timbercorp's revenue almost tripled to $129.1 million, predominantly due to increased revenue from the sale of non-forestry products such as olives or almonds. Similarly, Great Southern, which listed on the ASX in 2000 (having been founded in 1987) reported a 93 per cent increase in sales to $94 million. Those results were somewhat misleading though, with the Ralph Review requiring sales from 1999 and 2000 to be reported in the same year.

Regardless, Great Southern's share price performance was impressive—listing at $1.00 per share in July 1999, its scrip reached $4.80 the following March, before dropping in line with the general market. Briefly, Great Southern founder John Young's stake in the company would be worth $200 million.

The MIS players were also making friends in high places. When an article critical of the plantation forest industry appeared in the *Australian Financial Review*, the colourful then Minister for Forestry and Conservation, Wilson Tuckey, penned a lengthy defence of agribusiness schemes, noting that the industry had a 'negligible history of tax evasion schemes. These have now been reduced to nil'.[2]

Tuckey's logic was convenient; the reason that the schemes had a negligible history of tax evasion was because the tax laws permitted deductions—so why would anyone need to act illegally? Tuckey's comments were much like the government decriminalising theft and later boasting that there hadn't been any unlawful robberies during the year. (Of course, Tuckey had a vested interest of sorts; much of Great Southern's WA timber plantations were located in his O'Connor electorate.)

After a euphoric year, the MIS twins had a more difficult time in 2001—sales dropped as investors feared for the preferred tax status of the schemes. Great Southern would blame 'misinformation' and 'incorrect facts' for the concern. During the year Great Southern's share price plummeted to only 35¢ (down more than 90 per cent from its earlier peak) due to poor market sentiment surrounding forestry and agriculture schemes.

Despite their share prices being in the doldrums, neither Timbercorp nor Great Southern appeared to pay a great deal of attention to corporate governance issues. In 2001, Timbercorp's board of directors consisted of three executives and chairman Gary Liddell. Liddell could hardly be described as independent given his accounting firm was paid around $80 000 each year by Timbercorp to provide accounting services.

Almost comically, Timbercorp's audit committee included CEO Robert Hance, while Great Southern's audit committee consisted of managing director John Young. Given that—theoretically—the whole point of an audit committee is to ensure that management isn't cooking the books, one wonders why they even bothered.

Lesson #1: Committees are important

Investors should look closely at the composition of companies' audit and remuneration committees—these committees should consist of independent directors. The role of the audit committee is essentially to make sure that the financial statements prepared by the company are correct. The presence of an executive on an audit committee is a major warning that the company's corporate governance practices are substandard.

Continuing that theme, in 2001 Timbercorp appointed Bill Bessemer to its board. Chairman of small broker Austock, Bessemer enjoyed a similar conflict at Timbercorp as he did at ABC Learning Centres, with both companies being major clients of Bessemer's boutique brokerage house. In 2001, Timbercorp paid more than $2 million in fees to Austock.

Ignoring corporate governance concerns, sentiment towards the agribusiness sector turned for the better in 2002, despite both Timbercorp and Great Southern reporting lower sales and earnings figures. Great Southern was dubbed the premier yield stock on the ASX by *Shares* magazine. Meanwhile Timbercorp was building its non-forestry assets, with the sale of olive groves and almond orchards growing to be 60 per cent of the company's revenue.

Confidence in the sector was assisted by legislation being introduced into Federal Parliament allowing owner-growers to obtain a deduction for activities occurring the following year.* The ATO also confirmed the tax deductibility of Timbercorp and Great Southern's managed investment schemes. Happy days were here again.

---

* The effect of the tax law change, referred to as the '12-month prepayment rule', was especially beneficial for the agribusiness operators. This is because it allowed them to plant the trees or crops within 15 months of the 'sale' occurring to owner-growers. As a result, the promoters were able to sell as many units in the schemes as they could before having to buy or lease the land. This reduced the risk of the promoters having to acquire the land before actually selling the projects. (The rule would also have the effect of further 'bidding up' the price of land because promoters would desperately try to purchase land to fulfill obligations on pre-sold schemes.)

Lesson #2: Tax deductibility is just a bonus, not a reason to invest

Of all the reasons to invest in a financial product, tax deductibility should be one of the last considered. Aside from the fact that deductibility is at the whim of the government or Tax Office, any benefits from the tax deduction will be paid for in other ways. Usually, it will allow the manager or promoter to take a bigger cut for themselves.

Timbercorp's 2002 profit was boosted by the company revaluing its 'self-generating assets' upwards by $11 million. Without that rise (which was determined by Timbercorp management), profit would have been almost 42 per cent down on the prior year. (Increasing the value of self-generating assets was perfectly in accordance with accounting standards and was based on the fact that Timbercorp would often own a part of the underlying assets and would have an interest in the assets—say, olive groves—after the owner-growers' licence expired.)

SALES, SHARE PRICE AND RELATED-PARTY DEAL EXPLOSION (2003–05)

Both Great Southern and Timbercorp boomed in 2003. Great Southern's revenue doubled and the company's share price followed suit, leaping from 50¢ in mid 2002 to $3.25 two years later.

While its share price was rising, alarm bells should have been ringing for investors. That is because both companies' revenue (which is an accounting determination) was substantially higher than their cash receipts (which cannot be fiddled by management). One reason for the discrepancy was that the agribusiness companies would often receive a flood of new monies shortly before the end of the financial year and the cash would often be paid later on.

However, the predominant reason was that many owner-growers borrowed from the promoters to fund their investment.* This meant that owner-growers were only required to pay a small amount of cash.

---

* Many of Great Southern's owner-growers effectively borrowed from the company to fund their investments. Great Southern would then 'securitise' the loans (in basic terms, bunch them all together and sell them to a third party). Most of Great Southern's loans were purchased by Adelaide Bank.

Even though the company itself was providing a substantial proportion of the funds, it would report most of that money as 'revenue'. This was based on an accounting formula adopted by Timbercorp and Great Southern which considered revenue by reference to the proportion of work performed. This 'work' would include acquiring land and marketing and distribution activities.

Lesson #3: Cash don't lie

If a company's reported 'sales' are substantially less than its operating cash flows, it is highly possible the company is being somewhat creative with its financial reporting. 'Sales' are an accounting concept and subject to judgement and manipulation—unless a company is completely fraudulent, cash cannot be fiddled. If a company's 'sales' continually exceed cash inflows, stay away.

While the use of leverage made it easier for Great Southern to sell its managed investment schemes (investors needed less cash and it was more tax effective), the borrowing added a further layer of risk for those investors. Should anything happen to the underlying asset, owner-growers would still owe money on the loan taken out to fund their initial purchase but have nothing to show for it (other than a tax deduction).

Focusing more on longer term 'annuity style' income (such as harvesting, maintenance, finance and marketing services), Timbercorp's sales and revenue increased by approximately 20 per cent in 2003. Profit was, however, helped again by the company revaluing its assets upwards by $5 million.* Timbercorp would also for the first time report substantial related-party dealings with a company associated with Timbercorp co-founder and CEO Robert Hance and retired chairman David Muir.

---

* In its 2005 annual report, Timbercorp noted that 'although there is an intermittently active market for olive, almond and eucalypt trees, there is no suitable market evidence available to value the trees by reference to equivalent sales. Consequently, pursuant to AASB 1037 the trees are valued at market value based on net present value'. What this means is that the upwards revaluation of the assets by Timbercorp was not predicated on an actual 'market value', but rather on an assessment of the present value of the cash flows made by Timbercorp's directors. The problem with discounted cash flow models is that they are based on a number of assumptions which are highly discretionary. For example, by lowering the discount rate, the value of future cash flows, and by implication the value of the asset itself, would be substantially increased. Assumptions such as the relevant 'discount rate' adopted or expected future cash flows were determined by the company itself.

A company, known somewhat confusingly as Timbercorp WA Pty Ltd, was paid 'forestry harvesting' fees of $4 million and interest of more than $500 000 on a loan provided to Timbercorp. While possibly out of convenience, the name chosen by Hance and Muir for their private company may have inadvertently led some investors to believe that the company was not distinct from Timbercorp.

In mid 2003, Hance and Muir also tried to surreptitiously sell a large stake in Timbercorp. Hance and Muir owned their stake in Timbercorp through Timbercorp WA Pty Ltd. In May, Timbercorp announced a joint venture with Futuris to export three million tonnes of woodchips annually. Under the deal (which was announced in what appeared to be an intentionally vague manner), Futuris would contribute a Western Australian plantation business to the joint venture while Timbercorp would chip in existing plantations located in western Victoria. Crucially, Futuris agreed to pay $46.2 million for a 50 per cent interest in Timbercorp WA Pty Ltd. The sale would have allowed Hance and Muir to 'cash out' a substantial part of their interest in Timbercorp.

The agreed price appeared to be a very generous one. On 1 May, when the deal was made, Timbercorp was trading at around 70¢ per share—that meant that Timbercorp WA's stake in Timbercorp was worth around $43 million. However, Futuris had agreed to pay $46.2 million for a mere half-share of Timbercorp WA. This meant that Futuris would have effectively paid Hance and Muir a substantial premium for their stake.

Other Timbercorp shareholders would not see any of that money that was being paid to the company's two senior figures. It is for transactions like that one that companies have independent non-executive directors. However, in Timbercorp's case, their so-called independent directors were hardly independent. Timbercorp's board consisted of three executives, its long-time accountant, its investment banker (who was paid millions of dollars in fees) and a chairman who was technically independent but knew the CEO from horse racing circles.

Justifying the transaction, Timbercorp claimed that 'the cash paid to Timbercorp WA will then be invested by agreement... and may include the acquisition of further shares in Timbercorp Limited'.[3] Shareholders weren't fooled though. In November, Timbercorp quietly shelved plans to create the joint venture company, although this may have more to do with its share price rising to $1.40 than corporate governance and fairness issues.

Great Southern and Timbercorp continued to prosper in 2004 — Timbercorp's share price rose by 48 per cent, while Great Southern scrip leapt by more than 200 per cent on the back of a 140 per cent increase in earnings. In fact, Great Southern was the second best performed stock on the ASX over 2003 and 2004 as the company followed Timbercorp's lead and moved away from tree products and into horticulture with its first vineyard project.

Great Southern boss John Young gloated to shareholders in the 2004 annual report that the company had achieved sales of 'three times that of our nearest competitor' and had captured 'close to 40 per cent of the managed investment scheme market'.

But, as would be revealed, there is a big difference between sales and profit.

Given his optimism, shareholders would have been forgiven for being surprised when they heard that Young had sold almost 1.4 million Great Southern shares during the year. The revelation would have been even more of a shock given that Young neglected to lodge a change of interest notice with the ASX, as all directors are required to do when they buy or sell shares. The only way shareholders would have known that the company's largest shareholders had sold millions of dollars worth of shares would be by comparing the company's 2003 and 2004 annual reports. On top of his share sales, Young also received a substantial pay rise, taking home $2.14 million in 2004, including a $1.4 million cash bonus.

Despite its CEO's growing pay packet, digging a little deeper into Great Southern's results would have given even enthusiastic investors cause for concern. While the company reported strong revenues of $208 million, its cash receipts were only $88 million. Had it not been for Great Southern issuing $91 million worth of ordinary shares and a further $55 million in convertible shares, it would have been practically insolvent.

Timbercorp also enjoyed headline growth in 2004, with profit rising by more than 50 per cent to $41.1 million and annuity-style revenue increasing to $88.1 million. Timbercorp would in 2004 make more money from 'annuity-style' income (such as harvesting and maintaining its developments and providing finance to investors) than by actually selling MIS products.

Like his Great Southern counterpart, Timbercorp boss Robert Hance also appeared to be selling his shares while enthusiastically spruiking the group's prospects. In November 2004, Hance sold 12 000 000 Timbercorp shares, netting cash of more than $19.2 million. (Hance appeared to sell a little too early though — had he sold those shares six months later he would have received around $30 million for the same parcel.)

Hance was also reaping millions courtesy of a cosy deal between Timbercorp and his private company Timbercorp WA. During 2004 Hance's company was paid harvesting fees of more than $2.2 million and received interest payments of $360 000. Timbercorp, however, was an equal opportunity related-party transactor. Austock, whose chairman Bill Bessemer sat on the Timbercorp board, received $2.9 million in fees during 2004.

Timbercorp's profit rose again in 2005 as its share price rocketed. During the year, former real estate agent Rod Fitzroy joined the Timbercorp board. Fitzroy not only received directors' fees but also managed to negotiate a lucrative $400 000 per year consultancy fee. (In 2008, the Timbercorp board terminated Fitzroy's consultancy agreement and paid him a cash lump sum of $744 000. The payout was convenient for Fitzroy — he would have otherwise joined a long list of Timbercorp's unsecured creditors. Coincidentally, around the time the payment was made Fitzroy became Timbercorp's chairman.)*

During the year, Hance's stake in Timbercorp mysteriously fell by another 920 000 shares. Like Great Southern, Timbercorp also appeared to have difficulty adhering to the ASX Listing Rules regarding disclosure of director sales, forgetting to release a 'change of director's interest' notice informing the market of Hance's sales. Hance wasn't the only insider losing faith in Timbercorp — long-time director and former chairman Gary Liddell also sold a substantial portion of his holding, collecting almost $1 million from the sale of around half of his shares. At least Liddell did shareholders the courtesy of telling them about his share sale though.

---

* Timbercorp also paid $15 million to acquire a 50 per cent interest in a company called Almonds Australia Pty Ltd in April 2005 — Fitzroy was a director and major shareholder in Almonds Australia Pty Ltd.

A PONZI SCHEME EXPOSED? (2005)*

Until 2005, the MIS twins had reported reasonably consistent annual profit and sales growth. They were able to sell schemes to investors on the basis of a nice tax deduction but also the promise of solid returns when the crops or forests were eventually harvested. The general expectation was that investors would expect to receive an effective annual return of between 5 and 15 per cent. Not enough to make one a millionaire, but better than a term deposit.

The sales pitch had proved effective. In 2004, John Young made his debut on the *BRW* Rich List with an estimated wealth of $140 million.

The following year Young again cashed in part of his shareholding in Great Southern. He would do so by selling $32.5 million worth of shares into an underwritten institutional placement at $4.65 per share.

While Great Southern's share price was hitting record levels, it masked a sordid truth that would eventually destroy the company — quite simply, its tax-effective schemes were not profitable. Fortunately for Young, no-one actually knew that yet. And he sure as hell wasn't going to be telling anyone.

Great Southern's first timber projects were planted in 1994. It takes 10 years for the forests to be harvested and the revenues to be paid to investors. Great Southern's early forests were therefore set to be harvested in late 2004. The only problem was at some stage (and the timing is unclear, but it was likely well before 2004) Great Southern would have realised that the amount it would earn from selling woodchips would not even cover the costs of managing the scheme. In short, instead of making 5 to 10 per cent returns, the owner-growers would actually lose some of their investment. The loss in real terms would be even worse because investors had their money tied up in the various timber schemes for a decade. The figures for the 1994 crop were frightening—investors pumped $3.7 million into the project, and the sales 10 years later would equal $3.4 million. (As a comparison, by simply investing $3.7 million in a term deposit

---

* This section is partially based on the excellent investigative work undertaken by the *Australian Financial Review*'s Angus Grigg in his article entitled 'How Timber Chief Cashed in his Chips', *Australian Financial Review*, 10 June 2009.

yielding 6 per cent, investors would turn their initial capital into $6.6 million in 10 years.)*

When Great Southern realised that the yields for its early forestry investments were negative it appeared to become very concerned. Great Southern's business model relied on selling investment products to city folk who were keen not only for a tax deduction but who also required a satisfactory return on their 10-year investment. If owner-growers became aware that the schemes were losing money, it would be difficult or even impossible for Great Southern to sell future projects.

To overcome this hitch, Great Southern devised a scheme which was at best highly immoral and at worst fraudulent. What it did was create a new company, wholly owned by Great Southern, called Great Southern Export Company (GSEC). GSEC appeared to serve no useful purpose other than as a vehicle to mislead owner-growers. GSEC purchased timber products from Great Southern's 1994 project at highly inflated prices. This allowed Great Southern to give owner-growers the false impression that its 1994 project was profitable. GSEC would then sell the woodchips to Japanese paper mills at the current (much lower) market rate. Because it was paying above market rates for the timber, GSEC would lose a lot of money. GSEC losses were borne by Great Southern shareholders (remember, GSEC was a wholly owned subsidiary of Great Southern).

It would take a very shrewd investor to realise what was going on. Great Southern did not exactly advertise the fact that its projects were losing money and its entire business model was a fraud. Buried on page 86 of its 2005 annual report, in the 'contingent liabilities' section, the company noted:

> On 29 July 2005 Great Southern Export Company Pty Ltd (GSEC), a wholly owned subsidiary of the company, purchased all of the timber from the 1994 Project for $6.4 million. GSEC acquired the timber from the 1994 Project investors, primarily driven by efficiencies this option provided in timing of shipping and GST related issues...this resulted in an after tax expense of around $3 million being included in the results for the year ended 30 June 2005.

---

* Assuming one investor purchased the entire $3.7 million project and this person was paying a 40 per cent marginal rate of tax, the benefit would be a deferral of $1.5 million in tax for 10 years, worth about $1.1 million assuming a 6 per cent 'discount rate'.

In short, Great Southern shareholders spent $3 million subsidising its dud projects to ensure that the company was able to continue selling other dud projects to new investors—all the while, its founder was greedily pocketing $30 million from selling shares.

At the time of the placement, Young claimed that the company's timber projects were still expected to yield investors a return of around 5 per cent. This would arguably make Young either not entirely honest or a fool, given the company of which he was CEO was feverishly planning to subsidise a project to the tune of $3 million. (In addition, Great Southern admitted that it would subsidise future projects by $12 million.)

Great Southern's actions were even more suspicious when you consider the timing of GSEC. Great Southern registered GSEC in March 2005, not long after Young sold his shares to institutions. However, plans were afoot to create GSEC well before then. In fact, it is understood that Great Southern sought legal advice regarding GSEC as far back as August 2004, well before the 1994 project was harvested.

This gives rise to the question—when exactly did Great Southern become aware that its projects were not as profitable as promised? According to Great Southern, it only dawned on the company that the 1994 project would be a money loser in 2005—after Young had sold his shares (otherwise, the poor yields would have had to have been disclosed to investors, meaning that Young would have received less money for his shares). To this, Great Southern's executive director Cameron Rhodes would claim that returns cannot be determined until harvesting is completed.

However, forestry experts stated that a 'fair indication' of a project's yield should have been able to have been determined within seven years of planting the trees by analysing their by size. Based on that, it is likely that Great Southern should have been aware that the yield from its 1994 project was set to be poor as early as 2001. That theory is backed up by the fact that Great Southern would make provisions for losses to its 1995 and 1996 projects in 2004.

This notion was supported by the fact that in 2007 Great Southern changed its accounting model to allow the company to recognise $17 million worth of fees for services provided between 1998 and 2003. Great Southern stated that it could recognise the additional revenue because it could 'reliably measure' the proceeds of plantations four years prior to their harvest. If it only takes approximately four years for Great Southern to realise how profitable a timber project will be, it should have been informing owner-growers (and shareholders) back in 1998, rather than waiting until 2005 before breaking the bad news.

The full board of Great Southern allegedly became aware of the shortfall and the GSEC issue in early June 2005. When they heard the details, several independent directors were not impressed. Former solicitor and chairman Peter Patrikeos and accountant Jeffrey Mews both tendered their resignations almost immediately. It is believed that Patrikeos and Mews were furious at the lack of disclosure provided by Great Southern and the creation of GSEC. Patrikeos would vote against its creation while Mews did not attend the board meeting at all.

Perhaps Patrikeos and Mews were following the advice of Warren Buffett, who would once note that:

> If the owner/manager is mediocre or worse — or is over-reaching — there is little a director can do about it except object. If the directors having no connections to the owner/manager make a unified argument, it may well have some effect. More likely it will not.
>
> If change does not come, and the matter is sufficiently serious, the outside directors should resign. Their resignation will signal their doubts about management, and it will emphasize that no outsider is in a position to correct the owner/manager's shortcomings.[4]

GSEC had effectively turned Great Southern into a virtual Ponzi scheme. When Great Southern sold a new project to investors, those monies would be paid to the company itself. Great Southern would then use some of those funds paid by the new investors (via its wholly owned subsidiary GSEC) to pay satisfactory returns to investors in its earlier projects. The company was effectively using new capital to prop up the returns earned by earlier investors. The best explanation Great Southern could come up with for its behaviour was that GSEC would buy timber for an inflated price due to 'efficiencies ... in timing of shipping and GST related issues'. Great Southern's excuse would not have fooled anyone — efficiencies save money, they shouldn't cost shareholders $15 million over three years.

While Great Southern would contend that the profitability of its projects would improve as it gained more expertise, the foul odour of Charles Ponzi would continue to hang over the company until its eventual collapse four years later.

IGNORING THE OBVIOUS: THE GOOD TIMES CONTINUE TO ROLL (2006–07)

The growing Ponzi scheme at Great Southern wasn't the only problem that the company's shareholders were facing. Great Southern's operational cash flow continued to provide timely warnings that all was not well. In 2005, receipts from growers totalled $80 million. By contrast, 'securitisation of loan receivables' amounted to $178 million. That meant that of Great Southern's $318 million in sales, its customers were only providing around a quarter — the remainder would come from banks lending money to owner-growers and some accounting chicanery.

Courtesy of that accounting wizardry, 2006 saw continued headline growth for the MIS twins; revenue and earnings grew solidly at both companies.* Amazingly, Great Southern's share price once again recovered, reaching $4.20 in April 2006 (having fallen to $2.66 the previous September when the GSEC scam was revealed to shareholders). Timbercorp's share price also strengthened, hitting an all-time high of $4.10 in June 2006.

Not only were investors ignoring that Great Southern's projects didn't make any money, but they were also turning a blind eye to the fact that both Timbercorp and Great Southern were going deeper and deeper into debt. In 2006, Great Southern's borrowings rose from virtually zero to more than $400 million, while Timbercorp's interest-bearing liabilities would amount to $570 million. There were several reasons for the dramatic increase in debt, especially at Great Southern.

First, an accounting change meant that quasi-equity instruments such as preference shares were now considered debt (preference

---

* Great Southern would once again rely on debt funding to assist owner-growers — cash flows from investors was $232 million compared with securitised loan receivables of $403 million. Great Southern's cash flows were bolstered once again by borrowings ($204 million) and the issue of further convertible securities ($125 million).

shares have both debt and equity characteristics). Second, accounting changes also required securitised loans to be brought 'on balance sheet'. Finally, in Great Southern's case, it had increased the number of horticulture projects under management. Horticulture projects are far more capital-intensive, and therefore demand additional debt.

While its balance sheet had become far more leveraged, Great Southern continued to crank up its Ponzi scheme, noting in its 2006 annual report that 'GSEC, a wholly owned subsidiary of the company, has purchased all of the timber from the 1995 Project for $9 200 000'. GSEC (which in actual fact was a proxy for Great Southern shareholders) would make a loss of $3.3 million on the purchase and would foreshadow a $6.7 million loss the following year.

However, the rapidly growing debt piles and Ponzi schemes would be ignored when, in December 2006, Timbercorp and Great Southern shareholders received an early Christmas present after the federal government announced that upfront tax deductibility for investments in forestry products would be allowed to continue.

However, the MIS twins' glee would soon turn to horror. Their business would be devastated by a government announcement of another kind.

THE TAXMAN COMETH (2007–08)

It is a sad indictment on Australia's investor community that it took a federal government tax ruling to finally dent investor confidence in the MIS twins—one would have thought negative cash flows and the fact that their projects didn't make any money would have been more important. But confidence in the agribusiness MIS sector remained until February 2007, when the federal government reversed its earlier views on the tax deductibility of the initial investment made by owner-growers in horticultural schemes. (The deductibility of investments in forestry schemes was confirmed the previous year by the government.)

In simple terms, the new rules provided that the so-called 'fees' paid by investors were actually 'capital' and that a tax deduction could not be claimed. While implementation of the ruling would not occur until 2008 (and the decision would eventually be overturned by the Federal Court), the move devastated confidence in the sector.

The day after the announcement was made, Timbercorp shares slumped by 28 per cent and Great Southern (which managed mostly forestry assets) dropped 13 per cent.

The decision to remove the tax deductibility of non-forestry MIS schemes, flagged in the previous budget by the federal government, was largely inspired by public anger at what were largely considered tax-avoidance schemes. Another criticism was that agribusiness schemes led to inflated land prices and an oversupply of agricultural products. (Great Southern appeared to have a long memory—in the lead up to the 2007 federal election, the company would donate $40 000 to the Australian Labor Party shortly after it released a pro-MIS policy, but nothing to the federal Liberal Party, which was responsible for the adverse taxation changes.)

Allegations were also made that the MIS promoters had effectively forced up the price of water rights for irrigators. While the Murray River in Victoria and New South Wales experienced substantial reduction in flow in the early 2000s, Timbercorp, which was the largest operator in the Sunraysia district, utilised taxpayer-funded capital to construct 10 dams. Rival farmers would later accuse Timbercorp of flooding the market with cheap produce, and planting new crops in a drought while absorbing the losses.[5]

The unnatural effect of tax deductions also had an impact at an operational level—on occasion, MIS promoters would cultivate areas prior to the end of the financial year to obtain taxation advantages. The only problem was, the new financial year in some areas coincided with the wet season, which meant that heavy rain would lead to significant erosion.

While the ATO decision affected Timbercorp to a greater extent than Great Southern (Timbercorp had moved more aggressively into non-forestry products, and by 2006 had more than 60 per cent of its sales related to horticulture), investors would deal with both companies harshly.

Timbercorp and Great Southern's share prices continued to fall throughout 2007. Courtesy of growing annuity-style income, Timbercorp was still able to report record revenue for 2007; however, its alleged sales figures would once again have little relation to the amount of money that Timbercorp was actually bringing in the door. From its actual operations, Timbercorp burned $45 million cash. Gearing was also higher, with Timbercorp telling shareholders it would rely on asset sales to reduce debt. This was a pretty stupid idea in a credit crunch.

> **Lesson #4: Beware a company bearing gifts**
>
> If a company has to sell assets to survive it probably won't succeed in selling assets or surviving.

Great Southern's performance worsened in 2007. Earnings fell by 46 per cent as the company wrote $40 million from the value of its horticulture projects and continued to fund its flailing timber projects. Perhaps John Young knew what was coming—in December 2007 Great Southern's founder and major shareholder resigned as CEO of the company.

Looking closely, it appeared that Great Southern's 2007 financial results were being massaged like a fine piece of Kobe beef.

During the year, Great Southern received $124 million cash from investors and securitised a further $470 million worth of receivables. In real terms, that meant investors were placing only 20 per cent of their own money into Great Southern's schemes and borrowing the remaining 80 per cent. This is an extraordinarily high loan-to-valuation ratio. (While residential property will occasionally see LVRs upwards of 90 per cent, for share purchases it is not advisable to gear the investment by more than 50 per cent. Leverage in excess of 50 per cent places an investor under severe risk of being 'margin called' out of the holding.) However, 2007 was the height of the asset and leverage bubble and there were few better examples of debt-funded stupidity than retail investors borrowing four times their initial outlay to fund a scheme which was primarily designed to minimise their tax and would not provide an actual return for years.

Not only was Great Southern's revenue being goosed by lending to owner-growers, it would increase reported earnings through an accounting sleight of hand. This was achieved the old-fashioned way—by unilaterally writing up the value of its fixed assets, particularly its investment property. Because it would usually own the underlying land upon which the schemes were run, Great Southern owned a substantial amount of investment property on its balance sheet. It valued this investment property using a discounted cash flow model (DCF).

A lengthy explanation of the DCF model is beyond the scope of this book. In simple terms, it is a common way to value an asset or business. A DCF model will derive an asset value based on the expected future cash flows which the asset or business is expected to generate over its life (this is an educated guess of how much cash the business or asset will spin off) and a 'discount rate'. The discount rate is effectively the 'opportunity cost' of owning the asset or business.* Basically, the lower the discount rate the more valuable the asset, and the higher the discount rate the less valuable the asset.

In 2007 Great Southern chose to reduce the discount rate it used. This may seem innocuous to many investors, but it had the direct effect of increasing the value of its investment properties by $46 million and boosting profit by $32 million. Effectively, Great Southern was reporting earnings that were 80 per cent more than they actually were due to a change in how it accounted for property.

Lesson #5: Watch out for dirty accounting tricks

When companies use accounting methods to increase earnings, it is not a good sign. Profits that come from accounting changes rather than increased sales or lower costs are usually not sustainable and can even be an indicator of far deeper problems.

Those Great Southern investors who weren't concentrating would soon pay a steep price. In 2008, Great Southern reported a loss of $64 million, largely caused by asset write-downs. The company also warned that there may be doubt as to whether it would be able to continue to operate as a 'going concern' if owner-growers refused to

---

* Financiers usually determine the relevant 'opportunity cost' as being the weighted average cost of capital—a riskier or more volatile asset or business will have a higher 'cost of capital' (that is because investors and lenders would demand a higher rate of return for the higher level of risk involved) and therefore a higher discount rate should be used.

accept Great Southern's last-ditch plan to exchange shares in the company for their interest in various MIS projects. However, the scheme was too little, too late. By December 2008, the company's share price would fall to only 12¢—a drop of 97 per cent in two years.

Timbercorp was having problems of its own. Its share price fell to only 9¢ despite the company stating it made a profit of $44.6 million. Timbercorp would again claim Alice in Wonderland sales figures which bore virtually no resemblance to its cash flows. The company also claimed that it had net tangible assets of $1.30 per share—well below its prevailing share price.

However, it didn't really matter as investors had long ago lost faith in Timbercorp—the resignation of founder and CEO Robert Hance and chairman Kevin Hayes did little to boost confidence. It appeared that Timbercorp's non-executive directors, like a jilted wife, were the last to find out the truth. That the directors felt it appropriate to hold a mere 12 meetings during the year indicated they were not overly concerned about the company's ill-health or were simply unaware of its dire predicament. Or perhaps the board simply couldn't find the time between their extensive Spring Carnival horse racing commitments. (Timbercorp chairman Rod Fitzroy was also the chairman of the Victorian Racing Club, the body which runs the Melbourne Cup. Previous chairman Kevin Hayes was a former chairman of the Melbourne Racing Club. Timbercorp would spend tens of thousands of dollars sponsoring horse races in 2008 while its share price was tumbling.)

The relaxed attitude of the Timbercorp directors was especially strange given the company's auditor had stated that the group's earnings before interest and tax breached its loan covenants, and if the 'sale of selected assets and the consequent repayment of debt do not proceed as planned there [was] material uncertainty in relation to the Group continuing as a going concern'.[6] That view was possibly based on the fact that Timbercorp had a current asset deficiency of around $430 million.

It appeared that the only people who weren't worried about Timbercorp's dire financial health were its directors.

They would be in for a rude shock.

COLLAPSE (2009)

In April 2009, even the Timbercorp board realised its fate was sealed—unable to meet debt obligations which exceeded $900 million, they surrendered and appointed administrators. A month later, Great Southern would follow suit and enter voluntary administration.

While there were several straws which caused the twin collapses, the main reason was simple—the agribusiness projects didn't make enough money to pay a reasonable return to investors, especially given the fees which were charged by advisers and managers.

In some cases it appeared the schemes didn't make any money at all.

Timbercorp and Great Southern spent a decade pumping money into the schemes and further weakening their own financial positions, but eventually the dam would burst. It wasn't only Great Southern's schemes that weren't profitable. Analysts would note that Timbercorp's earlier olive projects and the citrus and table grape schemes were almost certainly money losers.

The Tax Office ruling that removed deductibility of investment in non-forestry schemes was not the cause of the collapses, but merely another factor which hastened the fall. In the end, the difficulty in obtaining debt financing and the inability to sell assets caused the groups' rapid insolvency. Timbercorp's executive director Sol Rabinowicz stated that 'from mid-2007, all of our funding sources, our equity, debt and an ability to sell assets [were] essentially... shut down'.[7] In April 2009, just before it slid into administration, Timbercorp would unsuccessfully try to sell its eucalyptus, almond and olive plantations.

Timbercorp and Great Southern's problems resembled the dilemmas faced by Allco, Babcock and MFS—paying too much for assets using large amounts of debt during the credit boom. When credit dried up, the value of those assets (be it infrastructure or agricultural) plummeted from their debt-inflated boom-time prices. In the space of months, not only were those companies unable to roll over their short-term debt, but the value of assets that had underpinned the leverage had dropped dramatically. When the financial engineers tried to sell assets to reduce gearing, they found that no-one would buy those assets for anywhere near what they had foolishly paid.

Shortly after its collapse, Timbercorp's administrator Mark Korda, of KordaMentha, stated that 'the responsible entity, TSL [Timbercorp Securities Limited], can't continue as the responsible entity because it is hopelessly insolvent, with the costs of running the olives and almonds projects at $300 million over the next 12 months. TSL is broke and cannot fund them. It has no cash and no access to new cash'.

The other problem was the fee-laden structure of the business model. Promoters (and often financial advisers) received fees from investors throughout the life of the various projects (which could last for more than a decade), while also receiving fees for performing as the responsible entity and, often, as the manager of the actual project. Meanwhile, owner-growers would bear all associated risks such as demand weakness, oversupply or externalities such as drought or floods.

As previously described, the structure of the schemes resembled a Ponzi scheme.* Ponzi schemes, as described earlier, involve paying investors out of capital contributed by new investors, rather than actual earnings. Even before Great Southern's GSEC fiasco, what the MIS companies did was a variation on this theme — investors paid a large initial amount which would be used to cover the establishment of trees or crops. The promoter would then pay annual maintenance costs and the investor would (usually) not need to pay any more fees until the product was eventually harvested.

The problem with this model is that new investor monies were effectively required to cover the yearly costs. (This was before Great Southern even started using shareholder monies to inflate the returns being paid to owner-growers.)

Without the continued influx of fresh capital, the promoters were unable to pay for the regular upkeep of the projects. Even ASIC would note that it was common practice for Timbercorp and Great Southern to divert investor fees to the companies' working capital, rather than quarantine funds for the specific project. Unsurprisingly, when equity and debt markets eventually dried up in late 2007, the promoters had a big problem.

---

* Some claimed that agribusiness projects weren't technically 'Ponzi' schemes because there was a meaningful economic enterprise involved, being the growing of horticultural products. Semantics aside, it appeared that in reality the projects bore many similarities to a pyramid or Ponzi scheme given they used new capital to repay earlier investors.

By 2009, many of Great Southern's schemes were believed to be unsustainable. A consultant investigating the feasibility of the company's vineyard projects would report that poor grape prices and high irrigation costs meant that the majority of vineyards operated by Great Southern were not viable. Great Southern's receiver, acting on behalf of secured lenders, claimed that all 43 of Great Southern's projects had run out of money, making basic maintenance tasks impossible.[8]

OWNER-GROWERS GET SHAFTED

The MIS twins were unique in the sense that not only did creditors and shareholders lose out, but so did owner-growers. In a submission made to the Australian Parliamentary Inquiry on Timbercorp's and Great Southern's collapses, ASIC stated that in the last three years of their existence the average amount invested in Great Southern's schemes was $50 447, while an average $71 318 was poured into Timbercorp's schemes.

Those investments were usually highly leveraged (through the use of 'margin loans' provided by the promoters). This would place many owner-growers in an especially tough spot—not only would the value of their investment fall to nearly zero, but they would still be liable to pay off the margin loan which they took out to supercharge their stakes.

By the time of its collapse, Timbercorp was the responsible entity for 34 schemes and had funds under management of more than $1 billion. Great Southern was larger, managing 43 schemes and with investor funds of approximately $2 billion.

When directors of a company believe that the entity is insolvent (that is, it is not able to pay its debts when they fall due), they are obliged to appoint administrators (or face personal liability for debts incurred). The administrators effectively act on behalf of the company's creditors and try to sell assets or businesses (or continue to run the business in some form) to maximise the amount that creditors receive. When this happens, regular shareholders (and often the preferred equityholders and unsecured creditors) receive practically nothing. (After administrators are appointed, receivers will usually be appointed by secured creditors to protect their priority interests.)

In Timbercorp's case, KordaMentha was appointed as administrators of both Timbercorp (the company which was listed on the stock exchange) and also Timbercorp Securities Limited (TSL). TSL was a subsidiary of Timbercorp and acted as the responsible entity (which is a fancy way of saying the manager) of the managed investment schemes.

Similarly, at Great Southern, Ferrier Hodgson was appointed as the administrator of both the publicly listed company and Great Southern Managers Australia—the responsible entity of Great Southern's various schemes

The appointment of KordaMentha and Ferrier Hodgson as administrators of both the listed and responsible entities in certain cases gave rise to a problem. That was because the interests of Timbercorp and Great Southern's creditors and those of owner-growers (to whom the responsible entity owed a fiduciary duty) were in conflict.

For example, it was in the interests of secured creditors for the managed investment schemes to be wound up. If that happened, the receiver or administrator would be able to sell the underlying asset (the land or crops) with less redress to the owner-grower (who still owned the crops growing on the property). The administrator would then be able to provide a greater return to some creditors while the owner-growers, who arguably still owned an asset of some value, would be left to battle for a greater share through the courts.

This was especially a problem with regards to the horticulture assets as the plants were a year-to-year proposition and the owner-growers arguably owned only a contractual right to the fruits of the plants rather than the plants themselves (for forestry assets, the problem wasn't apparent as it was clear that the owner-growers retained ownership of the trees themselves).

The administrators argued (not without merit) that it would have been almost impossible to sell the land if it remained beholden to the interests of thousands of owner-growers who owned the crops. The only way they could sell the land was to sell it with the crops attached and then apportion a part of the proceeds to the owner-growers. This argument did appear to make sense, but it did little to appease owner-growers who had watched the value of their investment evaporate.

Others claimed that owner-growers who largely invested on the basis of receiving a tax deduction got what they deserved. Given the treatment of the owner-growers in the administration of Timbercorp and Great Southern, one doubts anyone could be convinced to invest in such schemes again.

To overcome this conflict in the future, the Joint Senate Committee investigating the collapse of the agribusiness schemes suggested that the government amend the Corporations Act to require ASIC to appoint a temporary responsible entity when a registered managed investment scheme becomes externally administered or a liquidator is appointed.[9]

In the end, the problem was partially averted after the administrators of Timbercorp and Great Southern were able to sell the groups' various forestry and horticulture assets. The bad news for owner-growers was that the administrators received barely enough money for some of the projects to cover associated debt.

In October 2009, Timbercorp's administrator sold its olive plantations to Boundary Bend (the manager of the projects) for $59.5 million, its blue-gum plantations for $345 million to a US-based forestry manager and its almond projects to Singapore-owned Olam International for $128 million. (In June 2009, investors in Timbercorp's mango and avocado projects sacked KordaMentha as the schemes' administrator and appointed Huntley Management to act as the responsible entity for the schemes. The change appeared to bear fruit, with Huntleys predicting positive returns after stripping millions from Timbercorp's budgeted costings.)

In the case of Timbercorp's forestry assets, owner-growers would lose upwards of 80 per cent of their original investment (after being paid $198 million after the sale of the forests as a 'going concern'). For Timbercorp's almond and olive assets, owner-growers would be left with almost nothing other than their initial tax deduction after investing more than $800 million in the various projects, although the final amounts, if any, would be negotiated with the new buyer of the projects.

And, of course, in many cases the owner-growers were still left holding a massive debt which would also need to be repaid. In May

2009, Timbercorp's administrator issued 'final demands' to investors who had fallen significantly behind on their repayments. Timbercorp's loan book contained 14500 loans worth an average of $50000.*

THE VILLAINS

The list of villains in the Timbercorp and Great Southern sagas is a lengthy one.

Financial planners, accountants and representatives of the promoters were largely culpable for instructing their clients to invest billions of dollars into Great Southern's schemes. The majority of investors were advised by financial planners who received commissions of between 5 and 10 per cent of the monies invested. Almost a quarter of owner-growers were actually advised by representatives of the company itself. These advisers must have been very convincing, or their clients very naive. Even in 2005, after it had been revealed that Great Southern was artificially inflating its yields, the company still managed to sell $458 million worth of managed investment products to investors.

More than three-quarters of Timbercorp investment products were sold by commission-based financial planners who usually received 10 per cent of funds invested, with the commissions rarely being 'rebated' back to the client. (A growing number of financial planners provide rebates to investors for commissions paid by funds or promoters and charge the client on a fee-for-service basis. This model is being promoted by the Financial Planning Association of Australia and removes the substantial conflict which exists where planners are incentivised to promote products that provide them with the highest levels of commission.)

Financial planners would also receive what are known as 'soft commissions' from promoters. Soft commissions include access to events, marketing allowances and other fringe benefits, sometimes even extending to 'override payments' or 'strategic partnership agreements' which represented cash sums paid to financial planners. While these cash payments depended on the planner selling agribusiness

---

* Some investors refused to pay the outstanding amounts, arguing that Timbercorp failed to adequately disclose its financial problems even as recently as 2008 when those investors took out fresh loans to cover various management fees. See P Hopkins and R Williams, 'Investors Feel the Heat on MIS Loans', *The Age*, 27 May 2009.

products, because they were not directly linked to any particular sale they did not need to be disclosed to clients in product disclosure statements or financial services guides.*

In 1998, Timbercorp went so far as to grant share options to financial advisers. Those share options would vest if the financial advisers sold a specific amount of Timbercorp investment products in the coming three years. With such financial incentives on offer, financial planners and accountants would have been especially incentivised to push Timbercorp's products onto clients, regardless of the substantial risks and hazy returns.

The gravy train did not end there though—financial planners would also encourage clients to lever up not only their initial investment in the schemes but also, if applicable, borrow to pay the annual management fee. While using additional leverage provided further tax advantages to investors, it also vastly increased their risk. More importantly, it would provide an additional stream of fees to financial planners, already becoming obese from the all-you-can-eat Timbercorp and Great Southern fee buffets.

Lesson #6: Big commissions equals small returns

Investors should ask their financial planner exactly what commission they are receiving—10 per cent commissions should ring alarm bells. If a product requires such a hefty commission for advisers to sell it, it probably isn't a great investment.

Journalist Alan Kohler, a long-time critic of commission-based financial planners, stated that 'financial "advisers" flog [agribusiness schemes] hard because they provide wonderful cash flow for their businesses, and the investors end up being under-capitalized because of the ferocious scoop off the top at the start'.[10] That is an important point. If 10 per cent of the investment is skimmed off the top at the outset, the actual amount invested is substantially reduced, making it far more difficult to provide a reasonable rate of return. For example,

---

* One financial planner, Professional Investment Services, is understood to have received soft commission cash payments of more than $70 000 in 2008–09 alone. The same firm was also implicated in the collapse of property investment scheme Westpoint. See S Washington, 'Duo's Collapse Threatens Financial Planning Giant', *The Sydney Morning Herald*, 17 July 2009.

after the 10 per cent rake, to provide an investor with an annual return of, say, 7 per cent, the investment would really need to yield 7.8 per cent.

Financial planners were also largely responsible for a shift in the agribusinesses' fee model. In the early days of agribusiness schemes, promoters charged a lower initial fee and then levied annual fees for the upkeep of the crop. This structure made sense as it mirrored the amounts which needed to be paid by the manager. However, this structure didn't suit financial planners who needed to chase up annual payments and received a lower initial fee. Beholden to financial planners for revenue, Timbercorp and Great Southern agreed to convert to a 'no-ongoing-fee' model which maximised adviser commissions, even though it harmed the ongoing viability of projects upon which its clients were investing their savings.[11]

While financial planners and accountants were not responsible for the collapse of Timbercorp or Great Southern, they were certainly accountable to the thousands of investors who trusted them to provide impartial advice as to the potential risks and returns of an agribusiness investment. In that regard, they clearly failed.

Where the financial planners didn't fail was in keeping hundreds of millions of dollars of mouth-watering commissions. Since Timbercorp's and Great Southern's collapse, legal action has been initiated against financial planning firm Holt Norman Ashman (the largest seller of Timbercorp products) in August 2009 by disgruntled investors (in a strange twist, those same investors are also being sued by Timbercorp's administrator over unpaid loans owed to Timbercorp).

Another culpable group was the leading research houses which provided so-called expert advice to financial planners. Financial planners relied on the recommendations of experts including AAG, Lonsec and Adviser Edge to give added credibility when suggesting agribusiness products to clients (a common pitch would run along the lines of, 'you should consider this Olive investment run by Timbercorp; not only do you get a tax deduction, but it has been rated four stars by Adviser Edge').

The problem was these independent experts were not really independent at all. They received virtually all their income came from the likes of Timbercorp and Great Southern—the very promoters whose schemes they were independently assessing. If the advisers gave a negative outlook on a scheme, it was highly possible that the promoters would simply not ask them to rate other schemes in the future.

As it turned out, perhaps coincidentally, the leading advisers very rarely proffered any negative views on schemes managed by Timbercorp and Great Southern. Even with Timbercorp's and Great Southern's share prices slumping, the independent experts remained ebullient in their praise of the agribusiness schemes.

For example, Adviser Edge rated Timbercorp's 2008 Olive Project four out of a possible five stars, with the expert telling investors that 'with net assets exceeding $519 million and a focus on investment in key industries with significant opportunities for domestic and export growth, Timbercorp remains well positioned to take advantage of expected consumption growth of its core products, albeit with considerable risks remaining'.[12] Adviser Edge also stated 'ongoing fee revenue should be sufficient to sustain project operations'.[13] In June 2009, a year after Adviser Edge made those optimistic forecasts, Timbercorp's administrator determined that the company's almond and olive projects would have negative cash flow for three years even after the proceeds of the 2009 harvest were considered.

Similarly, in mid 2008 Lonsec Agribusiness Research deemed Timbercorp's 2008 Olive Project a 'recommended' investment (a rating above 'investment grade'). Lonsec stated that 'the project attained its highest major determinate rating for Business Strategy and Corporate Resources. Timbercorp Securities Limited is one of the largest and most experienced agribusiness project managers in Australia and has a sound record in establishing agricultural projects'. A year later Timbercorp's administrator deemed TSL 'hopelessly insolvent'.

The importance of the 'independent' research houses should not be underestimated—Timbercorp told shareholders in its 2004 annual report that 'the return of investor confidence to the sector has also been assisted by credible independent research…Timbercorp received strong product ratings across all its projects, and achieved investment grade ratings from all research providers'. Perhaps Timbercorp had forgotten that those so-called independent research providers were being paid by Timbercorp.

However, research houses weren't the only conflicted 'experts'. As part of the disclosure process to MIS investors, Timbercorp and Great Southern employed surveyors to assess the suitability of soil. The promoters provided minimal detail regarding their choice of experts in the product disclosure statements given to investors. Further, the promoters neglected to mention that they would be paying the experts' bill. It would not be outrageous to suggest that any soil expert who provided unfavourable opinions about a project may find themselves struggling for work in the near future.

While financial planners and the independent experts take some blame for the monies lost by owner-growers (and to a lesser extent shareholders), it was the management of Timbercorp and Great Southern who bear most responsibility for the businesses' collapse.

Not only did the MIS twins operate highly leveraged schemes which required constant capital inflows, but their profits appeared to be regularly inflated by asset revaluations and dubious accounting practices. Most notably, revenues were largely calculated using accounting valuations which judged 'probable economic benefits'. From 2005, Great Southern would resort to propping up its schemes because they were simply not making any money for investors.

The fee-based nature of the schemes also encouraged the agribusiness companies to bid up the prices of assets. Similar to Allco, Babcock and MFS, the MIS twins would pay too much for assets such as farming land only to witness the value of those assets slump and refinancing debt become virtually impossible thanks to a global credit crunch.

It should be remembered that simply running a business badly is not in itself a crime. For many years entrepreneurs have been protected by a common law principle known as the 'business judgement rule'. The rule provides that company directors are not held liable for business decisions, no matter how foolhardy, as long as they were acting in good faith. One could argue that such was not always the case with Great Southern and Timbercorp.

While all that accounting funny business was going on, Robert Hance at Timbercorp and John Young at Great Southern were cashing in their chips while at the same time promising growth and profits to shareholders and owner-growers.

In 2004 and 2005, Young sold more than $33 million worth of Great Southern shares. Young was paid more than $10 million in remuneration between 2000 and 2008.* While Young claimed that he shared the pain suffered by minority shareholders, his discomfort was somewhat tempered by the $43 million extracted from Great Southern before its collapse. The timing of Young's share sale was especially suspicious, occurring shortly before Great Southern announced that its early timber plantations were not profitable.

Similarly, Timbercorp founder Robert Hance collected more than $20 million from share sales in 2004, as well as $4 million in remuneration and $6.2 million in fees which had been paid to his private company Timbercorp WA over the years. Former Timbercorp chairman Rod Fitzroy collected millions from a lucrative consultancy deal which was paid out in full not long before the company's collapse.

Not only did Robert Hance walk away a wealthy man, his son Tony Hance, who was employed by Timbercorp, was also able to extract a few extra dollars before the company collapsed. Weeks before Timbercorp was placed in administration, Tony Hance, who worked in the company's sales and marketing team, was made 'redundant'. The rest of the marketing team had been sacked the previous year but the younger Hance remained in his role, presumably still being paid. Hance's termination and redundancy payment was certainly fortuitous — other Timbercorp employees who were not so lucky and kept their jobs not only didn't receive a cash redundancy payment but also risked losing a portion of their entitlements as Timbercorp's debts significantly exceeded its assets.[14]

John Young used the proceeds of his Great Southern share sales to acquire an expansive Perth mansion in the elite suburb City Beach. The property, like many of the other assets owned by characters in this book, is safely tucked away, legally owned by Young's wife, Sheila.

The Australian Securities and Investments Commission did not indicate whether any charges would be laid against any person involved in the collapse of Great Southern or Timbercorp. (ASIC was certainly not blameless itself; the regulator was warned about

---

* In 2008, despite having only served as Great Southern's CEO for six months, John Young was paid $1.2 million. During the year, Great Southern's share price fell by almost 80 per cent.

Great Southern being a Ponzi scheme more than a year before its collapse, but failed to properly investigate the claims.)

Similarly, the ASX never took any action against either MIS company for lack of disclosure, although it did question Great Southern about disclosure of the poor yields from its 2005 crop. The ASX were a little late on the scene though, commencing their interrogation of Great Southern in June 2009—four years after the alleged incident occurred and after the company had collapsed. The ASX's response was a bit like the police arriving to try to stop a murder from occurring just after the victim had been cremated.

A lonely civil action against several Timbercorp directors was initiated in August 2009. The claim against Gary Liddell, Robert Hance and Sol Rabinowicz relates to inadequate disclosure of Timbercorp's precarious financial position.

The collapses of Great Southern and Timbercorp caused widespread financial pain across Australia. From investors to shareholders to creditors to farmers and especially taxpayers, almost everyone was a loser. Well, except the companies' most senior executives.

Epilogue

YOU MAY have been horrified at the behaviour of many of the executives and company directors mentioned in this book; I certainly was when writing it.

However, at the time of publication, of the characters and companies studied, only directors from one—fund manager MFS —have been charged by Australia's corporate regulator, ASIC. (ASIC is also pursuing current and former directors of Centro Property Group, another victim of the global financial crisis, for misleading investors.)

In November 2009, ASIC announced that five former directors and executives of MFS will face civil (but not criminal) charges relating to the falsification and backdating of documents in order to repay lender Fortress Credit Corporation, a US hedge fund, in 2008. ASIC also claimed that MFS officers caused a managed fund, PIF, to pay the obligations of various MFS subsidiaries. Pursuant to its civil action, ASIC is seeking $147.5 million from former MFS managing directors Michael King and Phil Adams, as well as former CEO Craig White and CFO David Anderson. The charges are being defended.

While ASIC is understood to have investigated ABC Learning Centres, Babcock & Brown and Allco Finance Group, no civil or criminal charges have yet been laid. Nor have any charges resulted from the twin collapses at agribusiness companies Timbercorp and Great Southern Plantations, despite a Parliamentary Inquiry into the MIS twins. (The actions at Village Roadshow, Telstra and Toll/ Asciano, while an affront to shareholders, will almost certainly not give rise to either civil or criminal actions.)

The slow response of ASIC contrasts the relatively decisive action taken in the United States. Former Nasdaq chairman Bernie Madoff, who admitted to running a US$65 billion Ponzi scheme, was jailed for 150 years in March 2009, having been arrested only four months earlier. Similarly, two Bear Sterns hedge fund managers were charged (but later exonerated by a jury) with conspiracy, securities fraud and wire fraud within a year of the firm's collapse. Similarly, lawyer Marc Dreier was charged with fraud in December 2008, and within seven months was sentenced to 20 years prison.

Not only are few Australians ever charged with white-collar offences, there is often a significant lag between the alleged offence and the laying of of charges. (ASIC's unsuccessful action against One.Tel executives and directors took almost a decade to prosecute.) Further, in recent times the regulator has opted for civil, rather than criminal, proceedings, largely due to the lower burden of proof required.

While corporate collapses go unpunished, the federal government continues to avoid taking meaningful action to combat the scourge of excessive remuneration. While draft reports were produced in 2009 by the Australian Prudential Regulation Authority and the Productivity Commission, little real change is likely. However, the government was successful in introducing new legislation which limits the quantum of termination payments that can be provided to directors without shareholder approval to one year's fixed salary.

One of the overarching themes which traversed many of the companies covered was the apparent absence of responsibility and diligence taken by non-executive corporate directors. It was the job of these directors—most of whom are respected members of the Australian business community—to represent shareholders' interests and minimise agency costs; that is, the costs associated with employing managers whose interests were not aligned with smaller shareholders.

In virtually all cases, non-executive directors failed to properly undertake their trusted roles. Over the past decade, executives have been able to run their companies like personal fiefdoms—while directors did little or nothing to curb their largesse and institutional shareholders did virtually nothing to exercise whatever minimal power they had.

If the companies studied in this book teach us anything, it is that corporate governance and executive restraint are issues which must not be ignored by investors, non-executive directors or governments. A failure to address them in a meaningful way can lead to catastrophe.

Adam Schwab
Melbourne, Australia
December 2009

NOTES

Chapter 1

1   R Webb, 'Super Salesman Answers the Call', *The Age*, 12 June 2005.
2   I Verrender, 'Telstra's Monopoly Has Been Smashed at Last', *The Sydney Morning Herald*, 8 April 2009.
3   G O'Leary, Parliament of Australia, Parliamentary Library, 15 September 2003.
4   AAP, 'Telstra CEO to Step Down', 1 December 2004.
5   S Bartholomuez, 'Sol's Been Reading His Own Telstra Papers', *The Sydney Morning Herald*, 17 June 2005.
6   Accessed from <www.bizjournals.com/gen/executive.html?excode=3E814CC5ADCC479 9B86A4799D3935357&market=sanjose>.
7   J Borland, 'US West Under Fire for Poor Phone Service', *CNET*, 18 August 1999.
8   B Butler, 'Lines Run Hot Over Telstra Phone Service Complaints', *Herald Sun*, 6 April 2009.
9   S Steers, 'Colorado Missed the Call', *Denver Westword*, 6 July 2000.
10   K Askew and M O'Sullivan, 'How Sol Struck Pay Dirt', *The Sydney Morning Herald*, 26 August 2007.
11   C Kruger, 'Heir to the Phone', *The Sydney Morning Herald*, 11 June 2005.
12   M O'Sullivan, 'A Case of Déjà Vu', *The Sydney Morning Herald*, 4 October 2006.
13   AAP, 'Howard Slams Telstra Executive's Warning', 2 September 2005.
14   M Sainsbury, 'Telstra Report Costs $54m', *The Australian*, 28 September 2006.
15   ibid.
16   J Porter, 'Telstra Bosses on $1.3 million Trip Before Sending Staff Packing', *The Sydney Morning Herald*, 2 February 2006.
17   J Garnaut, 'Alcatel Memo a Prop', *The Sydney Morning Herald*, 29 May 2006.
18   M Sainsbury, 'Trujillo Phones a Friend for a Deal', *The Australian*, 13 October 2007.
19   M Sainsbury, 'Telstra Pays Premium for Handsets', *The Australian*, 12 October 2007.
20   M Sainsbury, 'Trujillo's Surprise Seat on US Bank Board', *The Australian*, 16 March 2009.
21   ibid.
22   K Askew and M O'Sullivan, 'How Telstra Conceals Its Sweet Executive Deals', *The Age*, 13 November 2006.
23   'Australian Prime Minister Assails Telstra Chief's Salary', *International Herald Tribune*, 27 September 2006.
24   K Askew and M O'Sullivan, 'How Sol Struck Pay Dirt', *The Sydney Morning Herald*, 26 August 2007.
25   J Hogan, 'Telstra Boss Rings up $11.8 Million Pay', *The Age*, 10 August 2007.
26   AAP, 'Trujillo Remuneration Totalled $11.78 Million', Ninemsn, 9 August 2007.
27   M Sainsbury, 'Trujillo's Song and Dance over Salary', *The Australian*, 29 October 2007.
28   M O'Sullivan, 'Telstra's Shareholders Wary of Exception for Trujillo', *The Sydney Morning Herald*, 12 March 2008.
29   S Washington, 'Executive Rewards Wake Sleeping Giant', *The Sydney Morning Herald*, 12 November 2007.
30   E Alberici, 'Shareholders Oppose High Pay for Telstra CEO', *ABC News*, 7 November 2007.
31   K Askew and M O'Sullivan, 'How Sol Struck Pay Dirt', *The Sydney Morning Herald*, 26 August 2007.

32 I Hundley, 'Inquiry Into the Regulation of Director and Executive Remuneration', Submission, Productivity Commission, May 2009.

33 M O'Sullivan, 'It Takes Two to Tango', *The Sydney Morning Herald*, 9 January 2009.

34 ibid.

35 M Davis, 'Revealed: Telstra's Secret Plan to Bust Unions', *The Sydney Morning Herald*, 14 August 2008.

36 M O'Sullivan, 'Telstra's Amigo Nears His Use-By Date', *The Sydney Morning Herald*, 18 July 2007.

37 M O'Sullivan, 'It Takes Two to Tango', *The Sydney Morning Herald*, 9 January 2009.

38 AAP, 'Trujillo "World-Class" in Making Enemies: Switkowski', 24 July 2009.

39 Telstra, 'Telstra CEO Sol Trujillo to Depart Company on 30 June', media release 040/2009, 26 February 2009.

40 A Schwab, 'A Bit Rich: Australia's CEO Payout Shame', *Crikey*, 3 March 2009.

Chapter 2

1 C Kruger, 'End of a Fairytale', *The Sydney Morning Herald*, 6 September 2008.

2 A Horin, 'When Making Money is Child's Play', *The Sydney Morning Herald*, 4 October 2003.

3 B Hills, 'Cradle Snatcher', *The Sydney Morning Herald*, 11 March 2006.

4 J Koutsoukis, 'Former Howard Minister Shares in the Pain', *The Age*, 2 March 2008.

5 B Hills, 'Cradle Snatcher', *The Sydney Morning Herald*, 11 March 2006.

6 'A.B.C. Learning Centres Limited to Acquire 3rd Largest U.S.A. Childcare Centre Operator', 16 November 2005, accessed from <www.asx.com.au/asxpdf/20051116/pdf/3t93n9q4qdj33.pdf>.

7 M West, 'The ABC of Lawyering', *The Sydney Morning Herald*, 22 July 2008.

8 V Carson, 'Rug Pulled from ABC Learning', *The Sydney Morning Herald*, 27 February 2008.

9 ASX, 'ABC Enters Joint Venture with Morgan Stanley Private Equity', 5 March 2008.

10 A Kohler, R Gottliebsen and S Bartholomeusz, 'KGB Interrogation: Eddy Groves', *Business Spectator*, 6 March 2008.

11 C Nader, 'Chief of Troubled ABC Learning Resigns', *The Age*, 1 October 2008.

12 J Gillard (Minister for Education, Employment and Workplace Relations), 'ABC Learning—Administration and Receivership', media release, 6 November 2008.

13 L Walsh, 'Under Scrutiny', *The Courier-Mail*, 3 October 2006.

14 ibid.

15 C Kruger, 'How the Numbers Stacked up in ABC's Labyrinthine Structure', *The Sydney Morning Herald*, 6 September 2008.

16 L Walsh, 'Inside the ABC Childcare Empire and Eddy Groves', *The Courier-Mail*, 31 March 2008.

17 *Australian Financial Review*, 1 September 2008.

18 C Kruger, 'End of a Fairytale', *The Sydney Morning Herald*, 6 September 2008.

Chapter 3

1 A Kohler, 'MFS's Gruesome Hour', *Business Spectator*, 18 January 2008.

2 A Klan, 'MFS' Roots in Solicitors Scandal', *The Australian*, 25 January 2008.

3 C Cummins, 'Flood of Cash on Its Way, so LPTs Open the Hatches', *The Sydney Morning Herald*, 6 September 2006.

4 K Hagan, 'Elderly Face Eviction in Retirement Village Dispute', *The Age*, 17 April 2007.

5 A Kohler, 'MFS's Gruesome Hour', *Business Spectator*, 18 January 2008.

6 S Rochfort, 'Market Aghast at MFS Share Issue Plan', *The Sydney Morning Herald*, 18 January 2008.

7 ibid.

8 S Washington, 'MFS Fiasco Adds to Woes', *The Sydney Morning Herald*, 21 January 2008.

9 *Australian Financial Review*, 2008.

10   A Klan, 'Peacock led Finance Company Freezes $770 Million in Investments',
      The Australian, 30 January 2008.
11   A Marx, 'Public Trustee of Qld Turns to Wellington Capital', *The Courier-Mail*,
      11 May 2009.
12   A Main, 'Go Figure: Even Auditors can Flunk Maths', *The Australian*, 29 December 2008.
13   Agilis Global, 'About us', March 2009, accessed from <www.agilisglobal.com/Uploads/
      Documents/20090312AboutUs.pdf>.
14   ibid.
15   S Rochfort, 'MFS Executive Nets Almost $1m', *The Age*, 12 October 2009.

Chapter 4
1   W Frew, 'Village: Ziegler's Full Demands', *The Sydney Morning Herald*,
      25 September 2003.
2   B Hills, 'Prime Bank Fraud: How Village Roadshow Was Scammed of Millions',
      The Sydney Morning Herald, 17 March 2001.
3   J McConvill, 'Schemes of Arrangement, Selective Buy-Backs and Village Roadshow's
      Preference Share Tussle: Entering the Matrix', *Macquarie Journal of Business Law*, 2005.
4   W Frew, 'Hunter Joins Protest Over Village Divvies', *The Sydney Morning Herald*,
      27 March 2003.
5   Australian Securities & Investments Commission, 'ASIC Concludes Enquiries into
      Village Roadshow', media release 03-173, 2 June 2003.
6   E Sexton, 'Village Shows a Preference for Intrigue', *The Sydney Morning Herald*,
      31 July 2003.
7   C Catalano, 'Court Rule a Setback for Village', *The Age*, 28 February 2004.
8   Grant Samuel Group, 'Independent Expert's Report', in Village Roadshow's Scheme
      Booklet, September 2003.
9   W Frew, 'Village Buyback Hits the Dust', *The Sydney Morning Herald*, 24 January 2004.
10   ibid.
11   C Webb, 'Now Showing: The Biggest Loser', *The Age*, 4 February 2007.
12   L Gettler, 'Biffo in the Boardroom', *The Age*, 3 December 2005.
13   C Catalano, 'Village Broke Promises: Ziegler', *The Sydney Morning Herald*, 27 April 2005.
14   C Webb, 'Now Showing: The Biggest Loser', *The Age*, 4 February 2007.
15   W Frew, 'Village Investors Didn't Know the Gun was Loaded', *The Sydney Morning
      Herald*, 27 September 2003.
16   C Catalano, 'Dividend Deal Sends Village Roadshow Shares Soaring',
      The Age, 16 November 2005.

Chapter 5
1   J Chessell, 'The Big Takeovers of 2005', *The Sydney Morning Herald*, 24 December 2005.
2   S Rochfort, 'Corrigan Derides $4.6b Bid', *The Sydney Morning Herald*, 19 October 2005.
3   K Askew, 'Looking Back on the Shipping Blues', *The Sydney Morning Herald*,
      13 May 2006.
4   ibid.
5   E Knight, 'Toll Demerger to Get Green Light, Despite the Vibe', *The Sydney Morning
      Herald*, 2 February 2007.
6   L Wood, 'How the Two Titans of Transport Collided', *The Age*, 22 October 2005.
7   S Washington, 'The Scramble for Brambles', *The Sydney Morning Herald*,
      22 September 2007.
8   S Rochfort, 'Asciano Clears Track for Recovery', *Brisbane Times*, 12 December 2007.
9   ibid.
10   S Rochfort, 'Asciano in Shock $71m Loss', *The Sydney Morning Herald*, 4 March 2008.
11   Asciano, 'Sale of Brambles Shareholding', 3 April 2008, accessed from
      <www.bourseinvestor.com/bi4/pdfnews/default.asp?d=00828886&f=20080403>.

12   M O'Sullivan, 'Bid for Asciano Well Short of the Mark', *The Sydney Morning Herald*, 6 August 2008.

13   M West, 'Debunk Notion of Paid "Independent" Wages Consultant', *The Age*, 31 October 2008.

14   AAP, 'Asciano Gives Positive Outlook', 21 September 2009.

Chapter 6

1   L Murray, 'Sydney's Niche in Global Finance', *The Sydney Morning Herald*, 27 April 2005.

2   S Washington, 'Allco Tries to Make Amends', *The Sydney Morning Herald*, 26 October 2007.

3   A Main, 'Mini-Mac Model Runs Out of Steam for Allco', *The Australian*, 8 November 2008.

4   L Murray, 'Sprung: Allco Finance Fiddles the Numbers and Makes Them Fit', *The Sydney Morning Herald*, 27 September 2006.

5   A Schwab, 'Dreams Averted a Qantas Nightmare', *The Age*, 5 May 2009.

6   F Norris, 'When a Public Offering Goes Bad Down Under', *New York Times*, 7 December 2007.

7   S Washington, 'Subprime Lender Mobius Worst Performer', *The Age*, 4 October 2007.

8   Explanatory Memorandum for the buyout of Rubicon by Allco, 5 November 2007.

9   Grant Samuel Group's independent expert report on the Allco acquisition of Rubicon, 2007.

10   Explanatory Memorandum for the buyout of Rubicon by Allco, 5 November 2007.

11   S Rochfort & S Washington, 'Deadlines Could Doom Allco', *The Sydney Morning Herald*, 26 February 2008.

12   L Wood, 'Kazakhstan Was to be Allco Jewel', *The Sydney Morning Herald*, 18 March 2008.

13   S Washington, 'Shareholders Cop Risks of Deals with Allco Bosses', *Brisbane Times*, 9 March 2008.

14   V Burrow, 'Allco's Toxic Fallout Lands on Innocent Party', *The Sydney Morning Herald*, 11 March 2008.

15   J Chancellor, 'Unreality Bites as Harbour Lures $47m Buyer', *The Sydney Morning Herald*, 18 September 2008.

Chapter 7

1   L Murray, 'B&B Knocks MacBank Model', *The Sydney Morning Herald*, 25 August 2006.

2   R Hughes, 'Love & Hate', *Ruby Sapphire*.

3   Accessed from <www.riskmetrics.com/system/files/private/RMG_Infrastructure_Funds_080326.pdf>.

4   RiskMetrics, 'Infrastructure Funds: Managing, Financing and Accounting — In Whose Interests?', April 2008.

5   Babcock & Brown, 'Notice of Meeting', 12 April 2005.

6   ibid.

7   T Fullerton, 'Babcock and Brown Wind Partners CEO Discusses Company Reform', *7:30 Report*, 13 March 2009.

8   D John, 'From Green into the Red', *The Sydney Morning Herald*, 23 August 2008.

9   M West, 'B&B Lures Legal Eagles', *The Age*, 19 December 2008.

10   E Knight, 'Hindsight Makes Bad Deals Worse', *The Sydney Morning Herald*, 23 October 2008.

11   S Washington, 'Fundies Query Tricom–B&B Dealings', *The Sydney Morning Herald*, 27 April 2007.

12   M West, 'A Sense of Irony Helps at Babcock', *The Sydney Morning Herald*, 3 March 2008.

13   I Verrender, 'Feeling Pain on the Margins', *The Sydney Morning Herald*, 11 March 2009.

14   M West, 'B&B's "Culture of Greed"', *The Sydney Morning Herald*, 6 August 2008.

15   D John, 'Brokers Slam B&B Warning', *The Sydney Morning Herald*, 13 August 2008.

16   D John, 'The Fall and Fall of Babcock & Brown', *The Age*, 21 September 2009.

17   I Verrender, 'Ex-Babcock Boss Looks at Having a Lend', *The Sydney Morning Herald*, 22 September 2009.

18   D John, 'Former B&B Chief Faces Probe over Tricom', *The Sydney Morning Herald*, 15 August 2009.

Chapter 8

1   I Verrender, 'The Sound of Two Schemes Failing', *The Sydney Morning Herald*, 19 May 2009.

2   W Tuckey, 'Letter to the Editor', *Australian Financial Review*, 16 June 2000.

3   Timbercorp, 'Clarification of Proposed Acquisition by Futuris of Interest in Timbercorp', media release, 1 May 2003.

4   W Buffett, Letter to Shareholders, 2003.

5   R Sexton, 'Rights Bring a Bitter Harvest to the Murray', *The Age*, 29 April 2007.

6   Timbercorp, 2008 Full Year Results, 2009 Outlook and Strategy, 27 November 2008.

7   L Battersby, 'Timbercorp Hopes Felled', *The Age*, 17 April 2009.

8   C LaFrenz, 'Great Southern Hopes Wither', *Australian Financial Review*, 13 October 2009.

9   Parliamentary Joint Committee on Corporations and Financial Services, 'Inquiry into Aspects of Agribusiness Managed Investment Schemes', September 2009.

10   A Kohler, 'The Trouble With Fee Huggers', *Business Spectator*, 6 May 2009.

11   M Newnham, 'Investors May See the Wood from the Trees', *The Age*, 1 May 2009.

12   Adviser Edge, 2008 Timbercorp Olive Project, p. 6.

13   Adviser Edge, 2008 Timbercorp Olive Project, p. 8.

14   A Schwab, 'Founder's Son Gets Timely Timbercorp Payout', *Crikey*, 21 May 2009.

INDEX

Printed in Australia
03 Jan 2019
694644